SELECTED PAPERS

of

HOMER CUMMINGS

A Da Capo Press Reprint Series

FRANKLIN D. ROOSEVELT
AND THE ERA OF THE NEW DEAL

GENERAL EDITOR: FRANK FREIDEL
Harvard University

Selected Papers

of

Homer Cummings

Attorney General of the United States

1933-1939

Edited by

CARL BRENT SWISHER

DA CAPO PRESS • NEW YORK • 1972

Library of Congress Cataloging in Publication Data

Cummings, Homer Stillé, 1870-1956.
    Selected papers of Homer Cummings, Attorney General of the
United States, 1933-1939.
    (Franklin D. Roosevelt and the era of the New Deal)
    Reprint of the 1939 ed.
    "Includes addresses, articles, letters . . . from personal and official
files." — p.
    CONTENTS: The Nation's largest law office. — Crime control. —
The courts, the Constitution, and the New Deal. [etc.]
    1. U.S. Dept. of Justice. 2. Justice, Administration of — U.S. 3.
Crime and criminals — U.S. 4. Law enforcement — U.S. 5. U.S. —
Constitutional law. 6. Civil procedure — U.S. 7. U.S. Supreme
Court. I. Swisher, Carl Brent, 1897-1968, ed. II. Title. III. Series.
KF213.C8S9   1972   353.5   79-168392
ISBN 0-306-70329-7

This Da Capo Press of the *Selected Papers of Homer Cummings* is
an unabridged republication of the first edition published in New
York in 1939. It is reprinted by permission from a copy of the original edition in the Library of Case Western Reserve University.

Published by Da Capo Press, Inc.
A Subsidiary of Plenum Publishing Corporation
227 W. 17 St., New York, New York 10011
All Rights Reserved
Manufactured in the United States of America

SELECTED PAPERS OF HOMER CUMMINGS

Attorney General of the United States

1933-1939

SELECTED PAPERS

of

HOMER CUMMINGS

Attorney General of the United States

1933-1939

Edited by

CARL BRENT SWISHER

NEW YORK

CHARLES SCRIBNER'S SONS

1939

Printed in the United States of America by
National Capital Press, Inc., Washington, D. C.

PREFACE

The public papers of Attorney General Homer Cummings, together with those of the President and of other officers in policy-making positions in the federal government, will be necessary to the presentation of an accurate picture of the development of governmental agencies to deal both with the depression which began in 1929 and with permanent reforms for which there was a crying need. We have been negligent in the preservation and publication of such records in times past. Even in the case of Presidents, only formal records have been consistently preserved, save as selected papers have been chosen and published from collections remaining after a lapse of years. The plan for the immediate publication of a number of the important papers of President Franklin D. Roosevelt is unique, and is not likely to be extended to the officers of the cabinet. Nothing like a complete collection of the papers of any cabinet member, at least in recent years, is available. This volume of selected papers of the man who was Attorney General from 1933 to 1939 is chosen from a number of sources and types of materials as described in the Introduction. It suggests the value of a more extended collection if such were possible, and the value of similar collections of the papers of other statesmen of the period.

Many persons have aided in the selection and preparation of materials for this publication. To all of them the gratitude of the editor is expressed. Attorney General Cummings has taken no part in the selection or arrangement of materials or in the drafting of editorial notes to explain their significance. The preparation of the book indeed has been arranged entirely without his knowledge, though some months ago he permitted the editor to have free use of all files for the study of current legal development and administration.

CARL BRENT SWISHER

Baltimore, Maryland
January 3, 1939

CONTENTS

PART THREE

THE COURTS, THE CONSTITUTION, AND THE NEW DEAL

PART FOUR

REFORM OF FEDERAL PRACTICE AND PROCEDURE

PART FIVE

JUDICIAL REFORM

PART SIX

ADMINISTRATION OF FEDERAL JUSTICE

APPENDIX

BIOGRAPHICAL NOTE

Homer Stillé Cummings was born April 30, 1870, the son of a distinguished inventor, manufacturer, and writer on technical subjects. He was educated at the Heathcote School in Buffalo and at Yale College and Law School, and in 1893 was admitted to the bar of Connecticut, where he maintained his home during his career as a practicing lawyer and a leader of the Democratic Party.[1] He participated in the civic life of his community and state—as mayor of Stamford at the age of 30, twice re-elected and President of the Mayors' Association of Connecticut, President of the Stamford Board of Trade, and member of the State Council of Defense for the mobilization of industry in one of the nation's leading industrial states during the World War. In 1909 he organized the firm of Cummings and Lockwood which engaged in a growing and diversified practice.

At the appointment of the local courts, he served for a decade as state's attorney. In his capacity as a prosecutor, he tempered professional zeal with humanity and a search for truth which found its most widely-known example in the story of *State v. Harold Israel.*[2] In Fairfield County, only a few miles from the borders of New York and not a great distance from Rhode Island

[1] For biographical and personal material, see: Kelly, *Homer Cummings, A Biographical Sketch,* Journal of the New Haven Bar Association, January 1934, p. 13; Creel, *The Tall Man,* Collier's Magazine, January 4, 1936; Soderholm, *Early Days in Buffalo,* the Buffalo Evening News, October 22, 1938.

[2] Wherein, despite a confession, ostensible evidence, and local feeling, the prosecutor became convinced of the innocence of a bewildered defendant accused of murder (see *The State* v. *Harold Israel,* 1924, 15 J. Crim. L. 406, 415; the same in pamphlet form, 1932, with a foreword by William M. Maltbie; and an edition of 1936 with an introduction by Brien McMahon). It has been widely reproduced or commented upon in such diverse publications as Borchard's *Convicting the Innocent* (1932, p. xviii); the report of the (Wickersham) National Commission on Law Observance and Enforcement, on *Lawlessness in Law Enforcement* (1931, pp. 184-185); *The Human Side of the People's Case* (staff magazine of the New York County district attorney's office, May, 1937, pp. 4-5); and the *Shanghai Police Gazette* (September, 1937, p. 4). In June, 1938, Mr. Cummings undertook to discover the subsequent conduct of Harold Israel. In July the Federal Bureau of Investigation reported him as an apparently respected citizen of Pennsylvania, married, with two children, living in a neat residence in a respectable neighborhood, with good credit, employed for the last twelve years as a competent miner of good character, and a member of the Methodist Church.

and Massachusetts, he observed the interstate operations of criminals while enforcing the peace of his community. His report as a special commissioner for the study of prison conditions in Connecticut [3] has been widely used by students of penology. Thus at first hand, he met three phases of society's war on crime— detection, prosecution, and penal treatment.

In 1900 he became Democratic National Committeeman from Connecticut, a position which he resigned twenty-five years later. He was one of the Democratic leaders in favor of the Wilson candidacy, and the active director of the Democratic speakers' bureau in the Taft-Wilson campaign of 1912, where he met young Franklin D. Roosevelt who was to become Wilson's Assistant Secretary of the Navy. He became vice-chairman of the Democratic National Committee in 1913, and served as head of the speakers' bureau in the 1916 presidential campaign. In this position he resorted to the unusual strategy of establishing a branch bureau in the crucial state of California—a step which may have been one of the decisive factors in the campaign, since California turned the election from Charles Evans Hughes to Wilson. At the request of President Wilson he accepted the nomination for United States Senator from Connecticut, but continued to give his time to the national campaign and failed of election by a narrow margin. During the pre-convention arrangements, he urged the abandonment of the notorious "two-thirds rule," a step not taken, however, until twenty years later at another convention in which he participated.

When he became chairman of the Democratic National Committee in 1919, he took the course, unprecedented on the part of a Democratic chairman, of traveling west of the Mississippi in a survey of party conditions. Long identified with the progressive wing of the Democratic Party, he had become closely associated with President Wilson, who let it be known on several occasions that he would like to have Mr. Cummings in the cabinet. In 1920 the ailing President handed him a code to be used in transmitting confidential reports of the forthcoming national conven-

[3] See Bates, *Prisons and Beyond* (Macmillan, 1936), pp. 19-20.

tion, remarking dryly, "Col. House used to have this. He won't need it any more."

As temporary chairman of the Democratic National Convention at San Francisco in 1920, he delivered a celebrated "keynote" address defending the record of the Wilson administration, and he was selected to deliver the address at Hyde Park, New York, at the notification ceremonies for the vice-presidential nominee, Franklin D. Roosevelt. In the conventions of 1920 and 1924, Homer Cummings himself received substantial votes for the presidential nomination. In 1925 he resigned his position with the National Committee [4] to give his whole time to the practice of law. The political acumen and experience thus gained were, however, to stand him in good stead when federal legislation was needed in the field of law enforcement and legal administration a decade later.

He continued to head one of Connecticut's largest and leading law firms, and, as a recognized leader of the bar, he became trial counsel in notable litigation in many jurisdictions. As a bank director, he had long been concerned with monetary problems. The legal problems of monopoly,[5] the defense of civil rights, the pitfalls of procedure, and the methods of commerce and finance became familiar topics to him in the arena of the courtroom and in business relationships.

After a seven-year retirement from national politics, he announced his support of Franklin D. Roosevelt for the Presidency and became an influential participant in the nation-wide Roosevelt pre-convention campaign in 1932. To this task he gave the greater part of his time. As a delegate-at-large to the Chicago Convention, he was a floor leader for Governor Roosevelt and delivered one of the seconding speeches—as he did also at the 1936 Convention at Philadelphia.

Upon the election of Franklin D. Roosevelt to be the thirty-

[4] The outline of these activities and the text of his addresses are to be found in the proceedings of the Democratic National Conventions and of the Democratic National Committee, 1900-1925, 1932-1936.

[5] See, for example, *Haskell* v. *Perkins,* 28 F. (2d) 222 (1928), 31 F. (2d) 53 (1929), 279 U. S. 872 (1929).

second President of the United States, Homer Cummings was often mentioned for various cabinet positions, including that of Attorney General. On his own part, he urged that Senator Cordell Hull, who had likewise been one of the few experienced leaders active in the pre-convention campaign, be made Secretary of State.

In the early months of 1933, the President-elect telephoned Homer Cummings from Florida, urging him to become Governor General of the Philippines, to replace Col. Theodore Roosevelt. Franklin D. Roosevelt, a former Assistant Secretary of the Navy like his cousin, was not satisfied with conditions in that far outpost in the Pacific. Mr. Cummings accepted and promised to try to be ready to depart in thirty days. Senator T. J. Walsh of Montana agreed to become Attorney General and, not aware of the Philippines arrangement, urged Mr. Cummings to become the chief Assistant Attorney General in charge of judicial and executive appointments.

The events of March, 1933, are not without their drama, particularly in the light of later history. On March 2, Senator Walsh, on his way to the inauguration, was found dying in his railway compartment. Regarded in Washington as the prospective "balance wheel" and "elder statesman" of the new administration, the 74-year-old Senator had conferred with Attorney General Mitchell on a "smooth transfer" of the reins. Otherwise, he seems to have anticipated no great problems. After the inauguration, he had planned to take a "two months or ten weeks" vacation to show his bride of a few days the beauties of the West with, perhaps, a visit to her home in Cuba the next autumn.

On the same day, March 2, Mr. Roosevelt asked Homer Cummings to delay his departure for the Philippines and head the Department of Justice temporarily. A month later the President announced at a cabinet meeting that the appointment would be permanent. Suddenly handed the job of chief law officer of the national government, and for a precious month without thought of permanent tenure, with no warning, no plans, no selected assistants, Homer Cummings of Connecticut turned his steps to the musty building on Vermont Avenue in Washington where the headquarters of the Department of Justice were located. This volume records in some measure the problems and duties he faced, how he faced them, and with what methods and what results.

He took the view that his office called for leadership rather than passive administration under old statutes and ready-made policies. Beyond the mere necessities of the day, he conceived a program to refurbish the rusty machinery of national justice. In order to see his plans brought to a permanent stage of achievement, he served nearly six years—the longest term of any Attorney General in more than a century, and the second longest in the history of the federal government. Twenty-eight different men held in succession the fourteen ranking positions under him. Of those in office December 30, 1933, after his original reorganization of the Department, only the Director of the Federal Bureau of Investigation remained in the same position five years later. Two divisions had each been headed by four different men. In some divisions the same rapid turnover had taken place among subordinate personnel.

Throughout the period the Attorney General himself constituted a unifying factor within a rapidly changing organization. He quickly made himself at home in the problems of his Department and impressed upon its work his own conceptions of policy. His ready sympathy, warmth in dealing with subordinates, and interest in the work of each unit of the Department of Justice drew about him a staff which served with an unbounded loyalty which was distinctive in an administration subject—as all national administrations are subject—to many personal feuds and conflicting private aspirations.

As 1938 drew to a close, the reforms to which Attorney General Cummings had committed himself had largely been achieved. In the fields of crime control, of procedural reform, and, to some extent, of judicial reform his work was done. As his task became one of routine, his resignation, postponed from time to time for other than personal reasons, was to no one an occasion for surprise when announced on November 15 to become effective in January 1939.

INTRODUCTION

The papers of Attorney General Cummings are important partly because of the conception of public duty and policy which they disclose and partly because they show the imprint of that conception upon the activities of a great department of the government. The papers of any cabinet member have a more than routine significance in that, however quiet the movement of public affairs and however methodical the activities of the head of a department of the government, his position makes him a participant in matters of unquestioned importance. He becomes a significant factor in the unfolding of the nation's history and in the development of governmental machinery for dealing with the nation's problems.

In times of crisis or transition for the nation as a whole or of development and change in the department involved, the man and his records become particularly important. The public papers of Attorney General Gregory, for instance, who headed the Department of Justice during the World War, would be of great value for a study of law enforcement in war time. The papers of Attorney General Wickersham, covering an important period of antitrust law enforcement, would be of value to students of that subject. The papers of Attorney General Bates, judging from his diary which has been published by the American Historical Association, would yield materials of great value for a study of the Civil War administration.

Attorney General Cummings served through the period of a crisis no less serious than war, during which the Department of Justice underwent transitions of fundamental importance. The interest of historians and students of government generally could be served best by the publication of a number of volumes which would include all the significant documents in the Department of Justice files. Facilities for such a broad publication program are not now available. On the basis of judgment exercised as explained below, a number of papers have been selected to illustrate the problems and tasks of the period and the steps taken by or under the direction of Mr. Cummings for dealing with them. In a sense this compilation brings forward the history of the office of Attorney General and of the Department of Justice as told in a volume entitled *Federal Justice,* prepared in joint authorship by Attorney General Cummings and Assistant Attorney General Mc-Farland and published in January, 1937.

The fact that this present compilation tells a rounded story is in itself significant. Aside from routine, the fifty-three men who, prior to March 4, 1933, occupied the position of Attorney General have left no voluminous archives. Few have made even a small number of public addresses or statements of aim in the all-important business of federal justice; and even then much that they have done has been lost. As lawyers, too, their public papers suffer from the obscurity of technicality or the anemia of legal caution. Moreover, the way of the law leads through unrecorded oral arrangements, consummated only by formal and oftentimes unrevealing documents—leaving a fading or lifeless record.

Homer Cummings, the fifty-fourth Attorney General of the United States, has, however, left an unusual number of documents which must some day be fitted into the historical mosaic of the time. The broad program of the administration of President Franklin D. Roosevelt brought unprecedented problems of law, justice, and administration to the desk of the Attorney General. The increasingly critical dilemmas of the criminal law, which had harried recent administrations and were bequeathed to the administration which took office in 1933, were the peculiar province of the nation's chief lawyer. The fact that the Department of Justice for the first time occupied a permanent home of its own was conducive to the planning and organization of its work. The spirit of change and the determination to adjust public institutions to the needs of the day invited study and curative action throughout the whole field of justice. Mr. Cummings used these opportunities to secure needed adjustments in the federal legal establishment, bringing to bear the mellowed experience of forty active years in public affairs.

His papers, peculiarly his own in style and thought, reflect something of the genesis and execution of a comprehensive undertaking. Some are in his personal possession. Others are scattered through tons of routine matter in the Division of Records of the Department of Justice as well as through the reports and hearings of congressional committees and in the *Congressional Record*.[1] Some appear in magazines and newspapers. Two books record his observations in government, law, and history.[2] The present volume includes addresses, articles, letters and telegrams, reports, legal arguments, statements for the press, memoranda, briefs, opinions, orders, and testimony at legislative hearings, from personal and official files. Public addresses or portions of addresses are used to knit together in concise statements the subject matter of extensive administrative undertakings. Many letters and office memoranda are included because of their pungency of statement and because they take the reader to the heart of problems as they were seen when they were as yet unfinished business. Departmental orders issued for the management of the Department of Justice itself, circulars issued to give general directions to United States attorneys and marshals in the field, and releases or statements for the press are included to illustrate their use as well as to present the contents of particular documents. Unless otherwise indicated, all materials reproduced or referred to in the text or notes are writings of the Attorney General.

A minimum of matter elsewhere published has been included —and then only to round out the story. An attempt has been made to eliminate trivia, repetitions, irrelevancies, and unneces-

---

[1] Many of Attorney General Cummings' addresses before various types of audiences and on a variety of subjects are to be found in the *Congressional Record* (see v. 77 [1933], p. 3347; v. 78 [1934], pp. 312, 851, 3677, same 4104, 5831, 7118, 9317; v. 79 [1935], pp. 4252, 9035, 10592, 10594; v. 80 [1936], pp. 59, 553, 6261, 7092, 7663, 9322; v. 81 [1937], App. pp. 7, 217, 604, 975, 1833; v. 82 [1937], App. p. 263; v. 83 [1938], pp. 23, 8672, App. 72, App. 2051, App. 2133, App. 2418, App. 3305).

[2] *Liberty under Law and Administration* (Scribners, 1934), is a collection of lectures at the University of Virginia. *Federal Justice—Chapters in the History of Justice and the Federal Executive* (Macmillan, 1937), produced in collaboration with Assistant Attorney General Carl McFarland, is a history of the Attorney Generalship, the Department of Justice, and federal legal administration generally.

sary details. In order to meet the limitations of space, only the central thought has been reprinted from each document. Behind each such general statement have been debate, planning, success and occasional defeat. At the most the selection of the documents and excerpts here collected is a mere sampling of the written record of the Attorney Generalship during the six-year period. Much of the activity of the Department of Justice has of course never been reduced to writing and can not be reproduced. No attempt is made to cover completely the vast field of litigation even though many cases not mentioned have had a degree of notoriety. Some legal proceedings are left unmentioned because they have been primarily the responsibility of other federal officers and agencies.

The arrangement of the selected papers has been made with a view to throwing light on all the major groups of problems with which Attorney General Cummings had to deal from 1933 to 1939. The several Parts vary greatly in length, arrangement, and subject matter, but each tells a story or presents a series of significant facts, from Part One, which shows the Department of Justice moving into its new home and functioning as the central law office of a great nation, to Part Six, which suggests something of the modes of performance of the complex duties allotted to the several divisions, bureaus, and offices.

Part Two, on Crime Control, covers such a broad field that most of the material is necessarily culled from addresses which summarize phases of the program. Part Three, on the struggle over constitutional interpretation, covers an even broader range of both litigation and policy. It has been arranged, therefore, in units built around explanatory and interpretative statements. It has been necessary to divide the documents on the President's recommendations for judicial reorganization between Part Three and Part Five—since the proposal to offset or replace the aged judges on the Supreme Court and other federal courts with new members was vitally related to the general subject of improving the personnel and functioning of the Judiciary as a whole, in which

Attorney General Cummings was perhaps even more deeply interested. Part Four, the successful undertaking to reform and make uniform practice and procedure in the federal courts, is largely built around addresses since the other materials are highly technical. Part Five, on Judicial Reform, is composed of statements, reports, and testimony, dealing with proposals for constitutional or legislative changes.

Part Six is composed of materials indicating the routine and methods of legal administration. It illustrates in a variety of ways the tasks performed by the Department of Justice in the several branches of its activity at home and in the field. The materials on the enforcement of the antitrust laws indicate something of the shifts of policy or emphasis which took place during the period. Materials on personnel terminate in comments on the resignation of Attorney General Cummings himself, as the culmination of personal plans which were in the making from the time it became apparent that the period of rapid, dramatic, and sweeping changes throughout the broad field of governmental activity had come to an end. The Appendix contains excerpts from addresses on the variety of occasions at which a cabinet officer, and particularly the Attorney General, is called upon to speak as an incident of his public office.

The papers have historical significance from several points of view. They throw light on the spirit of dealing with persons and problems. They reveal the aims and policies involved in important measures. They show something of the interrelations with other executive agencies, and the contacts of the Department of Justice with the Congress and the President. They will leave some questions. For instance, at least until the President's papers are published, there will be speculation as to the more precise role of Attorney General Cummings in the formulation of the so-called Court Plan (Part Three) generally attributed to and acknowledged by him. The papers, nevertheless, present significant facts, and show a definite implementation of the powers of the courts in the formulation of rules of practice and procedure, and an attempt to preserve judicial independence through the surrender by the Department of Justice of certain administrative powers over the courts.

Popular knowledge of the Department of Justice and its officers is usually limited, and understanding is often confused. While there is at times a recognition of achievement, old controversies have left an attitude of skepticism among many groups and interests. The turmoil over the enforcement of the antitrust acts since 1900, the legal opinions in the Ballinger-Pinchot dispute of the Taft administration, Attorney General Palmer's anti-radical crusade in the closing days of the Wilson administration, and the scandals and anti-labor actions under Attorney General Daugherty in the Harding administration have produced misgivings and have made law enforcement more difficult.

The Attorney General, as chief law officer of the federal government, is inevitably embroiled in many struggles. Great domestic changes are debated in the courts of justice, as well as in the Congress and the press. Other governmental officers and agencies call for legal aid or create local problems of diplomacy when the protective or enforcing arm of the law is withheld from them. Thousands of lawsuits, pending and imminent, in which hidden dangers may lurk, require quick judgment—for courts and litigants wait for no ponderous turning of official wheels. Administration of a vast organization engaged in divergent endeavors takes its toll through the steady grind of routine, however slight each item may be. A government whose diverse problems, deeds, and misdeeds filter through the Department of Justice on their way to or from the courts, lays a heavy burden on the Attorney General, whoever he may be. The struggle on a thousand fronts to find the facts, apply the law, and deal fairly with competing agencies and persons, public and private, is a task which has become with the years an almost impossible burden.

When the administration took office on March 4, 1933, more than three years of the worst depression in the nation's history had worked their smothering effects upon the land. The wheels of industry turned with sluggish motion or stood still. Unemployed workers walked the streets. Merchants cleared their shelves of old stock only at sacrifice prices. Farmers and home owners were unable to pay debts or stave off foreclosures. Banks found their funds tied up in loans they could not collect, backed often by securities which had little or no value. When panic brought the withdrawal and hoarding of deposits, banks were forced to close their doors.

The stress of hard times drove into crime people who might otherwise have remained within the law. The demand for forbidden alcoholic beverages, and the reward for supplying them, tempted large numbers into illicit manufacture, transportation and sale. It was a short step to kidnaping, racketeering, and extortion. The collapse of the stock market disclosed many wrongful business and financial manipulations, and caused still others on the part of men frantically striving to save themselves. The duty of enforcement officers was to enforce the law, yet the further destruction of confidence likely to result from publicity concerning the unsound conditions of banks and other financial institutions seemed a high price to pay for the punishment of a few men. The question of policy involved had to be answered by the new administration. Even in a field such as that of the enforcement of the antitrust laws, attitudes were similarly conflicting. Business was already fighting with its back to the wall. Public sentiment did not support action to prevent such cooperation among business firms as might be deemed necessary for survival. There was a demand for economy in government. Leadership and the definition of policy were needed in all these fields.

In the face of early retrenchment measures, the Department of Justice had difficult tasks before it. It had to prosecute prominent offenders of the financial world. It had to face, with a legislative program as well as with an enforcement program, the epidemic of crimes of violence throughout the country. It had to provide facilities for handling additional tax litigation transferred to it shortly after the administration came into power. It had to study the newly enacted emergency legislation, prepare for its defense before the courts, and work out jurisdictional lines between the Department and the several emergency agencies. It had to formulate an antitrust policy in conformity with the provisions and the intent of the recovery legislation. It had to be prepared to aid in the preparation of much new legislation desired by the administration. It had to handle an unprecedented increase in legal business in every field of federal activity. It had to render more opinions on legal questions in a single year than had been rendered during the entire previous administration.

The crisis in crime called for greatest concentration of effort in 1933 and 1934, while social disorganization due to the depression was still the outstanding characteristic of the times. In the public mind, to be employed by the Department was to be a "G Man." Persuading Congress to enact needed penal legislation was less dramatic than hunting down well-known criminals, but in the long run it was doubtless at least equally important.

Monetary legislation on the one hand, and regulatory measures such as the National Industrial Recovery Act and the Agricultural Adjustment Act on the other, involved distinct constitutional questions. The Attorney General gave personal attention in great detail to cases in the first category, and he successfully appeared in the Supreme Court as counsel for the government. Issues, facts, procedures, and cases in the other category were so diverse and numerous that he could exercise only supervisory and policy-making control. Throughout the period of government defeat in the Supreme Court in 1935 and 1936, the Attorney General sought ways to circumvent the hedge of nullifying decisions around the administration's social and economic program. Among other things, he thought much in terms of a constitutional amendment requiring justices to retire at the age of seventy. It was not until early in 1937 that, in lieu of the unwieldy device of constitutional amendment, he committed himself to the legislative device of adding new justices equal to the number of those sitting who were over seventy, or of replacing them if they should resign rather than see their courts increased in size. He called attention to the significant shift in the decisions of the Supreme Court after the reform measure was proposed and, however he may have felt about its ultimate defeat, he regarded the effort as amply repaid by the new line of decisions on social legislation.

Revision of procedure was too technical to interest the general public. It had none of the glamor of a war on crime or a series of battles over constitutional questions involving the immediate well-being of the people. While it had great long range significance for that portion of the public which might become involved in litigation, its immediate significance was largely for the judges and the bar. Attorney General Cummings brought to a successful termination a struggle for reform which had been carried on for many years, and he regarded his success in this field as one of the outstanding achievements of his administration.

His suggestions for judicial reform were interconnected outgrowths of study and experience in dealing with problems of law enforcement, constitutional interpretation, the reform of civil procedure, and the law's delays. The expansion of the work of the federal courts made necessary repeated additions to the number of judges. The nation had sought to secure a judiciary free from political and economic influence, but it had been unable to protect itself fully against stagnation or decadence on the part of judges entrenched by life tenure. Attorney General Cummings sought ways to eliminate or alleviate these related evils.

When the decisions of the Supreme Court seemed to make impossible any comprehensive control of business and industrial enterprise, deemed necessary under emergency legislation, emphasis was again placed on antitrust law enforcement to preserve a balance of power among business and industrial units, or at least to eliminate certain practices from the conduct of competitive warfare. A new line of policy was devised for enforcing the existing laws against monopolistic and unfair practices, and, as a result in part of influence exerted by the Attorney General, the Congress authorized an investigation as a preliminary step to revision of the laws.

Seldom in the course of American history have the people been in a state of mind to sanction readjustments on a comparable scale. Business conditions improved during the period, slumped, and improved again. The tempo of rapid change finally moderated in the consolidation of gains already made. Pressures abated and the work of the Department of Justice became stabilized in a more normal routine.

PART ONE

THE NATION'S LARGEST
LAW OFFICE

1. The Department of Justice Comes Home

[When Homer Cummings took the oath of office as Attorney General, the Department of Justice was centered in a leased building at Vermont Avenue and K Street, N. W., with groups of employees scattered among several other buildings in the city. In the latter part of 1934 the Department moved to its new home, a magnificent establishment of some 1,500 offices erected by the government in the area between Constitution and Pennsylvania Avenues and Ninth and Tenth Streets, N. W. The Attorney General's address at the dedication of the new building tells the story of the wanderings of the department. *Ed.*]

A succinct account of the establishment and wanderings of the office of Attorney General and the Department of Justice; from an address entitled "The New Home of the Department of Justice," delivered on the dedication of the new Department of Justice building, October 25, 1934, at exercises attended by the President, the Chief Justice, and other distinguished guests, as well as the officers and staff of the Department:

IT AFFORDS me great happiness to welcome you to the dedication of the new abode of the Department of Justice.

Truly, at last, we have come home and, in saluting this magnificent edifice, we indulge the hope that it may always be a house of Justice, a temple in which judgment, compassion, and understanding may ever find habitation and in which that fire "which burns at the heart of the world and whose name is Justice" may never die.

It is interesting to recall that during the greater part of its 145 years of existence the legal department of the United States has been a governmental wanderer, with no local habitation of its own and, for more than half that period, without an authoritative name. This has been due, no doubt, to the rather unusual manner of its development. Every other executive branch of the

3

national government was established by the Congress as a separate department at the time of its inception, but the Department of Justice is a product of the evolutionary process.

The post of Attorney General was created by the Judiciary Act of September 24, 1789; but it was an "office" that was created, not a "department." Edmund Randolph, of Virginia, became the first Attorney General. His compensation was fixed at the modest sum of $1,500 per year. Later he submitted various suggestions for the improvement of the service and, somewhat plaintively, pointed out the urgent need for at least one clerk. President Washington made these recommendations the basis of a special message to the Congress. The Committee to which the matter was referred reported favorably, but the Congress, evidently unimpressed, took no action. It was not therefore surprising that Attorney General Randolph described himself as "a sort of mongrel between the State and the United States; called an officer of some rank under the latter, and yet thrust out to get a livelihood in the former."

With the removal of the seat of government to Washington, the various departments were housed in nondescript buildings grouped about the President's house. No accommodations whatever were provided for the Attorney General. He was expected to furnish his own quarters, fuel, stationery, and clerk. He was "the forgotten man" of his day. President Madison, in a message to the Congress, movingly described the hardships which resulted from the failure to deal adequately with this situation. Nevertheless, the Congress, still unimpressed, took no action.

The suggestions which had been made by President Madison were renewed by President Monroe, and the Congress, in 1818, provided $1,000 for the employment of a clerk, and, in 1819, $500 for office rooms, stationery, and incidental expenses. In 1822 the Attorney General was furnished with his first official quarters—one room on the second floor of the old War Department building. There the office was maintained until 1839 when the Attorney General, whose staff now consisted of a clerk and a messenger, and who had acquired the nucleus of a library, moved into rooms located on the second floor of the Treasury Building.

Sixteen years later the office was removed to its third home, a brick building on the southeast corner of Fifteenth and F Streets. Here it remained until 1861, when, upon the completion of the south wing of the Treasury, a suite of rooms was provided on the first floor of the new addition.

Finally, after eighty-one years of existence, the office of the Attorney General had expanded to such an extent, both in functions and in personnel, that it became, in reality, one of the executive departments of the government. In recognition of this fact, the Congress enacted the law of June 22, 1870, entitled "An Act to establish the Department of Justice." This act provided that the Attorney General should be the head of the Department, created the office of Solicitor General, and provided for two Assistant Attorneys General. It gave to the Attorney General the direction and control of United States attorneys and all other counsel employed on behalf of the United States, and vested in him supervisory powers over the accounts of United States attorneys, marshals, clerks, and other officers of the federal courts.

After the creation of the Department of Justice, the Attorney General and his immediate staff remained in the south wing of the Treasury Building, while the Solicitor General and one Assistant Attorney General, with their clerical forces, were quartered on F Street, near Fourteenth, and the other Assistant Attorney General had to be content with a room in the cheerless basement of the Capitol.

In 1871, the Attorney General leased for a period of ten years the second, third, and fourth floors of the Freedmen's Bank Building on Pennsylvania Avenue and the entire Department occupied this space, with the exception of one Assistant Attorney General who still retained his gloomy quarters in the subterranean fastnesses of the Capitol. In 1882 the Congress authorized the purchase of the Freedmen's Bank building. This was the first real home of the Department of Justice. But it was not to be a permanent one. The Department remained there until 1899, when the Congress passed an act reciting that "the building now occupied by the Department of Justice is too small for its purpose, is unsafe, overcrowded, and dangerously overloaded, and has been pronounced unsafe, after examination by the proper officials of the Treasury Department." The sum of one million dollars was appropriated for the erection of a new building.

After the approval of this Act, the old building was abandoned and demolished to make way for the new structure. Meanwhile, the Attorney General and his personal staff took up their abode in the Baltic Hotel on K Street, between Vermont Avenue and Fifteenth Street. The other members of the Department were distributed in various parts of the city; and the library was placed in the old Corcoran Art Gallery. But, once more, the hope that the Department was to have a home of its own failed of realization, for it was found that a suitable building could not be erected for the sum provided; and the Congress promptly rescinded the appropriation.

After the lapse of several years, and to relieve an almost intolerable situation, the Attorney General leased the building at the northeast corner of Vermont Avenue and K Street. This building, until a few days ago, has been occupied by a major portion of the office force. It proved to be so inadequate in size that it was necessary to secure space in seven additional buildings.

I have indulged in this recital of the vicissitudes and wanderings of the Department of Justice that you may realize with what keen delight we, at last, take possession of our permanent home. You can easily visualize the growth and size of the Department by merely looking at this handsome and imposing structure.

We are grateful to the Congress for the foresight and thoughtful consideration which provided the funds for its erection. We salute, with profound appreciation, our immediate predecessors, as well as those who designed this beautiful building and all those who have had a part in its construction, for the care and wisdom which they brought to their difficult task.

Our thoughts turn, also, with abiding gratitude to the long

line of devoted public servants who, since 1789, have served in this Department and whose labors have ever been actuated by a lofty spirit of patriotism. * * * With us, at this hour, I seem to feel the quickening presence of those giants of other days—Edmund Randolph, William Pinkney, William Wirt, Roger Brooke Taney, Isaac Toucey, Caleb Cushing, Jeremiah S. Black, William M. Evarts, Richard Olney, Judson Harmon, Joseph McKenna—as well as a host of others whose high labors in the cause of justice have hallowed this spot. In literal truth this great building is their monument. With humble hearts and a certain sacred pride we take it from their hands and dedicate ourselves to the purposes to which they devoted their lives. May its doors never be closed to those who would do Justice, or to those who suffer from Injustice.

2. Chief Counsel for the United States

The traditional functions of the Attorney General and his staff as the representatives of the government of the United States in the courts and in matters of public law and legal administration; from an address in the National Radio Forum, April 24, 1933:

THE Attorney General of the United States, it has frequently been remarked, is at the head of the largest law office in the world. About nine thousand employees and officials fall within its direct supervision. It is a complicated organization dealing with questions affecting hundreds of millions of dollars and with the most sacred of human rights. Its functions have never been more important or more vital than they are today. * * *

There seems to be an impression in many quarters that the chief duty of the Department of Justice is to detect, and punish, violators of the federal criminal laws. This, of course, is one of its essential functions, but there are others of great importance. For instance, the Department defends all civil claims against the government. This involves the consideration of an endless number of cases dealing with suits based on contracts; claims made for the refund of taxes asserted to have been overpaid; and various other matters of a similar nature. In addition, the Department represents the United States in innumerable civil suits to recover moneys claimed to be due to the government; it proceeds in matters of land condemnations and in other types of litigation too multifarious to mention.

During the year ending June 30, 1932, there were commenced in the United States district courts alone 126,363 cases to which the government was a party, as compared with 22,541 in the fiscal year of 1914. While the prohibition law has undoubtedly brought about the greatest proportion of this increase, other factors have contributed in no small degree. New penal statutes, the enforcement of which devolves upon the Department of Justice, are constantly being enacted. The revenue laws are frequently changed, thereby raising new questions for judicial determination. The questions which can arise under the customs laws seem to be without end. Literally the suits there are legion. The engineering and construction projects of the government have multiplied enormously in recent years. Thus, there has been an inevitable enlargement of the functions of the Department of Justice. It has grown as the nation has grown. The new legislation enacted by the present Congress will undoubtedly, in due course, bring new responsibilities and duties to the Department of Justice.

Moreover, the Attorney General acts as adviser to the President and to the heads of the various executive departments in matters involving questions of law and is frequently called upon for both written and oral opinions. The services of the Department are invoked in connection with the drafting of new legislation, especially with reference to matters involving new and difficult problems. In a word, the Attorney General, together with the available machinery of the Department of Justice, is at the disposal of the government of the United States in performing the functions of attorney and counsellor at law. The client is the United States of America and this client receives advice from time to time and, when necessary, is represented in the courts of the land.

* * *

A vexatious problem with which I have to deal grows out of the enthusiastic manner in which many people endorse themselves for attachment to the public service. It must not be forgotten that the work of a lawyer employed by the Department is specialized to a very considerable degree, requiring intimate knowledge of the branches of the law peculiar to governmental administration. It is manifest, therefore, that there can be no indiscriminate removal from the service of those who are efficiently and faithfully discharging their duties. Such changes as are to be made will be designed for the betterment of the service and for that purpose alone.

One of the most important functions the Attorney General is called upon to perform has to do with the recommendation to the President of candidates for appointment as federal judges, United States attorneys, and United States marshals. These officials are concerned in a most intimate fashion with the rights, liberty, and welfare of our people in all parts of the country. In particular the members of the Judiciary (whose appointments run during good behavior and therefore in most instances for life) must be selected with the utmost care. So far as I am concerned, there will be no undue haste in making such appointments. Each person under consideration will be studiously investigated as to his character, capacity, knowledge of the law, and all other attributes which should be possessed by an upright, honest, and impartial judge. This particular responsibility lies heavily upon me. From personal knowledge I know, and in every fiber of my being feel, that the discharge of this duty is a solemn responsibility. Many mistakes may be repaired but an error in the selection of such an official leaves a permanent and almost ineradicable mark upon the structure of our government. I am not saying these things to magnify the tasks of the Department of Justice, but merely to state, in direct and simple language, what purpose it is we are supposed to serve and how we are endeavoring to meet the duties imposed upon us.

3. Early Problems

The legal problems raised by emergency legislation; from a radio address on "The Department of Justice and the New Deal," June 10, 1933:

UNUSUAL and difficult questions undoubtedly confront us. The field of administrative law, already clouded by much uncertainty, is being widely extended. The functions and limitations of the various departments and agencies of government have taken on new aspects; and the attainment of administrative unity in this vast complex of powers presents a fascinating problem. There is, for example, an increasingly intimate relationship between the Department of Justice and the other departments of government in connection with the extended administrative functions which recent legislation has created. * * *

My duty is not to make new law, but to construe and uphold the law and the Constitution as applied and interpreted by the courts. Equally, it is my duty to help give practical effect to the ends sought by the recent legislation and the policies of the administration. In this effort I shall hope to be governed by a sense of economic realism rather than by any narrow legalism— to be helpful and constructive rather than hypertechnical or reactionary; and to make the application and interpretation of these emergency laws fit not only into our established jurisprudence, but also into the new patterns of economic planning and broad statesmanship which these disturbed times demand.

From a second address in the National Radio Forum, January 10, 1934:

In numbers of opinions rendered, new legislation and executive orders reviewed, and in many other phases of civil activity, including gold hoarding, National Recovery Administration mat-

11

ters, tax cases, land condemnations, customs matters, and the vast realm of government litigation, this Department has been called upon in the last ten months to undertake a hitherto unparalleled volume of work.

Last year, among other functions, it was our duty to enforce the Volstead Act. Today a very different problem is presented. The federal government is no longer called upon to enforce a law which, in many sections of the country at least, did not have the support of public opinion; but it still remains the duty of the government to protect the dry states from the illegal importation of liquor. The Webb-Kenyon Act, the Reed Amendment, and the terms of the Twenty-first Amendment impose obligations which cannot and should not be avoided. This duty we accept and intend to discharge, so far as the available appropriations will permit. On December 5th, when the Prohibition Amendment was repealed, eleven states had constitutional prohibition and seventeen more had drastic laws preventing the sale of intoxicants. These twenty-eight states are clearly entitled to the support of the federal government in enforcing any laws on this subject which they may see fit to enact.

From Annual Report to the Congress, January 5, 1934, p. 1:

Under the terms of the executive order of June 10, 1933 (No. 6166, Organization of Executive Agencies), and subsequent executive orders, the work of the Department has been augmented and changed in many important respects. In addition to this, a great amount of legal work incident to the administration and enforcement of recently enacted legislation has placed a heavy burden upon the Department.

4. Organization for Federal Justice

[The present organization of the Department of Justice is the product of many decades of slow development. Only to a limited degree is it governed by statute. The Act of June 22, 1870, pursuant to which the Department was established, provided that the Attorney General was "empowered to make all necessary rules and regulations for the government of said Department of Justice, and for the management and distribution of its business." Aside from the limitations of appropriation acts, statutes creating the positions of the principal officers, and the act creating the Bureau of Prisons, the Attorney General is given a free hand in the organization of the Department. Changes from year to year and from Attorney General to Attorney General vary in terms of the problems of the time and the staff and organization needed for handling them. The following materials indicate the nature of the establishment as reorganized late in 1933. Additional materials with reference to personnel and related topics will be found in Part Six of this volume. *Ed.*]

From an address in the National Radio Forum, April 24, 1933:

IN TIMES of great prosperity, when things appear to run themselves, our people are inclined to take their government for granted. When trouble develops we appreciate more acutely the extent to which our welfare is dependent upon the proper functioning and economical administration of the various departments of the government. Such periods result in a sharp awakening of public interest. We are passing through such a period at the present time. Clearly there should be a thorough overhauling of every department of our government. This is a process which cannot be accomplished by a wave of the hand. It is going to require persistent, intelligent, and unrelenting efforts over a very considerable period of time.

From Order No. 2507 of December 30, 1933:

In order more effectively and expeditiously to carry on the work of the Department of Justice, it is hereby ordered:

The Department of Justice shall consist of the following

offices, divisions, and bureaus, the functions and subdivisions of which are set forth in Schedule A,* which is hereto annexed and made a part hereof:

The Office of the Attorney General
The Attorney General, Homer Cummings

The Office of the Solicitor General
The Solicitor General, James Crawford Biggs [1]

Administrative Division
The Assistant to the Attorney General, William Stanley [2]

Antitrust Division
Assistant Attorney General, Harold M. Stephens [3]

Tax Division
Assistant Attorney General, Frank J. Wideman [4]

Criminal Division
Assistant Attorney General, Joseph B. Keenan [5]

Claims Division
Assistant Attorney General, George C. Sweeney [6]

Lands Division
Assistant Attorney General, Harry W. Blair [7]

Customs Division
Assistant Attorney General, Charles D. Lawrence [8]

* The elaborate schedule assigning functions or classes of litigation is not included. It was modified by Orders No. 2790 of December 9, 1935; No. 2507 of January 20, 1936; No. 3001 of July 22, 1937; and other less formal designations of duties.
[1] Succeeded by Stanley Reed (1935-1938) and Robert H. Jackson (1938—).
[2] Succeeded by Harold M. Stephens (1935) and Joseph B. Keenan (1936—).
[3] Succeeded by John Dickinson (1935-1937), Robert H. Jackson (1937-1938), and Thurman W. Arnold (1938—).
[4] Succeeded by Robert H. Jackson (1936-1937) and James W. Morris (1937—). Created pursuant to Section 5 of Executive Order 6166 (see Circular No. 2494, November 9, 1933, and Order No. 2415, June 13, 1933).
[5] Succeeded by Brien McMahon (1936—).
[6] Succeeded by Angus D. MacLean (1935), James W. Morris (1935-1937), and Sam E. Whitaker (1937—). For the Alien Property Bureau of this Division, see Order No. 2575, July 2, 1934.
[7] Succeeded by Carl McFarland (1937—).
[8] Succeeded by Joseph R. Jackson (1934-1937) and Webster J. Oliver (1938—).

Office of the Assistant Solicitor General [9]
Assistant Solicitor General, Angus D. MacLean [10]

Division of Investigation
Director of Investigation, J. Edgar Hoover

Bureau of Prisons
Director of Prisons, Sanford Bates [11]

Bureau of War Risk Litigation
Director, Will G. Beardslee [12]

Office of the Administrative Assistant to the Attorney General
Administrative Assistant to the Attorney General, Charles
E. Stewart [13]

Office of the Pardon Attorney
Pardon Attorney, James A. Finch [14]

All necessary transfers of functions and personnel to conform to Schedule A are hereby authorized. All prior orders inconsistent with the foregoing are hereby superseded.[15]
This Order shall take effect as of January 1, 1934.

*The opening radio address of "The Cabinet Series," July 16, 1937,
summarizing the organization and services of a reconstituted Department of Justice:*

Today the nerve center of the Department of Justice is the
Washington headquarters, with its 2,184 employees, housed in

[9] Newly created by Act of Congress (48 Stat. 307-8, June 16, 1933) at the
recommendation of the Attorney General.
[10] Succeeded by Golden W. Bell (1935—).
[11] Succeeded by James V. Bennett (1937—).
[12] Succeeded by Julius C. Martin (1936—).
[13] Succeeded by Thomas D. Quinn (1937—). Reporting to and under the
direct supervision of the Attorney General (see Order No. 3022).
[14] Succeeded by Daniel M. Lyons (1936—).
[15] The Taxes and Penalties Division, later the Bond and Spirits Division, was
added, under Joseph Lawrence as Director (see Order No. 3074, January 20, 1938).
   In addition to the officers named, there is the Executive Assistant to the
Attorney General, Ugo Carusi, who is the immediate personal assistant and man-
ager of the Attorney General's office; the Special Executive Assistant in charge of
public relations (Henry Suydam, 1934-1937; Gordon Dean, 1937 —); and the
Special Assistant in immediate charge of legislative matters, Alexander Holtzoff.

the new Justice Building which was occupied for the first time in October, 1934.   Great changes have come since September 24, 1789, when the post of Attorney General was created.   Compare the spacious Justice Building of today with its well lighted courts, its muraled walls, its library of 80,000 volumes, with what William Wirt found when he succeeded to the post of Attorney General in 1817—a small office, no records, a meager supply of stationery. * * *   The picture today is far different even from that of June 22, 1870, when the Congress passed a statute establishing a Department of Justice.   Indeed, things have improved considerably since 1933 when the Department of Justice was housed in portions of eight widely scattered buildings in the city of Washington.

In the new edifice are the offices of the Attorney General, the Solicitor General, the Assistant to the Attorney General, the Assistant Solicitor General, and five Assistant Attorneys General who head divisions devoted to claims, taxes, antitrust matters, criminal cases, and lands.   Here also are the headquarters of the Bureau of War Risk Litigation, Bureau of Investigation, and the Bureau of Prisons.

From this point the activities of the field forces in the 93 federal districts are directed.   These include the 458 United States attorneys and assistants, and the 1,032 marshals and deputies, scattered from Shanghai to the Virgin Islands, from Alaska to the Canal Zone.   The 46 field offices of the Federal Bureau of Investigation are located at strategic spots throughout the country, as are 265 field attorneys, the staff of the Customs Division, the 173 probation and parole officers, and 2,000 employees of the Federal Prison Service.   All these comprise the field staff. * * *

Next in command to the Attorney General is the Solicitor General who has charge of all government interests in the Supreme Court, and who also authorizes or rejects the taking of appeals to the intermediate courts.   The heavy responsibility of this officer becomes apparent when it is understood that almost 40 percent of all litigation in the Supreme Court concerns the

United States. Many of the important cases in the Supreme Court are the climax of nation-wide litigation. For example, 2,000 separate suits were controlled by the decision of the Supreme Court invalidating the Agricultural Adjustment Act.

The third ranking officer in the Department is the Assistant to the Attorney General who has charge of all matters of administration, personnel, and legislation affecting the Department. This includes the laborious work of investigating all candidates for judicial office and all officers and employees of the Department including United States attorneys and marshals.

Next we have five divisions charged with work in particular fields, each under the supervision of an Assistant Attorney General. First, the Antitrust Division. This division receives and investigates each year hundreds of complaints of monopoly and restraint of trade out of which grow civil and criminal proceedings. Here, also, the orders and processes of the various federal administrative tribunals—Interstate Commerce Commission, Federal Trade Commission, Federal Communications Commission, and others—are defended or enforced. Labor cases and agricultural regulations are also for the most part referred to this division.

Pursuant to an order of the President in 1933, all tax litigation in the federal government was consolidated in the Tax Division of the Department of Justice. Cases handled during the fiscal year 1936 involved over 286 million dollars. In a single case recently decided, the government secured a judgment for twenty million dollars. But these sums, large as they are, do not begin to reflect the importance of the tax litigation, for the decision in one small test case, where the amount sued for is inconsequential, frequently results in a saving of many millions of dollars. You have heard a good deal lately of ingenious schemes devised to evade the federal tax laws. If the tax is due and the case comes to the courts, one of our tasks is to see that such schemes do not receive judicial blessing.

In the Claims Division of the Department are handled the countless money suits, both against and in behalf of the United

States. There is a theory of law well known to all lawyers that the sovereign cannot be sued in its governmental capacity without its consent. Ours, however, is a liberal government and in a long series of statutes it has submitted itself to private suits in many types of cases. These arise out of contracts for building battle-ships, erection of public buildings, dredging and improvement of rivers and harbors, the building and maintenance of dams, locks, drydocks, sea walls, army supplies, and the carrying of the mails, as well as suits for the alleged use and infringement of patented devices. The list is a long one.

The Lands Division handles all litigation in connection with public lands, which include the national forests, national monuments, reservations, and lands acquired for river and harbor and other governmental uses; irrigation and reclamation matters; federal power litigation; insular and territorial affairs; Works Progress Administration and Public Works Administration matters. This work involves condemnation proceedings, the securing of rights of way, the sale and purchase of land, and the giving of opinions on the validity of title before public funds may be expended. Indian affairs and property constitute a fascinating part of this division's work. In these Indian cases and in the land grant litigation there is unfolded the whole panorama of the West and the thrilling story of the expansion of the American people.

You may judge the volume of work of the Customs Division from the fact that 174,239 cases were pending when the last annual report was compiled.

A vast and heavy routine, you may conclude. Hardly that. Behind the routine of law work, hidden away in the file of virtually every case, there is drama and adventure. Law is a story of struggles, both petty and great. But always there is human interest aplenty.

This is particularly true of that phase of the Department's work dealing with crime. During the past few years this phase has received special emphasis. In 1933 there was a large group of persons tutored in methods born of the liquor traffic and hungry for new fields of lucrative crime. During prohibition crime paid and paid well. It was one of our tasks to see that in the newer fields of kidnaping, extortion, bank robbery, and racketeering crime did not pay.

Laws were enacted to reach criminals who played hide and seek with law authorities in the twilight zone—the neutral corridor—between state and federal jurisdiction. The Bureau of Investigation was strengthened. The number of agents was increased. They were equipped with firearms and greater powers of arrest. Training facilities were broadened. The finger-print file passed the 6,000,000 mark.

The first task, then, was apprehension, the next, prosecution. This latter work is performed by the Criminal Division of the Department and the United States attorneys. Last year these attorneys, stationed in every state, territory, and insular possession, secured convictions in over 94 percent of the cases brought in the federal courts. But the conviction record is not particularly important. There is inscribed on one of the walls of the Department of Justice building the following statement: "The United States wins its point whenever justice is done its citizens in the courts." That has been our guide.

But there is more to crime control than what transpires in the court room. Convicted persons divide into misdemeanants and felons, intelligent and dull, men and women, sick and healthy, dangerous and harmless, young and old, first offenders and repeaters—all different. Each must be classified, segregated, fed, housed, trained, and after a period of months or years returned to freedom. Here is a heavy responsibility. It falls upon the Bureau of Prisons.

Nineteen penal institutions are operated, ranging from jails and camps to the famous Alcatraz. The variety of detail involved is amazing. For example, at one of our prison farms last year I followed with almost maternal anxiety an experiment in egg production with hens whose coops are artificially lighted. With equal interest I found myself at work on parole surveys, the facts in a pardon application, and the opening of a Bureau of Investigation office in Puerto Rico.

There are other phases of the Department's activities which should be mentioned. The work of the Assistant Solicitor General calls for a particularly high degree of care and skill. In this office are drafted official opinions, executive orders and proclamations; and during the fiscal year 1936 action was taken by this official on 2,532 offers in compromise.

The Taxes and Penalties Division has been patiently at work collecting liquor taxes which were not paid during the dry era. Thousands of ex-bootleggers have been assessed and, I might add, with good financial results. Time prevents even a brief description of the work of the other officials and functions of the Department, such as that of the Alien Property Custodian, the Pardon Attorney, the Board of Parole, and others.

This great maze of duties is naturally confusing to many. And some Attorneys General, even in the days when life in the Justice Department was much less complex, found the work irksome. Attorney General Evarts in 1869 said: "I shall return to my business of farming and lawing and leave to the newspaper correspondents the conduct of affairs." Still, with all the buzzing of busy personnel and the ponderous turning of legal wheels, it is a department with a fine *esprit de corps* and with a unity which is remarkable.

PART TWO

CRIME CONTROL

1. Crime, Citizens, and Officers of the Law

[The name of the Department of Justice symbolizes in the minds of many people the enforcement of criminal laws. This indeed is one, though only one, of its important functions. Crime control, throughout most of the period of the nation's history, has been left largely to state and local governments. Federal criminal jurisdiction, traditionally, has been limited to such matters as violations of customs and internal revenue laws, postal laws, and legislation against counterfeiting. In the field of crime suppression, as in other fields, however, federal activities have increased with the spread of transportation and communication facilities and the expansion of industrial enterprise. A Criminal Division was set up in the Department of Justice a number of years ago, and an efficient Bureau of Investigation began to emerge out of a small investigatory unit. During the Hoover administration the "National Commission on Law Observance and Enforcement" produced significant materials of value for students of criminology.

When the new administration came into power in 1933, the subject of crime was of much more than routine importance. The era of prohibition, with the widespread disapproval and flouting of law which accompanied it, had been a breeding period for lawlessness as well as disrespect for law generally. Bootleggers, and the highjackers who preyed upon them, had become a serious threat to the preservation of domestic order. The depression brought hard times to prohibition criminals as well as to legitimate business men, and drove other men into crime in search of a livelihood. Ruthless groups of racketeers and kidnapers terrorized various sections of the country, often dramatizing their activities sufficiently to capture youthful imaginations and lead a new generation into crime. The end of prohibition meant the impoverishment of prohibition violators and their retainers, unless they could expand their activities into other fields.

It was clearly apparent that the nation faced a crisis in the field of criminal law enforcement quite as serious as the crisis prevailing in business and industry. Along with his other tasks, therefore, Attorney General Cummings gave earnest attention to working out a crime control program. *Ed.*]

*From an address entitled "A Twelve Point Program," delivered
before the Continental Congress of the Daughters of the American
Revolution, April 19, 1934:*

THE suppression of crime has become a national problem of
the first magnitude. Hundreds of millions of dollars are
expended each year in efforts to arrest, to prosecute, and
to restrain the criminal classes. Moreover, large sums are spent
annually by private individuals and corporations in the maintenance of guards and industrial police forces and for insurance
against loss by criminal acts. The yearly toll exacted of society
by predatory criminals, in the form of property destroyed, values
converted, money stolen, and tribute enforced, constitutes a
ghastly drain upon the economic reserves of the nation. Undoubtedly crime costs our country several billion dollars each
year; and it is conservative to say that there are more people in
the underworld carrying deadly weapons than there are in the
Army and the Navy of the United States.

Clearly the institutions and agencies upon which we have
relied for the enforcement of the law have not adequately performed their proper functions. In many localities there exists
an unholy alliance between venal politicians and organized bands
of racketeers.

Then, too, certain unworthy members of the bar maintain a
close contact with the criminal classes and prostitute an honorable
profession by resorting to improper practices in order to save their
clients from the legitimate consequences of their crimes. These
recreant members of the legal profession take skillful advantage
of the cumbersome and archaic procedural rules governing criminal cases which still persist in many of our jurisdictions. Trials
are delayed, witnesses die or disappear, and appeals upon frivo-
lous grounds are all too frequent. As Mr. Justice Holmes once
very shrewdly observed: "At the present time in this country,
there is more danger that criminals will escape justice than that
they will be subjected to tyranny."

In many parts of the country law enforcement officers are not selected primarily because of their training and general qualifications, but are given positions on a basis of political preferment. Where this is true, each change of political administration is accompanied by a reorganization of the local constabulary. It is impossible to build up an efficient and courageous force of officers so long as they are constantly subject to the whims of political fortune.

Another difficulty grows out of the unfortunate situations which result from a lack of cooperation so often characteristic of the activities of the various law enforcement agencies of the country. Still another serious phase of the problem has to do with the relative uncertainty which exists with respect to the dividing line between the jurisdictions of the federal and state governments. Here lies an area of relative safety—a twilight zone—in which the predatory criminal takes hopeful refuge.

At the time of the adoption of the Constitution of the United States there was little need for the federal government to concern itself with the problem of crime. Due to the isolation of different settlements, the operations of criminals were, of necessity, local in their nature. You will recall that when John Adams first went from Boston to Philadelphia, his wife, the famous and delightful Abigail Adams * * * made note of the fact that it took five weeks to receive a return letter from that "far country."

We are no longer a nation whose problems are local and isolated. The growing density of our population and the development of high speed methods of transportation have resulted not only in a large increase in our crime rate, but, also, have given to many offenses an interstate character. As a celebrated American jurist has said, "The maintenance of an organized society has come to involve much more than repression of local offenders against local laws. Where one hundred years ago the chief concern was the common defense against foreign aggression and savages, today it is rather a common defense against organized, antisocial activities extending beyond state lines, operating without regard to political boundaries, and threatening any locality where there is possibility of plunder or profit." Crime, today, is organized on a nation-wide basis, and law-breakers extend their activities over many states. In a well-remembered kidnaping case, which occurred during the past year, the operations of the criminals took place in seven states; and it was necessary for the agents of the Department of Justice to go into nine additional states before their efforts to solve the crime and bring its perpetrators to justice proved successful. The seven states referred to have an area of about 683,000 square miles, which exceeds in extent the combined areas of Austria, Denmark, France, Germany, Italy, Holland, Switzerland, England, Scotland, and Wales. This illustration indicates the extent of the difficulties involved and accentuates the need of a nation-wide approach to the problem. The federal government as a matter of fact has no desire to extend its jurisdiction beyond cases in which, due to the nature of the crime itself, it is impossible for the states adequately to protect themselves.

From "Criminal Law Administration—Its Problems and Improvements," an address before the Continental Congress of the Daughters of the American Revolution, April 15, 1935:

Much has been said about the importance of an informed public opinion. This aspect of the matter is not for a moment to be underrated; but all too often public officials are content merely to lecture the citizen for his alleged indifference to the duties which inhere in citizenship. This seems to me to be somewhat less than fair and an altogether too convenient escape from the responsibilities which rest upon the public officials themselves. Our people have placed such officials in key positions of power and trust, and have a right to expect that their high responsibilities will be faithfully and efficiently discharged.

Our experience has shown that what might have appeared to be public indifference was, largely, the apathy of the disillusioned, resulting from the frequent failure of public authorities to supply the service and the type of leadership to which the

American people are entitled. Once a reasonable course of action has been projected, and representatives of federal, state, and local interests have been brought together for concerted action, public opinion is inspiringly spontaneous in its support of the common objectives. * * *

The immediate and obvious action requires the employment of emergency techniques, and intensified efforts along accredited lines—the meeting, as it were, of force with force. And let no one imagine for a moment that militant methods are not necessary to curb the criminal depredations that threaten our common life. But I should like to stress a different, but equally important, line of procedure. I refer to the calm, dispassionate, thoughtful efforts which must be employed if the plague of crime is to be brought under permanent control. * * * They are not apt to be dramatic. Results will not soon be evident. They will be unspectacular, but it is worth doing and it can be done. * * *

One of the pathetic fallacies which misleads so many ardent friends of the movement to deal with crime is the idea that permanent results can be achieved through some kind of *tour de force.* We know, of course, that it cannot be done in that fashion. This may seem discouraging to some people, but our surest guarantee of success is to know, first, what the problem is, and, secondly, how it must be met. * * * The help that is needed to sustain this movement is not the sporadic efforts of zealous enthusiasts, but, rather, the assistance of earnest workers of practical experience, familiar with the obstacles that are certain to arise and everlastingly determined to overcome them.

* * *

There can be no higher form of patriotism, no greater contribution to the public good, than * * * to demand that the administration of criminal justice shall be modernized and placed upon a basis of maximum effectiveness throughout the United States; that the operations of courts, of prosecutors, of police departments, of prison officials and of parole boards shall be lifted above the swirling currents of politics; and that the detection, apprehension, trial, and punishment of criminals shall be confided to trained professional groups free to reach unhampered decisions and not forced to balance conclusions against the devitalizing and distorting considerations of political or personal interest.

The people of the United States want this job to be done. The law enforcing agencies of the country, whatever their jurisdictions, are in a more cooperative mood than at any time within memory. Moreover, there has been an acceptance of a measure of federal leadership that would have been deemed impossible only a short while ago. The signs are propitious and the time is ripe for a sweeping advance all along the line.

A crime control program is planned; from a radio address on "The Department of Justice and the New Deal," arranged by the Columbia Institute of Public Affairs, June 10, 1933:

There is here a large opportunity for constructive reform; and it is engaging my earnest consideration. * * * The campaign I have in mind, and which I expect to pursue, contemplates a steady, unrelenting, and persistent effort continued over a long period of time. No doubt there will be set-backs and disappointments and misunderstandings and, very likely, considerable criticism both just and unjust. That, however, is neither avoidable nor important. * * *

But neither the wisest leadership nor the best brains the government can summon to its aid, nor the most enlightened legislation it can devise, nor the most efficient administration its departmental heads can give, will alone solve our problems. What we can do is to shape and marshal and coordinate the constructive and recuperative forces of the nation; and legislate so that they can operate. But the government cannot put life into the dead nor courage into the coward. When all is said and done, the ultimate verdict rests with our citizens. * * * This is no narrow or partisan program. It is as vital as patriotism and as broad as America.

2. Alcatraz

[The suppression of lawlessness, in so far as the government and the individual criminal are concerned, leads through three, progressively simpler stages: detection and apprehension, trial and conviction, and the execution of imprisonment or other forms of sentence. Even imprisonment, the less arduous phase of law enforcement, faced the possibility of a breakdown in the early 1930's. Prisoners with the capacity for self-dramatization executed bold escapes. Serious prison riots and attempts to break from prison occurred. Prisoners of the prominent gangster type succeeded in gaining influential contacts outside prison walls. The move for relentless coercion of obedience on the part of confirmed and incorrigible criminals clashed with the objective of the reform of other prisoners who, with proper handling, might be made into good citizens.

The federal prison system, barely under way as a result of a reorganization in 1929-1930, might, by example, point the way to a satisfactory solution or become a miserable example of governmental impotency in the attempt to execute the sentences of those who failed to avoid detection and the subsequent steps leading to imprisonment. Accordingly, the federal government sought a model institution for the confinement of such prisoners as inciters of prison riots; of recidivists, "repeaters," and long-termers; incorrigibles, predatory criminals, and those of evil influence; of "escape artists," gangsters with outside contacts; and other vicious and dangerous types of prisoners. *Ed.*]

An idea; from an office memorandum to Special Assistant Joseph B. Keenan, August 1, 1933:

IN THE agenda of things to be considered, when we get around to it, would it not be well to think of having a special prison for racketeers, kidnapers, and others guilty of predatory crimes, said prison to be in all respects a proper place of confinement. * * * It would be in a remote place—on an island, or in Alaska, so that the persons incarcerated would not be in constant communication with friends outside. * * * Please think these things over.

Memoranda from Sanford Bates, Director of the Bureau of Prisons:

August 8, 1933

At your request, please find herewith estimate of the probable maintenance charges of the prison at Alcatraz Island if operated by the Department of Justice on the basis of 200 prisoners. * * * I am of the opinion that the removal of perhaps one hundred of the most desperate men in each Atlanta and Leavenworth would be a distinct benefit to those places and would aid in the prevention of threatened demonstrations. In accordance with your idea, however, Alcatraz should be reserved for desperate or irredeemable types of individuals.

October 2, 1933

Major Wheeler and Major Finley of the War Department called today. After discussion as to certain details which must be arranged coincident with the transfer of Alcatraz Island, it was agreed that Major Wheeler would proceed at once to prepare the formal papers for the transfer of the property and that he would submit the same to this Department for our approval as to form. He felt that the papers could leave him on Wednesday morning and that they ought to be signed by the Secretary before the end of the week.

A letter to the Secretary of War, George H. Dern, October 14, 1933:

Thank you for your letter of October 13th, transmitting two copies of a revocable five-year permit, granting to the Department of Justice the use of Alcatraz Island and the War Department installations, with certain provisions and conditions relative to movable property and service. * * * May I express appreciation of your prompt and cooperative action in arranging for the transfer of Alcatraz Island.

[Note: By act of Congress approved April 26, 1938, the permanent transfer of Alcatraz to the Department of Justice was authorized and later effected. *Ed.*]

An announcement; from a radio address on "The Recurring Problem of Crime," arranged by the National Anti-Crime Conference, October 12, 1933:

Our records demonstrate that a large percentage of the serious crimes are committed by men who have escaped from prison. These men operate in groups and make a study of methods by which to avoid punishment when they are caught. At large they prey upon the public, confined they plan and encourage prison outbreaks. Intimidation, bribery, and violence are their accustomed methods. The majority of the inmates of our prisons are comparatively well behaved, but a few desperate criminals among them present a menace to any penal institution. Relatives, friends, and fellow members of the gang congregate near the prison to be of help when a favorable opportunity is offered. This condition exists where large penitentiaries are located.

For some time I have desired to obtain a place of confinement to which could be sent our more dangerous intractable criminals. Such a place should be apart from the large centers of population, preferably on an island which would not be easy of access. It was not my purpose to find a prison in which the inmates would be subjected to any unusual or unreasonable environment, but rather a place which would be apart and inaccessible, so that the holding of the inmates would be assured and their influence removed from that of the better class of prisoners.

You can appreciate, therefore, with what pleasure I make public the fact that such a place has been found. By negotiation with the War Department we have obtained the use of Alcatraz Prison, located on a precipitous island in San Francisco Bay, more than a mile from shore. The current is swift and escapes are practically impossible. It has secure cells for six hundred persons. It is in excellent condition and admirably fitted for the purpose I had in mind. Here may be isolated the criminals of the vicious and irredeemable type so that their evil influence may not be extended to other prisoners who are disposed to rehabilitate themselves.

Order establishing a United States Penitentiary, July 1, 1934:

By virtue of the authority vested in me by the Act approved May 14, 1930 (46 Stat. 326), by the Act making appropriations for the Department of Justice for the fiscal year ending June 30, 1935, approved April 7, 1934, and by virtue of all other authority vested in me, I, Homer Cummings, Attorney General of the United States of America, do hereby order that a United States Penitentiary be and it hereby is established at Alcatraz Island, California; and that it is hereby designated as a penitentiary for the confinement of such United States prisoners as may be committed thereto by order of the Attorney General or transferred thereto from other penal or correctional institutions of the United States.

Given under my hand and the seal of the Department of Justice this first day of July, 1934.

Office memoranda to Sanford Bates, Director of the Bureau of Prisons:

September 17, 1934

As you know I was very deeply concerned as to the manner in which the transfers were to be made to Alcatraz. The arrangements, under your direction, were admirably made and carried out perfectly. I am greatly pleased and congratulate you and those who aided you in this admirable performance. A slip-up or mistake, or even an unfortunate happening of some kind, would have entailed very unpleasant reactions and consequences. It was a difficult job. I do not believe that very many people realized how ticklish a job it was. You are entitled to the thanks and applause of all who know anything about the subject.

October 28, 1935

You will recall that quite a long while ago I spoke to you about endeavoring to work out some system by which it might be possible for inmates of Alcatraz to graduate, as it were, from that institution. The subject is full of difficulty, but is well worthy of intensive study.

I do not want to do anything that will impair the distinct advantage we have gained by the establishment of Alcatraz and the discipline imposed and the conditions existing there, as I am satisfied that the deterrent effect has been very marked with reference to certain types of criminals with whom we had to deal with the utmost vigor. On the other hand, I am not quite prepared to write over the door of that institution, "Abandon hope, all ye who enter here."

An office memorandum from Executive Assistant Ugo Carusi, March 7, 1938:

In looking over the weekly report for the Prisons Bureau I ran across an interesting item. A survey indicates that the inmates of Alcatraz outshine the inmates of our other institutions in the matter of subscriptions to magazines. Not only is the percentage of subscribers the highest, according to population, but the magazines themselves are of the higher type. This may be accounted for by the fact that there are no direct commitments to Alcatraz, all of its inmates coming from other institutions; a kind of postgraduate situation!

Publicity; a memorandum from the Acting Director of the Bureau of Prisons, approved August 23, 1935:

We have been congratulating ourselves that Alcatraz Penitentiary is as inaccessible to the outside as any prison could be, but the Warden reports that he has just had a conference with a writer of the San Francisco *Daily News,* in which the latter states he has received a paper from a prisoner in Alcatraz through "subterranean channels," the substance of which is to the effect that several prisoners are insane, made so by cruel treatment; also

that we have had several suicides and attempts at suicide. * * *
While this may be nothing more than an attempt on the part of
the press to "smoke us out," it is the kind of transaction we may
anticipate as time goes on. * * *

As the Warden explained to the newspaper writer in this
particular instance, our policy at Alcatraz has been not to give
out information concerning prisoners, or to particularize, per-
sonify, or identify any of the prisoners for publicity purposes.
In no instance should we be put in the position of becoming a
disputant with a prisoner, or be drawn into a publicity article in
an attempt to answer any rumor or charge made to or through
newspapers. * * * The prisoner in Alcatraz should lose the place
in the public notice which attended his capture and trial.

Since this brings up an important administrative policy, I
recommend that the warden be advised that the Attorney General
is squarely back of him in the enforcement of the policy of "no
news relative to prisoners in Alcatraz," as explained above, and
that should any newspaper article appear, the Department will
neither affirm nor deny, unless it should seem advisable in the
interest of public policy to make some general statement of fact
not relating to any individual prisoner.

*A letter to Will H. Hays, President, Motion Picture Producers
and Distributors of America, Hollywood, California, August 27,
1937:*

My attention has been called to an article appearing recently
in the San Francisco *Examiner* indicating that there is to be a
Cosmopolitan production of a motion picture of Alcatraz. The
article, written by Dorothy Manners, quotes Mr. Bryan Fox, the
producer, giving the impression that the picture is to present an
authentic description of the federal government's penal program
at Alcatraz. I wish to protest most earnestly the production of
any motion picture on this subject and also to deny the inference
that the picture can have any authenticated details of the routine

of the institution. Such a picture could not possibly reflect accurately the objectives the department is seeking to attain at Alcatraz without our cooperation, and this of course we cannot extend. Our policy in this regard has been carefully thought out and seems to me sound and in the public interest.

While the institution at Alcatraz is an essential part of a unified and well-rounded federal penal system, nevertheless it contains only about 300 prisoners out of the nearly 16,500 in federal penal institutions. A production along the lines indicated will emphasize the difficulties of treating the few men we have at this one institution, will give a false impression of our whole penal program, and will create in the public mind a distorted picture which cannot but adversely affect our efforts to redirect and help worthy ex-prisoners in their efforts to become law-abiding and self-respecting members of the community.

I sincerely hope that the picture will not be produced and that I shall have your cooperation in this matter.

A letter to George Creel, Washington Bureau, Collier's Magazine, April 13, 1936:

There will be no objection at all to . . . a staff writer of *Collier's* seeing Warden Johnston of Alcatraz Penitentiary at his office on the mainland for the purpose of doing an article on him. I regret, however, that it will not be possible . . . to visit the prison itself inasmuch as the Department has declined to grant such permission to other writers and I do not feel that I should make an exception in this case.

3. A Legislative Program

From office memoranda to Assistant Attorney General Keenan:

February 10, 1934

HERE are two additional suggestions with reference to the suppression of crime.

First, that each large police department throughout the country should have what might be called a crime liquidation bureau which would have to do primarily, and perhaps exclusively, with crimes that had remained unsolved for say a period of sixty or ninety days. The argument is that a special department dealing with this particular follow-up method would get results whereas now many unsolved cases go into permanent cold storage.

Secondly, that some movement be instituted to encourage trial judges, both federal and state, to refuse to grant bail after conviction and sentence in the trial court unless there is very substantial reason for believing that there might be a reversal on appeal. This suggestion was made to me by former Secretary of State Stimson who said it worked very well in New York at a time when he was United States attorney.

I should be very glad to have you think this latter matter over and discuss it with me at some convenient time.

February 12, 1934

Following up my memorandum of Saturday in the matter of delay by appeal and the manner in which this subject has been brought home to us in connection with the Delaware County cases, it occurred to me that you might make some inquiry, or cause one to be made, which will answer the following questions, namely:

1. In what proportion or to what extent do U. S. district judges grant bail on appeals after verdict in criminal cases?

2. What proportion of these appeals are successful in the circuit court?

3. How often does the circuit court interfere in such matters in the manner in which the Circuit Court for the Third Circuit interfered with the Delaware County cases?

4. What are the statutory powers of the district judges and the circuit court judges in such matters?

5. Is any legislation required to meet any evil that these inquiries may disclose?

From an address entitled "A Twelve Point Program," delivered before the Continental Congress of the Daughters of the American Revolution, April 19, 1934:

In response to manifest necessity, and entirely within constitutional limitations, the Department of Justice is urging the Congress to pass certain important bills now pending before that body, as follows:

1. A law dealing with racketeering which will make it a felony to do any act restraining interstate or foreign commerce, if such act is accompanied by extortion, violence, coercion, or intimidation.

2. A law making it a federal offense for any person knowingly to transport stolen property in interstate or foreign commerce.

3. Two laws strengthening and extending the so-called Lindbergh kidnaping statute.

4. A law making it unlawful for any person to flee from one state to another for the purpose of avoiding prosecution or the giving of testimony in felony cases.

5. A law making it a criminal offense for anyone to rob, burglarize, or steal from banks operating under the laws of the United States or as members of the Federal Reserve System.

6. A law making it a criminal offense for any person to kill or assault a federal officer or employee while he is engaged in the performance of official duties, and a law to provide punishment

for any person who assists in a riot or escape at any federal penal institution.

7. A law to make the husband or wife of a defendant a competent witness in all criminal prosecutions.

8. A law to limit the operation of statutes of limitations by providing that such statutes shall not prevent the prompt reindictment and prosecution of a person after a prior indictment has been held to be defective, and a law to prevent dilatory practices by habeas corpus or otherwise.

9. A law to provide that testimony on behalf of the defendant to establish an alibi shall not be admitted in evidence unless notice of the intention of the defendant to claim such alibi shall have been served upon the prosecuting attorney at or before the time when the defendant is arraigned.

10. A law to repeal the statutory provision which has been held to prohibit comment upon the failure of the accused to testify in a criminal case.

11. A law to regulate the importation, manufacture or sale, or other disposition of machine guns and concealable firearms.

12. A law authorizing agreements between two or more states for mutual cooperation in the prevention of crime.

This is the twelve-point program of the Department of Justice.

Interpretation of the federal kidnaping act; from an office memorandum to Assistant Solicitor General MacLean, November 28, 1934:

I realize the force and implications of your very excellent memorandum dealing with the kidnaping statute. I have serious doubts, however, whether a court, bearing in mind that it is a criminal statute, would give it so sweeping an interpretation that it would include practically every kind of kidnaping except the one expressly excluded. Moreover, to make such an interpretation it would be necessary to take all the vitality out of the words "and hold for ransom or reward, or otherwise." In other words, this phrase would be sheer surplusage. I realize what was said by Senator Copeland and in other parts of the record, but at the same time it must be remembered that the same Congress declined to pass a law dealing with the general subject of lynching. It is difficult for me to believe that the Congress inadvertently passed an anti-lynching statute where kidnaping and interstate commerce were involved.

I imagine that the motive which actuates some of the complaints which have come in grows out of the hatred of lynching and the desire to have the federal government enter that field. * * * The crime actually perpetrated was murder, which is clearly not a federal offense. To say that the federal government cannot enter the case in its major aspects, but can enter the case in its minor aspects, presents, to say the least, a somewhat anomalous situation. * * * I also have in mind the possibility that if we should attempt to use the statute in an unusual manner we would not get any practical results and we might also raise difficulties and questions which might be embarrassing in connection with our general anti-crime program.

From "Criminal Law Administration—Its Problems and Improvement," an address before the Continental Congress of the Daughters of the American Revolution, April 15, 1935:

It cannot be too often reiterated that these statutes were designed to supplement, not to supplant, the law enforcement machinery of the various states. * * * The cases that have come to the attention of the Department since the enactment of the statute punishing the robbery of national and Federal Reserve Banks may be regarded as typical. In one case two defendants were indicted in the state courts. The defense attorneys, unjustly but successfully, attempted to turn the case into a trial of the state police officers and an acquittal resulted. The judge reprimanded the jurors. Later the state authorities appealed to the federal government for cooperation. The records of the state investigators were turned over to the federal authorities. The two defendants were brought to trial in the federal courts and were sentenced to fifteen years each.

In another case, involving four defendants, the local police department suggested that the federal government take charge of the prosecution—a suggestion due, in part at least, to a fear of the abuse of the parole system in that state. Three months later a verdict of guilty was secured as to three of the defendants and the fourth pleaded guilty. Each defendant was sentenced to twenty-five years on each of two counts in the indictment. This group constituted one of the most notorious bank robbery gangs in that region. Since these convictions there have been virtually no bank robberies in that section of the country.

In many other cases, while assisting in the detection and apprehension of the criminals, the federal government has cooperated with the state authorities in the prosecution of bank robberies in the state courts. In short, the two systems of law enforcement have worked hand in hand; and have worked successfully.

Another striking example of cooperation between the federal government and the states is found in the fugitive felon law. This law makes it a federal crime for a person to flee across state lines to avoid prosecution for certain major felonies. It is also a criminal offense for a person to flee across state lines to avoid giving evidence in a felony case. One object of this statute is to give to the states the benefit of federal removal machinery in instances where the ordinary interstate extradition procedure is unduly time-consuming or inadequate. The statute has been invoked in a number of cases to detain fugitives in distant states by federal process until the interested state could put in motion its own extradition procedure.

Further legislation; office memoranda to Assistant Attorney General Keenan and Special Assistant Henry Suydam:

May 7, 1935

What do you suggest should be done with regard to the pending crime bills and similar legislation in which the Department of Justice is interested? There are a number of bills which I had hoped would go through without serious difficulty. Perhaps we can do something to help these bills along. I should be glad to have your opinion on these matters and your suggestions.

Please let me know particularly about the firearms bill. From the last information I had on the subject this seemed pretty well stalled and had not even been introduced.

January 13, 1936

You will note that Governor Lehman has been very active in pressing the crime reform program in New York. Similar efforts have been made elsewhere, but he seems to be getting at it in a rather thoroughgoing fashion. I am hopeful that you and Mr. Miller * will analyze his program, as he has outlined it in messages and announcements, with a view to letting me know as soon as possible how it fits in with our general program.

A summary; from "Progress Toward a Modern Administration of Criminal Justice in the United States," delivered at the Annual Meeting of The North Carolina Conference for Social Service, April 27, 1936:

There was introduced in the 73rd Congress what has been termed the Twelve-Point Program of the Department of Justice, which ultimately resulted in the passage of twenty-one important enactments. The immediate result of these various acts and measures was to enable the Federal Bureau of Investigation and the Criminal Division of the Department of Justice to deal successfully with a series of outrageous kidnapings, and to put an end

* Special Assistant Justin Miller.

to the operations of many notorious murderers, gangsters, bank robbers, and hold-up men, whose activities had made American justice a subject of wonder to the rest of the world. * * * Encouraging as these events were, thoughtful persons realized that much remained to be done.

[Note: The process and program of corrective legislation in the criminal field was continuous. See final recommendations on disparity of sentences, public defenders, and other subjects, Items VIII, IX, and XI, Annual Report to the Congress, December 31, 1938. *Ed.*]

4. State and Federal Jurisdiction

[The enactment of new federal legislation for crime suppression immediately raised questions of constitutionality, based on federal encroachment upon the traditional activities of the states. The Supreme Court had previously upheld such federal statutes dealing with interstate crime as the Mann Act and the Motor Vehicle Theft Act, but the Attorney General of the preceding administration had been reluctant to assent to extension of federal activity in the criminal field. Faced with the growing seriousness of the crime problem, however, Attorney General Cummings deemed it necessary to extend federal control over the no man's land, the "unholy sanctuary" of crime, which lay between state and federal jurisdictions. Statutes were prepared with care. Developments were carefully studied. Moreover, the new crime program contemplated a minimum of federal interference with local enforcement and a maximum of assistance to, and cooperation with, state and local authorities. Generally, among lawyers, the validity of these measures has been assumed. *Ed.*]

From an address at "The Attorney General's Crime Conference,"
December 10, 1934:

T HERE was a time when, with a slow moving civilization, it was possible to treat crime largely as a local problem.

The sphere of federal criminal law enforcement related almost exclusively to highly specialized phases of governmental action, as, for instance, where the work of the Post Office Department or the Bureau of Internal Revenue was interfered with by criminal acts. Today the intricate web of improved highways, of railway lines, of telephone and telegraph service, to say nothing of the automobile, airplane, and the radio, have, for many practical purposes, erased the divisional lines between states and between their various local subdivisions. Where the stealing of a horse a generation ago was a matter to be handled by the local sheriff and the local courts, the theft of an automobile today is not only a matter of local law enforcement, but, in the event of interstate transportation, it becomes a federal problem as well. Examples could be multiplied indefinitely of the many and varied offenses which have become defined under the authority of the commerce clause and the postal provisions of the federal Constitution.

During recent years there has been an increasing demand for the extension of federal power under an apparent assumption that therein lies the remedy. Unfortunately, it is not a problem which can be so easily solved. Just how far the work of the federal department should go and just what the form of interrelation between the agencies representing the state and federal governments should be is, of course, one of the crucial questions which face us. Implicit in this phase of the matter there are constitutional questions and considerations of policy. Of this we may be sure—there is an urgent demand for an adequate solution, and an increasing necessity for the intimate and friendly cooperation of all official agencies in determining the best method of approach and in developing the most effective means of administration of which we are capable.

From "The Lessons of the Crime Conference," an address at the closing session of The Attorney General's Conference on Crime, December 13, 1934:

It is only fair to say that the vast extent of our country, the existence of state lines and the complicated and antiquated character of our law-enforcing machinery have presented problems of peculiar difficulty, especially in the face of an increasing population, with constantly multiplying social and industrial problems and interrelated in its contacts by the amazing developments in transportation and communication. To put it another way, America has outgrown its penal system. The difficulty all along has not been to diagnose the disease, but to find and apply the remedy. Much good work in the past has failed of its purpose because of the lack of an adequate follow-up system. Different groups have approached the problem from different angles. Progress has been made in one spot, only to be counter-balanced by losses in other places.

The whole movement against crime, in any national sense, has been sporadic, intermittent, disjointed, and totally lacking in correlation. With the amazing development in recent years of crimes of violence, perpetrated by criminals of a roving character who pass rapidly from the scene of their crimes into other jurisdictions, there has been presented, in very acute form, the question of the duty of the federal government. More and more it has become apparent that the Department of Justice, not only in the matter of discharging its own obligations, but for the purpose of securing some sort of national leadership in a national emergency, has been brought into a position of especial prominence.

An office memorandum to Solicitor General Stanley Reed, December 21, 1935:

At your convenience please let me know a little more definitely about the status of the case now on the way to the Supreme Court which brings in question the constitutionality of the Lindbergh law. Perhaps you could let me have a brief statement of how the case arises, what the background is, and what the precise question is that will be presented to the Court. Also, you might let me know what bearing a decision in this case might have on the whole crime program of the Department of Justice.

[Note: The case referred to was *Gooch* v. *United States,* 297 U. S. 124, 82 F. (2d) 534, 298 U. S. 658, in which the Supreme Court refrained from discussing the constitutional question. *Ed.*]

From "Progress Toward a Modern Administration of Criminal Justice in the United States," before the North Carolina Conference for Social Welfare, April 27, 1936:

The political philosophy dominant in this country at the time of the Declaration of Independence emphasized, as of primary importance, the individual rights of man as distinguished from the requirements of organized society. It was natural that this concept should have been uppermost in the minds of our forefathers. Government, in the countries from which they came, had been largely oppressive in character. The criminal law there administered was frequently employed as a whip to compel obedience upon the part of reluctant, if not recalcitrant, subjects. Most of the early colonists came to America to escape the compulsions of arbitrary laws which seemed to them unwarranted interferences with their religious, political, and social beliefs. Moreover, the country to which they came was a wilderness in which each individual lived largely on his own responsibility. In the small clusters of population which constituted the first communities, only the most primitive forms of governmental structure were possible. Until comparatively recent years there has always been a frontier beyond which the restless could find escape. It was natural, therefore, that in the building up of our laws—particularly those which related to crime and punishment—there should have been a sharp emphasis on the rights of the individual and a constant resistance to any form of social control which seemed to involve a limitation upon individual activity.

In the early days, the scope of criminal law was relatively narrow. The prevailing conditions of life made unnecessary the elaborate present-day structure of criminal statutes. Such crimes as were committed were, of course, matters of vital consequence to the localities in which they occurred. The court house was a center of community interest and court day was an occasion for the assembling of the populace from the far corners of the country. When a murder was committed it was of such general concern as to disrupt the quiet of the countryside and to warrant the calling out of all available resources for the capture and punishment of the criminal. In fact, it was a matter of such moment that, in the absence of an effective local government, vigilante groups were active and methods of hue-and-cry and outlawry were employed. * * *

There came to our shores a heterogeneous population. * * * The mere territorial extent of our domain, while affording opportunities for the assertion of the vigor of the pioneer, at the same time subjected the influence of law and order to a process of indefinite attenuation. Industrial and manufacturing communities, great centers of population and of enterprise, grew up, each with its particular texture, atmosphere, and standards of public morals. Between some of these large centers the greater part of Europe might have been superimposed with room still left for an almost uninhabited frontier. There came into existence forty-eight states, each sovereign within its own jurisdiction, each with its own capital, each with its own government, and each with a population drawn together through some common interest in the natural or human advantages of its peculiar environment. The federal government, established through fiat on the banks of the Potomac, isolated with conscious purpose from the great centers of population, trade, manufacturing, business, and industrial life, bore a relationship of limited and delicate character toward all of these. * * *

Between federal and state jurisdictions there existed a kind of twilight zone, a sort of neutral corridor, unpoliced and unprotected, in which criminals of the most desperate character found an area of relative safety. It was the unholy sanctuary of predatory vice.

From "Progress in Cooperation in Crime Control," address at the Third General Assembly of State Governments, January 22, 1937:

When the federal government in 1934 decided that the time had come, in view of a menacing crime condition, to assume responsibilities theretofore not acknowledged on an adequate scale, we kept in mind existing constitutional compulsions, the complex structure of our form of government, and the practical difficulties of what I might term our continental geographical situation.

The federal government sought to deal with crime in its interstate aspects. We have resisted, and we shall resist, all attempts to bring the Department of Justice into the sphere of state or local criminal activities. We have sought to develop in the Department a structure and a technique predicated upon cooperation with state and local agencies toward the accomplishment of our common aim—the progressive control of crime in the United States. * * *

But cooperation between the federal government, on the one side, and the forty-eight states, on the other, is but a part of the process, and it might even be considered the simpler part. What is of equal importance, and what is more difficult to achieve, is cooperation among the governments of the forty-eight states and, within each state, between the state government and local jurisdictions. But here also great progress is being made. The National Conference of Commissioners on Uniform State Laws has been engaged in preparing and sponsoring reciprocal legislation having to do with the administration of criminal justice. The American Law Institute, with its Code of Criminal Procedure recommended for adoption in 1930, has made an important contribution. Its offer to prepare another code, governing the whole field of criminal law and its administration, is one that should have our ardent support. Following the enactment in 1934 of congressional consent to compacts between the states for the purpose of controlling crime, there was established an Interstate Commission on Crime which contains in its membership an official representative of each state. Here again a number of measures have been recommended to tighten up and to facilitate the administration of justice in the criminal field. Not the least evidence of how the leaven of progress is working are the numerous state and regional conferences that have been held in all parts of the United States, some of them organized on a permanent basis, and all of them straining toward a series of objectives designed to bring about the kind of law enforcement essential to the welfare of our people. A more effective and wider exchange of criminal information, interstate supervision of parolees and probationers, the simplification of extradition, the facilitation of close, or "hot," pursuit of criminals from one state to another—these are some of the projects engaging the attention of those responsible for leadership in this inspiring enterprise. * * *

In short, the movement for a unified, integrated, consistent, and effective administration of criminal justice is making real strides. And while we shall meet with obstacles and make mistakes in this empirical process of accommodating modern law enforcement to the exigencies of our complex scheme of government, we can feel confident that the principles of our approach are sound.

5. A National Crime Conference

[The Attorney General convened a national conference on crime, December 10-13, 1934, which was attended by 600 representatives of national, state, and local institutions and organizations, public and private. The complete proceedings are published in a volume entitled "Proceedings of the Attorney General's Conference on Crime." *Ed.*]

Planning the conference; from an office memorandum to Special Assistant Gordon Dean, November 8, 1934:

I AM wondering if the subject of racketeering is being sufficiently stressed in our program. I pass this along for your consideration. Also might it not be well to have something on interstate compacts? * * * Also regarding the general subject of number games and lotteries generally, there seems to be so much discussion about it lately that some place on the program should be made for this subject.

Generally speaking, I should like to have the program as a whole so comprehensive that practically every aspect of the crime problem could be touched on at one time or another. More formal addresses could deal with the more important questions, but a whole lot of topics could be taken up in the part of the program devoted to open discussion.

I should be very glad if you would think this over carefully with a view to making our program so complete that it will touch every aspect of the problem. I am especially concerned about the open discussion periods.

From the opening address at the Crime Conference, December 10, 1934:

Let us sit down and reason together, in a non-critical mood, ready, impersonally and objectively, to consider a common problem, ready to admit error as well as to assert the validity of meth-

ods now in use, and prepared to collaborate in devising and setting up new procedures. In order to do this we must be patient
and generous. We must recognize, first of all, that it is impossible for us to cover, in the time allotted to this conference, all
the details of our varying interests. Many of us, by reason of our
experience, have been thinking largely in terms of particular problems and of specialized issues. Obviously, unless we can quickly
reach common ground, we are likely to spend too much of our
time discussing our own experiences and living over our own
ideas. * * *

The program which has been prepared will make it possible
to give consideration to all pressing phases of the crime problem;
for example, crime prevention, detection, apprehension, police administration, prosecution, court organization and administration,
pardon legislation, and others which will immediately occur to
you. An examination of the subjects which have been assigned to
the various speakers will reveal that the sessions have been arranged, not with the idea of having specialized discussions of
unique problems, but rather with the idea of presenting challenging issues as between different agencies and different objectives.
For this reason each session will cover a number of topics, each
one of marked interest to particular groups, with the hope that
there may be thus secured a wide interchange of views and a
searching analysis into the validity of assumptions made by one
group or another. * * *

The fate of this conference is in your hands. * * * There
is one point which I most emphatically wish to stress, namely,
that it is not intended that this conference shall meet, discuss, ad-
journ, and be forgotten. Nor is it intended that its sole product
shall be a group of pious resolutions. What we want are concrete proposals for action; constructive suggestions as to why and
how certain things should be done, and by whom.

Extract from "Progress Towards a Modern Administration of Criminal Justice in the United States," an address at the Annual Meeting of The North Carolina Conference for Social Service, April 27, 1936:

There was summoned to meet at Washington, D. C., in the winter of 1934, a conference on crime, based upon a new method of approach. Theretofore the public, expressing itself through conferences or otherwise, had appealed to the public authorities for aid in dealing with the menace of lawlessness. Now the process was about to be reversed—the government was to appeal to the public for its thoughtful advice, for its sustained interest, and for its active help.

Attended by six hundred delegates, each an expert in his own field, the conference sought to approach the question in as dispassionate, as objective, and as practical a manner as possible; to consider crime in the light of the experience of the participating groups, without at the same time getting into the field of particular crimes, specialized suggestions, and minute professional preoccupations.

This gathering, I believe, elicited an unusually valuable exposition of basic facts and was of great assistance in enabling the public to see the problem of crime in its broader aspects and to see it whole. Since that time a number of state conferences of a similar nature have been held. Many things are afoot. The psychology of our people has undergone a wholesome change. No longer does the public glorify the gangster. Its admiration and its gratitude go out to those who, daily taking their lives in their hands, seek to enforce the laws that are our common protection.

A national crime control movement emerges; from "The Lessons of the Crime Conference," address at the closing session of The Attorney General's Conference on Crime, December 13, 1934:

It would be idle, of course, to expect that the problem of crime could be solved by a single conference or, indeed, by a series of conferences, or, for that matter, in our generation. Crime conferences have been held before, bringing together people of high moral purpose, engendering enormous enthusiasm, and leaving behind but little in the way of tangible results. * * *

As I see it, many of these efforts have been relatively ineffective because of conditions over which their sponsors had no control. There was not available any clearing house for information, or any authoritative moving force for continued activity. It is this missing element which I believe it to be our duty to supply. It is an enormous responsibility; but, if I do not mistake the temper of this conference, it is a responsibility which its delegates desire the Department of Justice to assume; and, in behalf of that Department, I accept the responsibility. It is not the purpose of the federal government to usurp the functions of the state and local police units. It is not the desire to extend activities in violation either of constitutional limitations or the customs of our people. The motive is to attempt to meet a need which long has existed; and to assist, complement, and serve the law enforcing agencies of America.

When this conference passes into history, it will leave behind it concrete practical results that can be translated into effective action. I shall not deal in detail with the admirable resolutions which were adopted. It is enough to say that they contemplate the development of a permanent structure which will permit and secure the concentration and cooperation of forces which will make themselves felt in behalf of law and order, not merely for a few brief hours, but for three hundred and sixty-five days in the year. It is not the function of this conference to attempt to work out a detailed solution of delicate and intricate subjects. The time limit alone forbids such a course. It is, however, its province to suggest the erection of a suitable and permanent structure that will afford the means of working out these problems. Thus measured, this conference is a triumphant success. The keynote is cooperation, with all that it implies, and the permanent structure, not only for continued technical training and instruction but for the marshaling of the forces that affect and sustain public interest.

For convenience in thinking, and at the risk of laying myself open to criticism for inaccuracy, the problem, as I see it, breaks up into four major topics.

First: There is the question of devising and securing a proper law-enforcement system. This deals with federal activities, state activities, and local activities. It involves study and action in the whole field from the time a criminal act is perpetrated, through the processes of detection, apprehension, trial, conviction, punishment, probation and parole, to the time when the prisoner is returned to society. This includes, also, the matter of interstate compacts, legislation, and similar topics, as well as the scientific study of crime, methods of detection, schools of training, the improvement of our legal procedure, and the purging of the bar of those who debauch its high purposes.

Second: There is the question of personnel. No matter how effective a system may be, it is worthless in the hands of those not competent to operate it. We have come to realize that those who enforce the law and undertake to represent the public in this high relationship of trust and responsibility should not be men who look upon their occupation as a temporary job, but regard it in the highlight of an important and, indeed, a sacred professional undertaking. Allied with this topic there will be the questions of training, qualification, character, methods of appointment, tenure of office, freedom from the blight of partisanship or improper political or other influences, and related questions.

Third: There is the question of crime prevention. Herein lies the problem of the treatment of the juvenile offender, the first offender, and children who have begun to fraternize with the so-called gang. It will involve also aspects of social questions, far too numerous to mention.

Fourth: There is the question of public support. This will involve the proper interpretation of the work of officials to the public, so that the people may be informed of what is going on, and why, to the end that a healthy morale may be developed which will strengthen the arm of the law-enforcing agencies, encourage and stimulate the work of honest officials, and so affect the psychology of our people that there will be a universal abhorrence of crime and a fixed determination to eradicate it. * * *

The immense difficulties inherent in these matters must be apparent to all. We are in for a long-time program. It will require unremitting service, continued over a long period of years. The resolutions which have been adopted do not make the mistake of trying to do too much. They have the merit, however, of showing the way, and that is what we most imperatively need— a chart and a compass. * * *

This has not only been a conference, it has been a school. Review the program; read carefully the resolutions; note the names of those who have addressed you, both in the formal sessions and in the highly stimulating discussion hours; observe the wide range of topics discussed; consider the thought and labor that have been devoted to these extraordinary addresses, and you will agree with me that when our records have been compiled in permanent form, they will constitute an unfailing source of authoritative information upon every aspect of our difficult problem.

Following up the Crime Conference; from a letter to the President, February 1, 1935:

Sometime, before too many days slip by, I should like to have the opportunity of discussing the crime situation with you with a view to outlining some of the plans we are formulating. I recently designated an Advisory Committee in this matter. * * * This committee is set up for the purpose of advising in connection with the suggestions which grew out of the recent Crime Conference. * * * In general, our plans are working out exceedingly well, and I am greatly encouraged.

6. Enforcement Training

Police training under way; from "Progress Toward a Modern Administration of Criminal Justice in the United States," an address at the Annual Meeting of The North Carolina Conference for Social Service, April 27, 1936:

WITH respect to the practical recommendations of the Crime Conference of 1934, time does not permit me to offer a discussion, except to state that one of the important actions taken was that approving the establishment at Washingon, D. C., of a scientific and educational center to provide national leadership in the broad field of criminal law administration and the treatment of crime and criminals. The Advisory Committee appointed to consider this recommendation approved the creation of the proposed center within the structure of the Department of Justice, and it was decided to use the existing facilities of the Department for this purpose.

For several years, under the guidance of its skilled Director, Mr. J. Edgar Hoover, there had been in successful operation in the Federal Bureau of Investigation an excellent training school for the instruction of special agents. * * * It was decided to make that training course, with suitable adaptations, available to selected law enforcement officials throughout the United States.

The first Police Training School was held in the summer of 1935, and a second group of law enforcement officers was graduated a short time ago. Plant, technical equipment, scientific facilities, lecturers, and instructors are made available for this important work. The sole expense to those who take these courses is the cost of transportation to and from Washington, and of personal maintenance during the period of instruction. The Department cannot, of course, offer these advantages indiscriminately, but it can and does undertake to supply to a limited number of experienced police officials instruction in all of the manifold scientific and technical subjects in which special agents of the Federal

Bureau of Investigation are now trained.   In this way we both teach and learn.

We have followed the subsequent careers of the graduates of this school.   Many of them, promoted in rank and given increased compensation, are now passing on this instruction to their colleagues and subordinates in various state and local police jurisdictions.   The results, thus far, have been highly satisfactory.

* * *

In the selection of personnel, both at Washington and in the field, the Federal Bureau of Prisons has recognized the importance of professionalizing the service.   A comprehensive plan of in-service training for the custodial officers is now being put into operation and in the future all promotions and salary raises will be made upon the basis of the completion of the training requirements as well as the maintenance of satisfactory service records. Not only does the proposed scheme offer an opportunity for developing the best qualities in candidates for the position of prison officer, but it also assures to them something in the nature of a career service.

This training course for federal prison officials, now maintained under the experienced direction of Mr. Sanford Bates, Director of the Federal Bureau of Prisons, can, I hope, be made available under proper conditions to selected state and other officers in this field.   While this is a difficult arrangement to work out, it is being given serious study.

A letter to Henry F. Ashurst, Chairman, Senate Committee on the Judiciary, May 26, 1936 (Sen. Report No. 2111, 74 Cong. 2 Sess.):

Supplementing my oral statement to the Senate Judiciary Committee yesterday, with reference to S. 4673, permit me briefly to state the principal reasons for the passage of the bill, as follows:

Section 1 of the proposed bill would supply basic and specific authority for the following:

1. The maintenance of the system now in vogue in the Fed-

eral Bureau of Investigation in connection with the training of special agents.

2. The maintenance in the Federal Bureau of Investigation of the police school which has already met with great success and which should, in my judgment, be supported and strengthened. Under this system training of the same type and character as that given to our special agents is supplied to carefully selected representatives of various police departments. This is a highly important work, not only of instruction, but in furthering our program of cooperation as it affords intimate contact with police agencies throughout the country and tends to the dissemination of information as to the technique, qualifications, and system approved by the Department of Justice.

*   *   *

4. The maintenance in the Federal Bureau of Prisons of the present system of training guards and other members of its administrative staff, with authority to extend this type of instruction to selected and specially qualified groups.

*   *   *

S. 4673 does not contemplate any reallocation of authority in the Department of Justice, or any radical departure from the existing practices and program. It is a constructive measure designed to support and justify the activities already under way, to make them more effective, and to place the Department of Justice in a position to gather and supply information upon all aspects of the crime problem.

From "Law Enforcement as a Profession," an address before the International Association for Identification, September 30, 1937:

In the moving pictures and magazines of a few years ago the forces of law and order were usually symbolized by a rather clumsy policeman who spent most of his time chasing criminals, rarely catching anyone, and then usually the wrong one. The policeman was a favorite subject for ridicule. And similarly, until very recent times, detective work was symbolized by that creation of Conan Doyle—Sherlock Holmes. There was always a checkered cap, a large pipe and a magnifying glass. The members of the criminal element, on the other hand, were usually represented as shrewd individuals, equipped with the latest devices for the commission of crime and avoidance of pursuit.

Those of us connected with law enforcement naturally resented such portrayals. I am not so sure, however, that our resentment was wholly justified, for only recently has science been keeping pace with the criminal and matching his devices, his methods, and his equipment. When scientific crime detection, as such, first received public attention it was met in some quarters with skepticism by many experienced law enforcement officials who labeled themselves as "practical" men—men who boasted that an ounce of horse sense was worth a dozen microscopes.

This controversy within the police ranks is fast disappearing. Scientific crime detection has established its place and the men engaged in this work are securing for it recognition as a professional field. If I were to venture an explanation why the field of scientific crime detection has won its spurs, so to speak, I would say that it is because of the premium placed upon skill and the emphasis given to trained personnel. If these are essentials of effective identification work, I submit that they are equally indispensable to the other groups and agencies in the law-enforcement field.

If I were to name one of the outstanding deficiencies in crime control efforts today I would without hesitancy point to the need of greater emphasis on personnel. * * * Any study of characteristic failures in law enforcement reveals that in the large percentage of instances they are the result of faulty, unskilled administration of the law rather than of weaknesses in the law itself. * * * We have paid much too little attention to the skill of those who investigate, apprehend, prosecute, and mete out sentences. We have attracted too few men of merit to enforce the criminal laws which have been enacted by our legislators.

Often breakdowns occur in the administration of criminal justice. Sometimes they may consist of failures to arrest or failures to prosecute. Sometimes the evidence is insufficient although available. So-called expert witnesses quite frequently disagree on the given statement of facts. Juries sometimes acquit, despite overwhelming evidence of guilt. Delays occur between conviction in the trial court and decision by the appellate court. Persons who should not be released from prison are occasionally paroled and deserving men are denied release who are safe risks. In virtually all of these instances of breakdown, the failure could not have been averted by the placing of additional statutes upon the books. In these cases somewhere down the line there has been a defect in skill and character—a breakdown in people, not in laws. Some person—policeman, prosecutor, judge, juror, parole officer, prison guard—has failed to measure up.

We have been woefully lax in this country in establishing standards of performance and prerequisites for those who would make crime suppression a career. While such standards need not always be inscribed upon the statute books, it is nevertheless significant that in most states any person, regardless of his intelligence quotient or his training, can become a justice of the peace, a coroner, a prison guard, a parole officer, a sheriff. The medical and legal professions are waging a winning fight for standards; and other professional and trade groups have established higher standards of proficiency. In the field of law enforcement we have lagged far behind but in recent years we can safely report progress. One evidence in the federal system can be found in the requirements for admission established in the Federal Bureau of Investigation, the fourteen-week training course for agents and the system of promotion on merit. All of our prison officials are chosen by the Civil Service; and in both the Federal Bureau of Investigation and the Bureau of Prisons, career service is encouraged and employees have been granted retirement privileges. Much might be said of similar trends in the state and local governments. The establishment of regular training courses in connection with the police departments of many cities is a new and an encouraging development. I have no hesitancy in predicting that some day crime fighting will attain a professional status.

7. Scotland Yard and the Sûreté Nationale

[Attorney General Cummings spent some weeks in Europe in the summer of 1935, studying the law enforcement and procedure of several countries against the background of the operations of his own department. *Ed.*]

From an address entitled "The Crime Problem at Home and Abroad," in the National Radio Forum, October 28, 1935:

RECENTLY I have been engaged in examining the methods of criminal law administration in three of the countries of Western Europe—Great Britain, Belgium and France. I embarked upon this tour of study in the hope of obtaining information that might be utilized in the war on crime at home; to learn how the problem presents itself in other countries, and to ascertain what methods have been there devised to deal with it; and in the still further hope that, through a comparison of foreign methods with our own, I might have a more acute understanding of the reasons for our failures and a sounder confidence in the reasons for our successes.

The first place I visited was Scotland Yard. It is a virile and efficient organization, splendidly officered and admirably conducted. It is the coordinating factor in the varied police forces of England and Wales. The bulk of its work, however, is confined to policing London. Its investigative excursions outside of that area are infrequent, and assistance is not rendered to local authorities except upon specific request. It is under the general supervision of a cabinet minister responsible to Parliament.

The personnel of Scotland Yard numbers more than 20,000 men, including about 1,000 detectives assigned to the famous Criminal Investigation Department, the C. I. D. known to popular fiction. Its annual expenditure runs to about $35,000,000.

The new police training school recently established at Hendon is an institution of great promise and one of which they have every reason to be proud. It strikes a modern note of marked significance. It is patterned somewhat along lines which we have been following in the training of our agents in the Department of Justice.

During the visits I paid this great institution, I examined its technical facilities and equipment, its methods of training, its filing system, its scope of activities, and its general mode of procedure. Comparisons are ungracious, and I have no intention of entering upon them except to suggest that a study of Scotland Yard and of our own Federal Bureau of Investigation reveals the profound differences existing between the problem of crime in the United States and the same problem in Great Britain.

Quite apart from constitutional limitations, it is apparent at once that Great Britain—an island, relatively small in territorial extent, homogeneous in population, without conflicting sovereignties and jurisdictions—has a problem far less complex and difficult than our own. The roving criminal, who carries on his depredations across state lines and whose activities cover vast geographical areas, is unknown to Great Britain. That is the problem that brought our federal government upon the scene. Investigation of the Urschel kidnaping case, for example, extended over an area of nearly 700,000 square miles, which, if superimposed upon a map of Europe, would cover most of the countries in the western part of that continent.

I was interested to learn that the number of fingerprint cards filed each day at Scotland Yard is between 200 and 300, while the most recent report from the Federal Bureau of Investigation shows that the Department of Justice is receiving as many as 3,700 a day. These figures of themselves suggest the greater scope of crime in the United States, the vast geographical extension of criminal operations, the almost infinite possibilities of a criminal losing himself in a land where passports and other methods of personal identification are unknown, and the importance of having at least one focal point for the exchange of criminal information, such as is now represented by our Federal Bureau of Investigation at Washington.

My visit to the famous Sûreté Nationale in Paris was an intensely interesting experience. One could not fail to be impressed by the alertness of its representatives and their infinitely painstaking methods. One of the most difficult countries in the world in which to become lost, I should say, is France. Its wideflung method of personal check, its cards of identity, its registration through hotels and lodging houses, and "the concierge system" are of great assistance in police work, though hardly adaptable to the genius of our own institutions. It suggests, however, the advisability of extending the voluntary civil fingerprint system recently established in the Department of Justice, in which we already have recorded about 50,000 fingerprints of reputable persons in all walks of life. I predict that this method of recording identities will be resorted to more and more generally as its merits, as a protective measure for the benefit of the average citizen, become increasingly manifest.

The Police System of Belgium is not unlike that of France in its broad outlines; and it is highly effective. The School of Criminology at Brussels is an admirable institution and includes in its curriculum a course of instruction for magistrates. * * *

During the course of my trip I inquired concerning the number of prisoners in the countries I visited. I found that in England and Wales there are about 11,000 persons in penal confinement, in Belgium about 4,000, and in France between 30,000 and 35,000. How many prisoners do you suppose there are in the United States? The appalling answer is—about 220,000. In other words, on an adjusted basis of relative population the United States has seven times as many persons in prison as England, four times as many as Belgium, and more than twice as many as France. This is a staggering fact, a discreditable fact. * * *

The statistics I have cited are, of course, subject to certain explanations, but these explanations do not alter the ultimate fact. It has been suggested, for example, that certain acts are punished as crimes in the United States which are not thus dealt with on the continent of Europe, such as drug addiction, drunkenness, and certain sex offenses. It is further suggested that about five-sixths of all the automobiles in the world are in the United States and that offenses growing out of the misuse of the motorcar account for a substantial proportion of our crime. Again it is suggested that the problem of assimilating diverse strains into our citizenship is responsible to some degree for the situation under discussion.

Some foreign observers point to the fact that prison sentences in the United States are longer than those in foreign countries and thus our prison population accumulates. Others have suggested that our traditional insistence upon the rights of the individual has at times militated against control of persons of antisocial behavior. Another explanation offered is that apprehension and punishment are much more swift and certain abroad than in the United States.

Doubtless there is some truth in all of these suggestions, but the fact remains that we have an immense and disproportionate prison population which is increasing all the time. While I was at Scotland Yard a message came in to the effect that a pickpocket had snatched a woman's purse on one of the principal London thoroughfares. An immediate call was sent out. Before I left the Yard two hours later the criminal had been arrested. Later that same week I asked what the status of the matter was. This was the answer: "He's serving time." This was just 72 hours after the offense had been committed. * * *

While I was in Paris I attended a murder trial at the Assize Court for the District of the Seine. One man had killed another in a quarrel about a girl. The defendant claimed that it was a case of self-defense. There were three judges on the bench. There were twelve jurors in the box. There were five alternate jurors in attendance available to replace any who might become ill or otherwise incapacitated. The trial lasted less than three days. The judge's charge was completed in ten minutes. He submitted four written interrogatories to which the jurors, after a deliberation of 25 minutes, returned negative answers. The defendant was thereupon brought into court and informed that he had been acquitted. He bowed his acknowledgments, was assessed one franc in damages to be paid the family of the deceased, and—that was that. And let us note that he had been in jail since the crime was committed, and that even had his alleged offense been a lesser one, he would not have been out on bail.

I notice that in France and elsewhere there is no such abuse of bail as is all too common in the United States. When a man is charged with a crime and placed in detention until brought to trial, he is anxious to have his case heard. His attorneys are not interested in postponements and legal technicalities. In the United States when a defendant charged with a serious offense is admitted to bail, it is all too often a fact that public opinion becomes indifferent, witnesses disappear, die, or lose their memories, and the initiative of prosecution is dissipated. I do not suggest that the bail system be abandoned, but I do suggest that those who wish to improve the administration of criminal justice in the United States might well turn their attention to the outrages committed against justice in abuse of the privilege of bail— an abuse that so often has no other result than to permit persons guilty of crime to escape punishment. * * *

In the conferences which I was privileged to hold with cabinet ministers of European governments, with judges, and with police officials, I heard frequent expressions of incredulous surprise when I told them of the ease with which criminals in the United States are able to secure possession of .lethal weapons of offense. * * *

Of course, I have brought home from my visit abroad no magic formula for dealing with crime, nor do I ever expect to find one. It is a far-flung problem and the battle must be fought on many fronts. * * * We hope to do better and better work as the days go by. * * * In short, we are developing in the United States a method of dealing with crime that accords with our constitutional limitations, the genius of our political institutions, and the traditions of our people.

The need of controlling crime is one of the most exigent of our national problems. There can be legitimate differences of opinion concerning appropriate remedies for our economic and social ills, but there can be no room for such differences when the question is one of protecting our persons, our financial, industrial, and business structure, our families, and our homes from the predatory criminal and the menace of the underworld. Unless our lives and our homes are safe, unless there be a secure domestic peace in which great human problems can be thoughtfully dealt with, then all that we strive to accomplish for the betterment of our people rests upon the treacherous sand of disrespect for order and defiance of law.

8. In and Out of Prison

From an address on a national study of "Release Procedures," at the annual dinner of the Section of Criminal Law of the American Bar Association, Boston, Massachusetts, August 25, 1936:

WITH the advantage of a federal perspective on the sordid panorama of crime, it was inevitable that our attention should become focused on the subject of parole. During recent years there has been an increasing public challenge as to the validity of that procedure both in theory and in the manner of its administration.

The importance of this subject suggested to me several months ago that the time was opportune for a nation-wide examination of parole, related as it is to the proper administration of criminal law throughout the country. Because of the variations existing among the statutes and practices of the several jurisdictions, I became convinced that such a survey should include not only parole but all forms of release procedures. Thus was initiated the studies now in progress, concerning which I have been asked to give a brief report tonight. * * *

Only a few tentative and preliminary studies in small areas have heretofore been made of the operation of parole, but the problem is nation-wide in character and a survey to be useful must be nation-wide in scope. This need is readily apparent when we consider that there is not even common understanding of the meaning of the word "parole." In one jurisdiction it means release by the governor or other executive agency, under circumstances which resemble so closely the granting of clemency or pardon as to be indistinguishable. In other jurisdictions the word is used to describe the release of prisoners by trial judges under conditions which approximate the procedure generally known as probation. In a third group of jurisdictions parole means release following an investigation of the record of the prisoner, based upon some form of prediction as to the probability of success following release, and controlled by the supervision of the parole officer into whose custody the prisoner is placed. Even the third form just described has many variations, according to the administrative method in vogue.

So far as the general public is concerned it is quite immaterial by what route a dangerous criminal is released. For instance, if the work of investigation is so inadequately done that a defendant cannot be effectively prosecuted; if by reason of political interference at the arrest stage he is released by the police; if by reason of unintelligent analysis of facts no indictment is found by a grand jury; if by reason of poor prosecution such a criminal is not convicted—then the public suffers just as much in the one case as in the other. If an inadequate investigation has been made of a particular case and a dangerous criminal is thereby improperly released on probation, society suffers whether the release is granted by a trial judge, by the pardon of a governor, or on parole by a parole board. The public is not apt to draw fine distinctions between one method and another.

There are some who seem to assume that the way to solve the problem of crime is to keep convicted persons "locked up" for very long periods of time. The use of excessive punishment inevitably causes a revulsion of feeling upon the part of the people. It is well known that where heavy sentences are made obligatory by law, juries become notoriously tender toward accused persons and are reluctant to bring in verdicts of guilty. Moreover, long and severe sentences have often produced excessive executive interference by way of pardon and commutation.

Another reason which makes impossible an easy solution by long imprisonment lies in the fact that we have barely enough room in our penal institutions to guard those now incarcerated. Practically all of the penal institutions of the country are already overcrowded. The cost of maintaining prisons and supporting prisoners is a continual drain upon the resources of our country. Moreover, a large proportion of the prisoners who are confined in penal institutions leave dependents who must be supported at public expense. It is contended by many professional probation and parole officers that a state-wide system of supervision, control, and discipline for certain types of prisoners can be operated at a cost of approximately one-tenth of the cost of maintaining such prisoners in institutions, with as great protection to the public and with much more promising results so far as concerns rehabilitation and readjustment.

The various forms of release constitute a part of the general picture of penal treatment. So considered, what are the relative values of parole, probation, pardon, commutation of sentence, release following credit for good conduct, and the other devices which are used by the various judicial, executive, and administrative agencies? The correct answer to these questions is of the utmost importance to any integrated program for the control of crime, or for a modernization of criminal law administration in the United States.

To secure at least a partial answer to these questions, a fund for carrying on the survey was procured. * * * It is probable— in fact it is inevitable—that the survey will disclose a striking lack of uniformity among the various state jurisdictions. Such lack of uniformity is not in itself necessarily important, especially in the earlier stages of the development of a general plan. There is even some advantage in having so many laboratories at work. * * *

A proper understanding of the nature and purpose of probation and parole would remove many objections to their use. Still more convincing would be their proper administration. Not alone the general public, but, indeed, many officials have assumed that these procedures are forms of clemency. They should not be so regarded or so applied. Considered not merely as a method of rehabilitation but, in each case, as a method of punishment administered in such manner as actually to supervise, discipline, and control the offender, probation and parole would cease to be looked upon as a way of defeating the efforts of police and prosecutors, and would achieve a recognized position as important as imprisonment and other forms of penal treatment.

From an address entitled "They All Come Out," in the National Radio Forum, May 23, 1938:

The federal prison system is today the largest coordinated prison system in the world. Its story has never been fully told. Prison stories generally remain untold. From the beginning of institutional treatment, the public psychology has dictated that what transpires behind prison walls shall remain a mystery. There has been a definite demand that those who have transgressed be forgotten. * * *

It has only been in recent years—very recent years—that we have come to comprehend the challenge which prisons present in our culture. The awakening comes inevitably if we inquire about our prisoners. Who are they? What happens to them? They all come out! * * * Their children will associate with your children, their families will be a part of your community. * * * That is the challenge of the prison system. We cannot escape it and we simply must face it.

The institutions which come under the federal Bureau of Prisons of the Department of Justice have been called "Uncle Sam's barred cities." The people in them have one—and only one—thing in common. They have been caught, convicted, and imprisoned for some violations of the many hundreds of federal criminal statutes. There are forgers, auto thieves, kidnapers, smugglers, murderers, bank robbers, racketeers, narcotic addicts, confidence men—and some mountain-folk who neglected to comply with certain revenue requirements in the manufacture of moonshine. No two persons are alike. Some come from broken homes. Some are rich, others poor. There are the sick and the well, the morons and the geniuses. Every occupation, skill, profession, and religion is represented. They form an amorphous mass which must be broken down and analyzed before there can be intelligent treatment. Remember that, for better or worse, some day they all come out.

Classification thus becomes our first great task. Obviously 16,000 separate means of institutional treatment for 16,000 prisoners are out of the question. But we can make, and we have made, genuine attempts to separate the old from the young, the sick from the well, the good risks from the bad. Let me describe briefly this phase of the work.

Young offenders are placed in reformatories such as the one at Chillicothe, Ohio. Here they are educated and taught trades. Others who give evidence of an awakened sense of responsibility and who have no apparent ambition to escape are sent to our mountain camps, such as the one at Kooskia, Idaho, or the one in the Catalina Mountains of Arizona. The physical and mental defectives are sent to our hospital at Springfield, Missouri. The narcotic addicts are concentrated in specially equipped institutions. While only five percent of our prison population is made up of women, it has been necessary to maintain a special institution for them at Alderson, West Virginia. The habitual criminals are ordinarily sent to the older prisons, such as Atlanta and Leavenworth. For those with serious records of violent crime, or who are intractable in ordinary prisons, we have the institution at Alcatraz. It will be seen from this brief listing that each institution serves a separate purpose. The most recent attempt to secure a degree of specialized treatment is represented by the measure, recommended last week to the Congress, which would create a uniform system for dealing with immature delinquents. * * *

The greatest curse of prison life is the degrading effect of idleness. Each year in the prisons of this and other countries thousands of men are going through a process of mental, spiritual, and physical disintegration. Many of the men who are in prison were unable to meet the tests that modern existence imposes. We conceive it to be our duty to see that these misfits are not returned less fit than when they enter. During the past five years we have developed three new prison industries and increased the number of inmates employed in industrial occupations from 1,760 to 3,230. Approximately 80 percent of our inmates are kept busy at some kind of work. The goods manufactured are made only for the use of the federal government and we consequently eliminate any possibility that these products will reduce the wages of industry or the standards in private enterprise. In this way we have attempted, without injury to free labor, to remove the ancient curse of idleness.

Another challenge is presented in the health of these men. We have resolved that they shall not leave our institutions with the mark of prison pallor and the handicap of a sickly body. Men cannot fight their way back to respectability under such a burden. In the past five years we have doubled the medical staff of the federal institutions and during this period the number of out-patient treatments increased from 385,000 to 900,000. Special research in the treatment of drug addiction has been inaugurated at two of the institutions. Why should we expend all these efforts in behalf of men who have violated our laws, when often outside prison walls persons who have led orderly lives suffer for want of such treatment? * * * Because they all come *out*.

Another great task which confronts us may be characterized by the phrase "hope versus despair." Prisons breed bitterness. The whole atmosphere of prison life is conducive to the production of warped minds—long prison corridors, the lock step, the monotonous shuffle of marching men, the walls, the bars, the guarded towers. It becomes our duty in these surroundings to inject some note of hope, though at times I confess it is extremely difficult. To remove bitterness, rancor, and the pervading sense of defeat is a real task, but nevertheless an essential task which falls upon us. * * *

We have another obligation, however, and a primary one. That is to see to it that the sentence of the court is fully and faithfully executed, and that men leaving the institution do not leave by the route which is commonly described by the inmates as "over the fence." When a man goes to a federal prison he must realize that loss of liberty is the inevitable consequence of crime. Occasionally, of course, a few men escape. They are few indeed. During the last fiscal year, out of an average population of nearly 16,000, only 19 men escaped, usually from prison camps, and 18 of these were recaptured within a few hours.

Shortly after I assumed the office of Attorney General, I became convinced of the need in our prison system for an extra secure institution in which might be confined offenders of a well-understood type. It was this conviction which led me to take such a personal interest in the establishment of the penitentiary at Alcatraz in 1934. We needed some place where the "end product" of our law enforcement system could be incarcerated. We needed a place also for ingenious "escape artists," and for those who are intractable or impair discipline or seek to maintain contact with the underworld. We established such an institution. It was not only intended for the purposes named but also to improve the morale and release the tension in the prisons in which this type of prisoner had previously been confined. Firm discipline and minimum privileges without resort to brutality, these characterize what has picturesquely been termed "The Rock."
* * *

There are today upwards of 150,000 men and women in all of our state and federal prisons and reformatories. This does not include thousands of individuals confined in city and county jails. A little more than 18,000 of these, including inmates in narcotic farms, are in federal institutions. In addition, about 4,900 are serving parts of their sentences on parole or on conditional release. To these must be added about 30,000 men and women who have been placed upon probation by federal judges and who are under the supervision of federal probation officers. This makes a total of more than 50,000 federal offenders who are today under the supervision of the Department of Justice.

There is still one other group consisting of 5,000 federal offenders who are boarded out in local city and county jails awaiting sentence or serving short sentences. To insure proper housing for this group, it has been necessary for us rigidly to inspect all of the jails in this country which might be used by the federal government. Out of a total of more than 3,000 county jails in this country the Bureau of Prisons has approved less than 700. These inspections have served a highly useful purpose by drawing public attention to those that are inadequately equipped or poorly operated. The conditions which exist in many of them are deplorable. Such institutions frequently are virtual schools of crime. Ofttimes there is no attempt at segregation. Discipline is lax and the sanitary conditions are literally disgusting. Graft, corruption, and brutality are not uncommon.

Partly because of these conditions and also to serve as a demonstration of what standards should prevail in the operation of a modern jail we have provided for three new regional institutions: at Sandstone, Minnesota; Tallahassee, Florida; and Terminal Island, California. The California institution will be formally opened within the next two weeks. The other two institutions are almost ready for occupancy. They will also serve to take care of the growing number of federal prisoners who are crowding our institutions. Some of our institutions are greatly overcrowded. We hope to meet this increasing load by the construction of additional facilities as soon as funds become available.
* * *

I have reminded you, perhaps too often, that prisoners must some day leave our institutions. I have occasionally been asked why this is necessarily so. Why should not the great mass of offenders be kept behind the bars for life or for long terms? The answer is twofold. First, for many of our federal offenses, it would be unjust to impose long prison terms. In the second place, there are practical difficulties. The average time of confinement of an inmate of a federal prison is about twenty months. If this confinement period were extended to forty months, we would have to erect twice as many institutions at a staggering cost. And if this were done it would be very questionable whether we had made any particular contribution to the solution of our problem because after the forty months' period had been served the prisoner would still come out.

But we are presented with a real problem when it comes to the method of release. The basic question is this—shall a man leave the prison scot-free or shall he come out under supervision? We must not forget that he has to undergo an adjustment process. If people were to trace the footsteps of the average man who leaves prison today and goes in search of employment in an effort to fight his way back they would comprehend some of the difficulties which the prisoner faces in making this adjustment.

A well-regulated parole system whereby deserving prisoners may be permitted to leave their cells before the expiration of their terms, and get permanent work outside of the jail under the supervision of honest parole officers, has its place in any scientific program of crime prevention. Twenty-five percent of those who leave the federal institutions today go out under parole. The small percentage of those who fail is a tribute to the intelligent selection by the Federal Parole Board and the conscientious work of our federal parole supervisors. The Department of Justice rejects the idea that parole should be used for clemency, as an opportunity to review the sentence meted out by the trial judge, or for any purpose except to provide a scientific and helpful means of rehabilitating those cases in which reformation is possible and where law-abiding conduct may reasonably be anticipated. When parole systems do not do this, they are not deserving of the name "parole." Release without supervision is not parole. Our position is simply this—we believe in parole and constantly seek to improve its administration.

9. The Youthful Offender

A letter to the Chairman of the Senate Committee on the Judiciary and the Speaker of the House, May 12, 1938:

THE federal criminal law is lacking in any comprehensive provisions on the subject of juvenile delinquency.

Although many of the states have from time to time passed laws for special treatment of juvenile delinquents, the Congress has not enacted any statute on the subject. The result is that a juvenile offender against the laws of the United States is treated and prosecuted in the same manner as an adult. The only exception is found in the power conferred upon the Department of Justice by the Act of June 11, 1932 (47 Stat. 301, U.S.C., title 18, sec. 662a), to surrender a juvenile offender to state authorities if he has also committed a state offense or is a delinquent under the laws of a state that can and will assume jurisdiction over him.

Students of criminology and penology generally agree that it is undesirable, from the standpoint both of the community and of the individual, that all juvenile offenders be treated as criminals. Many of them can be reclaimed and made useful citizens if they are properly treated and cared for, and are not permitted to mingle with mature and perhaps hardened criminals. In order to achieve these purposes it is important that juvenile offenders should not become inmates of penitentiaries or other penal institutions in which adults are incarcerated. It is likewise advisable that a juvenile delinquent for whom there is some hope of rehabilitation should not receive the stigma of a criminal record that would attach to him throughout his life.

I, therefore, recommend the enactment of a federal juvenile delinquency act and enclose herewith a bill for that purpose.

*From an address on "Federal Law and the Juvenile Delinquent,"
delivered before the first convention of The Association of Juvenile Court Judges of America, Cleveland, Ohio, July 29, 1938:*

The juvenile court movement has come far in a short time.
What was regarded by many at the turn of the century as merely
a well-intentioned scheme to pamper wayward boys and girls has
ripened into an almost universally-acclaimed method of dealing
with a perplexing national problem. The pioneer efforts in this
matter, originating in Chicago and Denver, have brought rich
returns. Juvenile courts have been established in a large number
of communities, from one end of the country to the other.

To many persons, however, this method of dealing with
juvenile delinquents seemed to offer a satisfactory solution of the
complex problem of crime prevention. It was reasoned, and not
without apparent justification, that if we could eradicate juvenile
delinquency, the crime problem would gradually disappear. "Stop
crime at its source" was a taking phrase. The source was the
oncoming generation. The proposal was the essence of simplicity. It captured popular imagination. It was a cure-all.

The fact that the juvenile court was never regarded by its
most discerning exponents as more than a partial answer to the
crime problem is quite beside the point. It remains true that
many people looked upon it as such. Consequently, when Pro-
fessor Sheldon Glueck and Dr. Eleanor Glueck, of Harvard,
demonstrated through a most careful statistical analysis and case
study that 85 percent of the youngsters who passed through one
of our better juvenile courts continued their delinquencies for at
least five years thereafter, many socially-minded people were disillusioned and discouraged. The cure-all had cured only fifteen
percent. By some, the results of the study were resented, questioned, and even denounced. But the reminder, even for those
of us who needed no reminder, was a blessing. It brought us
back again more sharply than ever to the realization that any
single device in the baffling work of preventing crime has its
necessary limitations. * * *

We have not discharged our responsibility with reference to the juvenile delinquent in the federal system. It was not until 1931 that the federal government even recognized juvenile delinquency as a status calling for specialized treatment. Apparently we had learned but little from those sordid pages of history which record that children of eight and ten years of age were put to death for minor infractions of the law. As late as 1833 a death sentence was pronounced upon a child of nine who broke a glass and stole two penny-worth of paint. While it is true that American courts were not chargeable with such brutality, it is nevertheless amazing that we had profited so little from innumerable instances of the glaring inadequacy of our criminal procedure. In 1931, however, a statute was enacted which permitted the federal government to turn over to the state courts certain cases of federal juvenile offenders. The program was launched with optimism. The Department of Justice set out to perform its delicate task. It secured the assistance of the Children's Bureau of the Department of Labor in interpreting the policy and evaluating the local resources.

But after several years had passed we were faced with the fact that only about 5 percent of our juveniles under nineteen years of age were being diverted to local authorities. Manifestly, the system was not working. There were a number of reasons for this. We found in some localities that means for the care of juveniles were either inadequate or completely lacking. We found, also, that as our federal probation service improved it was preferable to the probation methods open to us in certain of the states, especially in the matter of institutional treatment. Even in advanced states where the facilities were adequate, we found that they were not permitted for the older offenders, particularly those eighteen years of age. While these were very compelling reasons why, in so many instances, federal juveniles could not be turned over to state juvenile courts, they were not reasons for subjecting these youngsters to indictment, trial, and imprisonment in the federal system. To persist in that process involved a complete abandonment of the whole theory upon which the juvenile courts were created. Juveniles had to be handled in one jurisdiction or the other. The state system was not working out and the federal system had no juvenile court.

This experimental period was not, however, a complete loss. We learned much and some progress was made. For example, we found that as the federal probation service improved and the number of probation officers increased, juvenile offenders against federal laws received more intelligent supervision than had been possible in earlier years. Federal judges made increasing use of probation in juvenile cases. In the year 1932 only 18 percent of such cases were handled through probation, whereas by June 30, 1937, the number had increased to 32 percent. Nevertheless, these cases were handled as criminal rather than chancery cases. The very structure of the federal courts made it impossible to provide the type and variety of treatment available in the better juvenile courts in the various states. The necessity of grand jury indictments, infrequent terms of court, the resort to detention in local jails pending trial, and other conditions imposed by an inflexible criminal procedure made it impossible to initiate reconstructive processes. It is not necessary for me to stress the damaging results which come from the detention of juveniles in the average county jail.

We were faced with two alternatives. First, we might establish a system of federal juvenile courts with separate judges and separate procedures; or, on the other hand, we might, by legislation, replace the old system of criminal trials with a flexible chancery proceeding. For practical reasons, which I do not pause to discuss, we decided upon the latter course as the only feasible alternative.

A measure was drafted and transmitted to the Congress on May 12, 1938. In almost record-breaking time it had become law. The principal features are as follows:

1. It applies to all persons under eighteen years of age.

2. It applies to all federal offenses committed by juveniles, other than offenses punishable by death or life im-

prisonment. However, the Attorney General is to be granted the option of prosecuting a juvenile on a charge of juvenile delinquency or for the substantive offense of which he is accused. The purpose of this provision is to make it possible, if it appears desirable, to prosecute the more serious juvenile offenders in the same manner as adults.

3. Juvenile delinquents are to be prosecuted by information and tried before a district judge, without a jury, who may hold court for that purpose at any time and place within the district, in chambers or otherwise. Informal procedure of this kind has been found in many of the states conducive to attaining the humane and beneficent objects of such legislation. The consent of the juvenile is, however, to be required to a prosecution for juvenile delinquency under the act. It has been held that minors may waive the constitutional right to a trial by jury in the same manner as adults.

4. It is proposed that in the event the juvenile is found guilty of juvenile delinquency, he may be placed on probation or may be committed to the custody of the Attorney General for a period not exceeding his minority, but in no event exceeding the term for which he could have been sentenced if he had been convicted of the substantive offense. The Attorney General is to be empowered to designate any agency for the custody and care of such juveniles. The purpose of this provision is to make possible the use of such state and local institutions and quasi-public homes as may appear to be suitable.

5. The Attorney General is to be notified of the arrest of any juvenile and may provide for his detention in a juvenile home. The purpose of this provision is to reduce the detention of juveniles in jails to a minimum.

6. The Parole Board is to be given power to parole a juvenile at any time.

7. A saving clause is contained as to the District of Columbia in view of the fact that the District has its own juvenile delinquency statute.

In making any appraisal of the new act, let me urge you not

to place too much emphasis upon its terminology. For example, in the statute we speak of such matters as offenses, trial, prosecution. The reason for this, which may not be apparent at first, is that while state legislation establishing a juvenile court system is based on the theory that the state should act as *parens patriae*, the federal government, under its limited powers, is not in any sense a guardian of juveniles, save in the event of a violation of federal criminal law. Another explanation lies in the fact that it was not deemed advisable to depart too far from strictly legalistic language, in view of possible opposition that might otherwise have developed, thereby imperiling the passage of the act. * * *

A development of recent years is reflected in the statistics which show that youth contributes more than its share to arrests for such crimes as homicide, robbery, burglary, auto theft, and aggravated assault. As the social agencies of a community become more active, there is left for the juvenile court the more difficult problem of coping with those youthful offenders who have committed the aggravated offenses. I think that probably this latter trend will be especially observable in the federal courts. Federal offenses are, for the most part, more serious and call for heavier penalties than the average run of violations of state laws or local ordinances. Kidnaping, extortion, bank robbery, interstate transportation of stolen property, white-slave violations— these are the matters which will come before our federal courts.

The task of the federal judges will not be easy. All in all, there is presented a challenge to the resourcefulness of federal officials and a strenuous test of the new Juvenile Delinquency Act.

10. Firearms Control

An office memorandum to The Assistant to the Attorney General,
Joseph B. Keenan, April 14, 1936:

YOU will, of course, keep me advised as to our firearms bill. I should like to make some progress with this matter if possible. It also becomes especially important in view of certain recent developments with reference to high-powered pistols and revolvers. The problem is becoming more rather than less important, it seems to me.

From "The Crime Problem at Home and Abroad," an address in
the National Radio Forum, October 28, 1935:

I can put the situation in graphic form when I state that this afternoon I obtained from the Federal Bureau of Investigation statistics on cases reported since January 1, 1933, to date, showing robberies and thefts from National Guard armories and other public institutions of government-owned firearms and ammunition, as follows: Number of firearms stolen, 2,047 (this includes pistols, rifles, automatic rifles, and machine guns); number of rounds of ammunition stolen, 273,326.

These figures seem to me to be appalling. While hundreds of these weapons have been recovered and while prison terms have been meted out to many of those who stole them, the fact remains that our great American underworld is armed to the teeth. It steals its heavier weapons and purchases its pistols. There is no legitimate reason on earth for an individual to have possession of a machine gun; nor do I believe that any honest citizen should object to having all classes of lethal weapons placed under registration. To permit the present situation to continue indefinitely amounts to a disclaimer of national intelligence.

82

Address entitled "Firearms and the Crime Problem," delivered before the Annual Convention of the International Association of Chiefs of Police, Baltimore, Maryland, October 5, 1937:

Charles Harris was convicted of murder in the District of Columbia and sentenced to death. After the conviction I ordered an investigation for the purpose of tracing, if possible, three weapons which were found in a secret compartment of the car used in the murder. I wanted to know where those guns had come from originally and through whose hands they had passed. An elaborate investigation was undertaken, which, so far as throwing light on the Harris case was concerned, proved unproductive.

But we learned this: A few years before the murder, a man walked into a sporting goods store in a Northern city, represented himself as a hardware dealer and, having given a fictitious name, purchased 30 weapons. Two of these eventually found their way to the secret compartment of the murder car. The list of 30 weapons included three 45 caliber Colt revolvers, three 45 caliber Smith & Wesson revolvers, twelve 38 caliber Smith & Wesson special revolvers, six 38 caliber Del Colt special revolvers, and six 45 caliber Remington derringers. The sporting goods dealer who sold the guns had no method of identifying the purchaser and thus the trail ended. But we did find this: some of the 30 weapons were later found on the scene of gang killings at Oak Park, Illinois; Newark, New Jersey; and Philadelphia, Pennsylvania.

I recite this incident because it is a startling testimonial to America's inertia in dealing with the traffic in firearms. At the same time it is typical of the ease with which weapons find their way to the underworld. * * *

If we are to be realistic in our approach to the problem of firearms legislation, we must recognize that firearms have legitimate uses, not only in the hands of law-enforcement officials but in the hands of the private citizen. Hunting is an American sport and the sportsmen of America are, by and large, a fine group of citizens; and to many it is a form of livelihood. In some communities the shotgun and the rifle are a traditional part of the American farmer's household equipment. There are well-organized rifle and pistol clubs, the members of which find a genuine diversion in target practice. There are outdoors men in limited number, such as trappers and guides, to whom a side-arm is as much a part of their equipment as a mackinaw or a pair of boots. There are institutions such as banks and trucking concerns, engaged in transporting large sums of money, which have legitimate use for firearms as protective devices. Mention should be made also of the collectors of firearms. Any measure for firearms control must of necessity make provision for these groups and the proper uses which they make of weapons.

On the other hand, firearms have illegitimate uses. Our homicide rate in the United States runs annually between 11,000 and 12,000 victims. The proportion of these deaths that are due to firearms is approximately 70 percent, a terrific toll and one that cannot be minimized by fine-spun rationalization. I might add, parenthetically, while making mention of this staggering figure, that deaths from homicide in this country are twenty times more common than in England and Wales, and ten times more frequent than in Canada. And I might add, parenthetically again, that while almost 70 percent of our homicide rate is traceable to firearms, Canada shows but 32 percent and England and Wales less than 12 percent. * * *

Any plan for firearms regulation must take into consideration the proper and the improper use of firearms. It must, so far as possible, recognize the first and curb the second. On the other hand, any regulatory measure will impinge upon certain groups and interests. Anything that appreciably throttles production of firearms will arouse the wrath of those who profit by a limitless market. Personally I see no necessity for the adoption of legislation which cannot both protect the legal use and curb the illegal use of firearms. But if the American people are ever definitely faced with the choice between protecting the luxury of pistol shooting on the one hand and dealing a smashing blow at the criminal traffic in firearms on the other, we can be sure what their choice will be.

In this country we have a background which partially explains our reluctance to curb the traffic in firearms. The Pilgrim fathers shouldered muskets as they made their way to Sunday worship. Prairie schooners crawled slowly across the plains to the new West under the watchful care of riflemen. The gun was a symbol of the turbulence which accompanied America's westward expansion. A man's home is his castle. In America, the land of opportunity, the castle of the homesteader was jealously guarded. Such, then, was our tradition and we find traces of this tradition today in our laws dealing with firearms.

Just how far have we gone in this matter? And to what extent has the tradition of our hazardous pioneer existence shaped the law of the modern state? In the first place, firearms control has been regarded as primarily a matter within the police power of the state. Each of the states has approached the problem differently and independently of the others, and the attempts at uniform legislation have been far from fruitful.

State statutes have pretty generally prohibited the carrying of concealed weapons. These statutes do not apply to the individual who carries a weapon openly. Some of the states have increased the penalty for a crime where firearms were used in its commission. In some states a license is required of those who deal in firearms. The fee is ordinarily not a large one and the license is available to virtually anyone who can pay the fee fixed by the statute. Some of the states require manufacturers and dealers to keep a record of sales, with the name and address of purchasers, but ordinarily no extensive identification is required—such as finger-printing or a check upon the applicant's criminal record. In a number of cities and in many states there are provisions in the law which require that anyone who wishes to carry a firearm on his person must secure a permit, usually from the police authorities of the municipality or the county.

For the most part, however, the traffic in firearms has been uninterrupted. This was the situation in 1927 when the Congress enacted a statute which prohibited the use of the mails for the transportation of concealable firearms. The statute, of course, was quickly circumvented by the simple device of transporting the weapons by express.

The president of one of the large mail-order houses in the United States which has discontinued the sale of firearms admitted that his company had done an annual pistol business amounting to $250,000. His statement is significant. "We found," he said, "that most of these pistols were being bought for unlawful purposes."

This was the situation then in 1934, when a bill based upon the tax power and patterned upon the Harrison Narcotic Act was prepared and submitted to the Congress. It came to be known as the National Firearms Act. The measure was not based on the commerce clause for the reason that the traffic in firearms is not always interstate. For example, we wanted a record of the guns which were shipped from Philadelphia to Pittsburgh, within the same state, and we wanted every owner of a firearm in both these cities to be subject to the terms of the statute.

The tax power, consequently, seemed the only basis upon which to frame a registration statute. Briefly, this bill did three things. First, it placed a tax on all manufacturers, dealers, importers, and pawnbrokers dealing in firearms and required records of manufacture and sale. A firearm was defined in the bill and did not include ordinary sporting weapons. Secondly, a tax was placed on the transfer of such firearms, and the act required from the transferee certain identification information, including fingerprints and photograph. Thirdly, the bill called for the registration of all such firearms which were in existence at the time the act went into effect. There was no charge made for the registration.

It should be made clear that we did not expect certain results from the act. We did not expect, for instance, that criminals possessing weapons would register them. Under this bill no person then possessing a weapon was to be deprived of that weapon unless he violated the provisions of the act, in which case there were provisions for forfeiture. The act did not require permits or licenses to *purchase* weapons. The act did not set up a system of permits or licenses to *possess* or carry weapons. These were matters, for the most part, beyond the control of the federal government. They fell within the jurisdiction of the states.

When the bill came on for hearing one of the witnesses opposed to the legislation, in order to show his good faith, stated that he had been advocating state legislation for fifteen years. The reply of one of the congressmen was, to my mind, significant: "Are you advocating that we play along for fifteen more years?"

I have indicated certain things that could not be accomplished by the act. Let me point out what the act did accomplish. In the first place, under its terms if the criminal did not register his gun and he was arrested with a gun he could be sent to the penitentiary for as many as five years. There was no necessity to link such a law violator with a kidnap scheme, a burglary, a robbery, or a murder. There was no necessity to try him on charges which would be difficult to prove. The statute provided a simple way of reaching the known criminal.

This question has been asked: "If a criminal is not going to register a gun, what point is there in having a registration of guns which are possessed by non-criminals?" The answer is this: "Tomorrow's supply of guns for the underworld is today in the hands of manufacturers and private individuals who *will* register under the act." Every weapon possessed by a law-abiding citizen and every weapon hereafter manufactured is a potential weapon for use by criminals. These guns in time are lost, or sold, or pawned. Under this act a criminal will not buy a weapon from an honest citizen or a registered dealer since in order to make a purchase he will have to submit his fingerprints. Legitimate firearms dealers and honest citizens will not be a party to such a violation. For this reason we want a registration of guns now legitimately possessed, as well as those which are to be hereafter manufactured. Of course the statute was not made applicable to law-enforcement officers.

When the bill was introduced in the Congress, interested

groups began their opposition with the result that pistols and revolvers were not included in the measure as it finally passed. With the ordinary hunting rifle and shotgun excluded, and with pistols and revolvers eliminated, the act for all intents and purposes became a federal machine gun act. The act has been in effect three years. During that time there have been registered 9,316 sub-machine guns, 11,520 machine guns and machine rifles, 16,456 miscellaneous weapons, and 769 silencers.

To supplement the statute, the Department of Justice secured from the distributors of the sub-machine gun an agreement that no sales should be made by them to other than law-enforcement agencies. In addition, by seizures and forfeitures a number of these weapons have been withdrawn from general circulation. Thus progress has been made in controlling the sub-machine gun.

But a disturbing situation has developed. The criminal's arsenal is today made up not only of pistols and revolvers, but of ordinary shotguns and rifles. These weapons continue to take their terrific toll. The high-powered rifle which will kill big game at tremendous distances is, unfortunately, equally effective against human beings. During the past two years improvements have been made both in hand-arms and the quality of ammunition, which have already rendered obsolete much of the protective equipment of law-enforcement agencies. We cannot longer remain blind to these facts. Are we altogether realistic when we require the registration of a shotgun with a barrel of less than eighteen inches in length and overlook the weapon which measures nineteen inches? Why should we require the registration of the short rifle and exempt the automatic pistol or the newer type revolvers? I am convinced of this—any practical measure for the control of firearms must at least contain provisions for the registration of *all* firearms. I submitted such a bill to the present Congress. So far I have not been able to secure an open hearing upon the measure. But I propose to fight this thing through to a finish despite the pistol manufacturers who have so far blocked every honest attempt to deal with this subject. * * *

I do not suggest that registration will disarm the criminal

but I do say that it is the first step in the control of the firearms traffic. Registration is a simple procedure—much simpler than the registration and licensing procedure applicable to automobiles. No honest man can object to it. Show me the man who does not want his gun registered and I will show you a man who should not have a gun. Registration under the proposed bill involves no expense to the owner, and the tax on subsequent transfers of firearms is only nominal. When the weapon is transferred, the purchaser will be required to supply his fingerprints, and you can be sure that this will be a cause for lament by the dispensers of pistols.

How many pistols are today in the hands of private persons in this country? No one knows. Perhaps five million, perhaps ten million, perhaps more. At any rate the number is large—too large. The time has come to take constructive steps to control the traffic and to direct it into legal rather than illegal channels. The federal government cannot assume the entire responsibility. But I am determined that it shall do everything within the constitutional framework that can be done. There will be bitter opposition.

[Note: For other statements, see testimony at hearings before House Committee on Ways and Means on H.R. 9066, 73 Cong. 2 Sess., pp. 4-26, April 16, 1934; and an article entitled "New Guns for Old," *The Commentator,* January, 1938. *Ed.*]

11. Prevention—The Next Step

From a radio address entitled "The Campaign Against Crime,"
November 22, 1933:

CRIME, in its wider aspects, requires consideration of the whole structure of our social life. For instance, a study of the records of more than one quarter of a million arrests for the year 1932, as evidenced by fingerprint cards received by the Department's Division of Investigation, reveals the menacing fact that there were more arrests at the age of nineteen than at any other age; and that a startlingly large percentage of serious crimes were committed by minors. Manifestly the problem of crime is not limited to detection, arrest, and punishment. It is a social question, with manifold ramifications touching environment, heredity, education, the home, the school and, indeed, almost every activity of life. Prevention is even more important than punishment.

From a radio address entitled "How the Government Battles
Organized Lawlessness," May 12, 1934:

In a radio address several months ago, I stated that the Department of Justice was contemplating the organization of a national institute of criminology. Since that time further consideration has been given to the matter, and plans are now being made which look toward its establishment. The functions of the new organization will be: (a) to assemble, digest, and translate into practical form reports of improvements in the various branches of the administration of criminal justice, such as police, prosecution, court organization and administration, probation, parole, peno-correctional institutions and experiments, and the pardoning function; (b) to educate civic organizations in different parts of the country as to the nature of these materials, their availability, and how they may be used locally to improve the administration of criminal justice and to help in the prevention of delinquency and criminality; (c) to conduct a training school where specially qualified officers, federal, state and municipal, may study scientific methods of crime repression and prevention. A primary concern of the proposed new unit of the Department of Justice will be the development of methods for dealing effectively with young predelinquents and delinquents, for the purpose of checking crime at the source.

From an office memorandum to Special Assistant Justin Miller, February 3, 1936:

I am persuaded that it would be unwise to attempt to secure, at this session, the passage of a bill establishing a Bureau of Crime Prevention. It simply cannot be done and an attempt in that direction might react against the plans we have in mind. I am very desirous of obtaining the $50,000 for training purposes, as requested and approved in the present proposed budget. * * * My purpose would be to arrange for the establishment of a bureau which could be merged, or expanded, into the type of bureau we really ought to have. * * * Suppose we think along these lines at present, and in the meantime concentrate upon getting the appropriation.

From "Progress Toward a Modern Administration of Criminal Justice in the United States," an address at the annual meeting of The North Carolina Conference for Social Service, April 27, 1936:

I am persuaded that as time goes on our national program must place an increasing emphasis upon crime prevention. Here is a great field which many people, either because of inadequate information or lack of imagination, are reluctant to enter. In this area, as in the matter of detection and apprehension, as well as of punishment and rehabilitation, the federal government owes a duty of leadership. With only a moderate extension of activities, the Department of Justice can be made a nerve center of helpful impulses and a clearing house of useful information. The chief reliance, however, will naturally be placed upon scientific groups, universities, and training schools, many forms of industrial, business, and social agencies, and the state and local governments. Here again cooperation is the key word if we are to have a unified and coordinated program.

During recent months there has been a tremendous increase in the activities of various agencies. In several universities courses of training have been provided for improving the personnel of police administration. Chambers of Commerce and municipal leagues have been engaged in similar programs. Fraternal and religious organizations, women's societies, the Boy Scouts, and other groups have been helpfully active. The movement to establish and extend boys' clubs, playgrounds, and the like is in line with the desired end. The American Bar Association, as well as the various state and local bar associations, have been carrying on an intensive program, particularly for the improvement of laws relating to procedure and administration. The important work of the American Law Institute in the preparation of a model code of criminal procedure is one of the most striking of recent achievements.

The American Judicature Society, the American Institute of Criminal Law and Criminology, the International Association of Chiefs of Police, the National Probation Association, the American Prison Association, and many other organizations have made substantial progress in forwarding their respective programs of action. The creation of juvenile courts and coordinating councils and proposals for state departments of justice and state police departments all merit careful attention and promise rich results. In short, we are slowly but surely developing a national program and an adequate public leadership. * * *

Such a program must include, among other essential elements, compassion for the unfortunate, instrumentalities to guide those in danger of anti-social contaminations, solicitude for first offenders, rehabilitation where rehabilitation is possible, progressively improved procedures, prompt detection and apprehension followed by the swift and inevitable punishment of the guilty, vigorous and understanding administration, unfaltering resistance to political interference, and the raising of the personnel in this great field of human relationships to unimpeachable standards of individual character and professional competence. Without such a program to guide us, progress, at best, will be intermittent and wavering, but with its aid the American people can put their house in order and go about their ways of living under conditions of domestic peace.

From "Federal Law and the Juvenile Delinquent," address before The Association of Juvenile Court Judges of America, Cleveland, Ohio, July 29, 1938:

In the Department of Justice we have naturally devoted our principal efforts to the traditional fields of departmental activity —investigation, prosecution, and imprisonment. We have sought to be effective in all three. We have developed new techniques and we have secured the passage of laws calculated to strengthen our hands. That these effects have met with widespread popular approval I have no doubt. But I must confess quite frankly to you that I have been troubled by the comparatively inconsequential advances in the basic matter of crime prevention. What can the Department of Justice—the national government's law office—do about it? What contribution can we make? What responsibility should we assume? Such questions are disturbing.

The origins of crime are primarily local, and the sources many. There will ever remain thousands of problems for thousands of separate communities. At the same time, I am convinced that the federal government has a definite responsibility which it cannot afford to shirk. It was this conviction that led me to advocate, over and over again, the creation of a crime prevention unit in the Department of Justice which would serve as a nerve center of helpful impulses and a clearing house of useful information. The Congress has not as yet seen fit to provide us with the necessary funds. The urgency of the problem does not seem to be fully realized. Nevertheless we have made an informal beginning with our present staff. It is a relatively feeble effort but, at least, it is a beginning. Some day the plan will materialize into something definitely worth while. Ultimately such a unit will be created and, in years to come, some person reviewing the struggle will make a vigorous speech expressing a well-warranted indignation that the step was not taken sooner. But we must not be too impatient. These things take time.

[Note: See Annual Reports to the Congress, January 3, 1938, and December 31, 1938, renewing previous recommendations in this field. See also a series of articles in *Liberty Magazine,* reprinted in pamphlet form with an introduction by Fulton Oursler, 1937. *Ed.*]

PART THREE

THE COURTS
THE CONSTITUTION
AND THE NEW DEAL

1. Extension of Federal Authority

[The special session of Congress which met March 9, 1933, pursuant to the call of the President to cope with the depression crisis, enacted at his request a number of broad regulatory measures. These included the Emergency Banking Relief Act, the Agricultural Adjustment Act, the Tennessee Valley Authority Act, the Securities Act of 1933, and the National Industrial Recovery Act. In these measures were included provisions for the regulation of industry, labor, agriculture, financial institutions, and the monetary system of the country. Appropriations for direct relief for the unemployed, for public works, and for the extensions of credit in a number of fields called further attention to the display of power on the part of the federal government as it girded itself for the task of promoting recovery. Broad grants of power were phrased in general terms. The press, even when fully sympathetic with the various enactments, referred to them freely as measures conferring "dictatorial" powers. *Ed.*]

From an address entitled "Modern Tendencies and the Law," delivered at a meeting of the American Bar Association at Grand Rapids, Michigan, August 31, 1933, anticipating the constitutional debates which were to reach their climax in 1937:

WE AMERICANS are much given to quick generalizations. We have a weakness for headlines. In a certain fashion we realize that we are apt to be misled by them, but that does not seem to shake our faith in them. We generalize our hopes, fears, vices, virtues, plans, and ideals—give them a name, and then think more of the name than of the substance. We talk of "economic law," "inherent rights," "fundamental liberty," "equality of opportunity," and "social justice" until these concepts register more as abstractions than as realities. For this reason we are apt to be bewildered when some movement like the "New Deal" comes along and seeks to treat ideas and principles as living and vital things.

It is interesting to note that already this movement presents, in some of its aspects, a slightly distorted picture, because of the mystic potencies and weaknesses of mere names. Would it assert new executive power, it becomes "a dictatorship"; would it compel needed changes, it becomes a "revolution"; would it put reliance upon the best intellects it can mobilize, it creates a "brain trust"; would it coordinate administrative functions, we behold "a supercabinet"; if it seeks to combat crime by attempts to bring the police agencies of the country into closer cooperation, we find that "Scotland Yard" has been transplanted to America. Many of the current criticisms, as well as the excessive hopes it inspires, spring, I apprehend, very largely from this passion to generalize and to see it in the abstract for that which it is not, instead of in the concrete for that which it is. * * *

Manifestly, local government has proved in many ways quite incapable of meeting present emergencies. In the banking crisis, which occurred at the moment of inauguration, it was to the nation's Chief Executive and to national legislation that the country had to look for relief. The colossal attempt under the National Recovery Act to spread labor and to raise wages and purchasing power, and, under the Agricultural Adjustment Act, to control crops and to make the farmer's product capable of supporting him, is a federal effort to which the states and the people are lending willing support. The Department of Justice itself is the subject of demands for the federal solution of problems hitherto thought the proper subject of local control—racketeering, kidnaping, and the whole problem of crime. * * *

Today almost every economic and social problem is both local and national. Manufacturing, merchandising, transportation, agriculture, mining, oil production, problems of employment and unemployment, of strikes and the settlement thereof, are upon a national scale, or, if local in scope, are national in effect. Child labor in one state may destroy an industry in another. Crime is organized on a nation-wide basis. Neither the vigilance committee of the Old West nor the metropolitan police force of today can cope with this problem without national aid. * * *

The theory of our government has not changed; but the times have changed and invention has altered the scope and tempo of our life. I think it is hardly to be doubted that the average citizen of today senses his participation in government more acutely and more personally than he has for a generation. In very truth, a Roosevelt and a radio have made a town meeting of America.

It is but natural that some of the legal aspects and implications of what is now going forward should disturb the more "static" members of the bar. I have had occasion to discuss these problems with many of my learned brethren who, while suppressing any public expression of doubt, are manifestly doing so with difficulty. Later on, all in good time, I suppose these matters will be argued out before our courts and disposed of in orderly fashion. To that hour I look forward with a knowledge of its certainty, and with considerable tranquillity of spirit. * * *

To my mind, the law is not a mere body of precedents. I visualize it as a living, vital, growing thing, fashioned for service and constantly being refashioned for further service. Its function is to serve. It changes and it grows. It is not, and it should not be, the unloved ruler of a reluctant people. It is, and it should be, a trusted servant ministering to the needs of mankind. It should serve to cement, and not to strain, the bonds of affection that exist between the people and the government they have erected. * * *

If, however, these emergency laws and constructive acts are to succeed, or are to accomplish lasting good, it will not be because of their coercive powers or their perfections of plan and detail, or the aggressive enforcement efforts of agents and officials, but rather because they correctly interpret, as I believe they do, the thought and spirit, the tone and rhythm of our day.

From "The Right Arm of Statesmanship," an address at a meeting of the Bar Association of the District of Columbia, December 5, 1936:

Economic and social problems, the consideration of which was postponed by the World War, have now recurred with fresh insistence. Ideas are loose in the world. We may run from them, but they will hunt us down. The American people have not abated an iota of their faith in our institutions, but they are in a mood to demand something more substantial than thin political gruel. * * *

Manifestly they think as a nation and in terms of a nation. It is idle, therefore, to assure them that agriculture is a state matter or a question for the farmers alone. They know that nature has decreed it otherwise. The winds and the dust and the drought do not heed state lines. They have unmistakable jurisdictions of their own.

Likewise, it is futile to assert that unemployment is merely a state or local affair. It has arisen to become a national problem of the first order. * * * Technological displacement, increasing population, and the new workers who have entered the labor market have been decisive factors. * * *

The great South African statesman and soldier, General Jan Smuts, some time back, took occasion to warn the people of all nations that the depression which had affected so many countries was not merely cyclical, but disclosed a complete change of world economy. Since that utterance was made, many of the governments of the old world have gone forward with their absorption of private industry, under conditions of absolutism and tyranny which a lover of American liberty contemplates with extreme distaste. Herein lies a warning for us.

We are a great creative nation. We have enormous accumulations of capital and, fortunately, we are coming to have a more enlightened view as to the trusteeship involved in the ownership and control of property. Power must not be employed to destroy the human beings it should serve. The products of child labor and the sweatshops must not be used to displace the toil of fathers of families endeavoring to live according to American standards. An evolutionary process is going forward. It is idle to stand in its way or to proclaim that it does not exist.

2. Gold Hoarding

[During the weeks preceding March 4, 1933, runs on the banks of the country had taken place and, in one state after another, they had been compelled to close their doors. In a mood of panic, depositors had demanded their deposits, often in gold or gold certificates, preferring to hoard their money rather than risk the custody of banks. On inauguration day, banks throughout the country were closed. The money crisis had to be met without delay. When the President had taken the oath of office and led the inaugural parade down Pennsylvania Avenue, Attorney General Cummings left the throng for a law library and began the preparation of his first legal advice to the President.

The advice given culminated in the proclamation of March 6, 1933, prescribing a bank holiday throughout the country, and the call for a special session of Congress to act on this and other critical matters. The Emergency Banking Relief Act of March 9, 1933, in addition to providing specific banking regulations, approved and confirmed the steps previously taken, and delegated broad powers over the currency including the power to prohibit export or hoarding of gold or silver coin or currency. The cessation of efforts to take money from the banks and the return of gold already hoarded was necessary for the resumption of banking operations and the control of the currency. Executive orders prohibiting the hoarding of gold and gold certificates were issued.

The Department of Justice had the task of enforcing obedience to the orders. Evidence of the strategy of the Attorney General is to be found in the statements given to the press from time to time. On May 5 he was reported to have said that it was the patriotic duty of those still hoarding gold to turn it in to the Treasury. He said further, "If I were a hoarder and had not made good, I rather think I should make haste to do so. The man who turns in his gold now may be a technical violator, but those who purge themselves forthwith are in a better position than recalcitrant violators." Subsequently he made reports of the numbers of persons who had turned in gold, as a result of interviews by representatives of the Bureau of Investigation with alleged hoarders. On June 9, the Department was working on a list of approximately 10,000 persons. He declined to say when action would be taken against hoarders whose names had been turned over to the Criminal Division of the Department of Justice, but declared that "they will be held up to scorn before their fellow citizens. * * * Somebody is going to be prosecuted; that is certain." On June 12 he said, "All of these will be run down and not one person who can be located will escape investigation. I am so

101

thoroughly committed to the necessity that all gold be returned to the Treasury that I have no patience with those who hold it out in defiance of their government, and I brand them as slackers." The stream of gold continued to pour into the Treasury. When on one occasion he was criticized for making repeated threats of punishment without carrying them into action, he was said to have replied: "Hell, I was looking for gold, not for victims."

The first instance of prosecution, for hoarding 27 bars of gold worth somewhat more than $200,000, gave rise to a considerable amount of litigation (see *Campbell* v. *Chase National Bank,* 5 F. Supp. 156; *Campbell* v. *Chase National Bank,* 71 F. (2d) 669; *Campbell* v. *Medalie,* 71 F. (2d) 671; *United States* v. *Campbell,* 291 U. S. 686; *Campbell* v. *Chase National Bank,* 293 U. S. 592). Before the completion of the litigation, Campbell, like most other hoarders, made a voluntary surrender of his gold to the government. *Ed.*]

From a press release, September 28, 1933:

THE campaign against gold hoarders is progressing satisfactorily. The first prosecution for violation of the executive order of August 28th relating to the hoarding, export, and earmarking of gold was instituted yesterday in the United States district court at New York City by the indictment of Frederick Barber Campbell, an attorney, for the failure to file a return with respect to his ownership of gold bars valued at $200,574.34.

As a result of investigation by special agents of the Department of Justice, the number of alleged gold hoarders is 116, or a reduction during the past week of 168 persons and the reduction in the total amount of gold outstanding in the possession of such persons of $74,108.00. The gold and gold certificates returned as a result of the President's executive order and the activities thereunder amount to $38,901,009.95.

The later phase; an office memorandum to Assistant Attorney General Brien McMahon, in charge of the Criminal Division, December 10, 1937:

As no doubt you remember, the Department of Justice did a lot of work in the early days of the administration in forcing into the Treasury hoarded gold pursuant to a presidential proclamation. The work went on over a long period of time. I do not have the figures before me but I seem to recall that as a result of these activities nearly forty million dollars in gold were turned in.

For a long time I have been anxious to write "Finis" on these proceedings. There were some cases in court, however, and the matter finally worked down to a rather narrow compass. Mr. Parrish* had charge of this, as I recall it. My thought is that we should dispose of these remaining cases some way, and as soon as possible, so that we may regard our work in this particular field as a closed chapter and so that I can submit to the President a final résumé of it.

A final report to the President, April 22, 1938:

A large number of investigations and a considerable amount of litigation have been handled by the Department of Justice in connection with violations of the statutes and executive orders relating to the hoarding of gold. You may be interested to receive this brief résumé of the work done by the Department of Justice in that connection.

As you of course recall, beginning with the act of Congress of March 9, 1933, executive orders and acts of Congress prohibited the withdrawal, hoarding, and exportation of gold, and required all persons to surrender gold bullion, gold coin, and gold certificates in exchange for other currency. Provision was made for the punishment of violators and the seizure and forfeiture of such gold unlawfully withheld, acquired, transported, exported, or earmarked.

After full opportunity had been given to all persons to comply voluntarily with the executive order of April 5, 1933, I instructed the Federal Bureau of Investigation of this Department to undertake a comprehensive investigation of failures or refusals to fulfill the requirements of the order. The result was the dis-

*Special Assistant and second in charge of the Criminal Division.

covery of numerous gold hoarders, many of whom, upon discovery, voluntarily surrendered their gold while others remained recalcitrant, making further action necessary.

In the course of their work, the special agents interviewed 5,629 persons. By September 28, 1933, when the investigations had been completed, the amount of gold which was returned and which can be attributed directly or indirectly to these activities was $38,901,009.95. Of this amount $8,700,597.26 was definitely due to the activity of special agents in particular cases. Thereafter legal proceedings, civil and criminal, were instituted to reach persons who remained obdurate.

In the aggregate, seventeen criminal prosecutions were instituted. In nine of them defendants returned their gold to the Treasury after the commencement of proceedings, and thereupon their cases were nolle prossed. Two cases were dismissed for lack of sufficient evidence. Five cases went to trial, in four of which there were convictions, one terminating in an acquittal. One defendant was fined $50; another was fined $10,000 and sentenced to 40 days' imprisonment in jail; one was given a suspended sentence of one year in jail and a fine of $500; and one was sentenced to imprisonment in jail for six months.

Three actions were filed to recover the double penalty provided by the Gold Reserve Act of 1934. All three were eventually dismissed. Ten libel proceedings were instituted under the Gold Reserve Act of 1934, against gold held by defendants named in such proceedings. Decrees of forfeiture were entered in nine of these cases, involving in the aggregate over $17,000. In the tenth case, which involved $200,000, a settlement has been recently consummated.

In two instances, the government intervened in equity suits between private parties involving title to a large amount of gold coin, which was eventually turned over to the Treasury.

Except for small cases which may occasionally arise, we may consider the matter brought to a close.

The aftermath; an office memorandum to Special Assistant Alexander Holtzoff, October 3, 1938:

From time to time, attorneys come to this office to ask what can be done with gold certificates. They usually come as the representatives of other attorneys who, in turn, either represent still other attorneys or undisclosed clients. Almost invariably I think these gold certificates are held in substantial amounts and have been so held for a number of years, and in many instances at least are the proceeds of illegal operations. The holders of these certificates are unable, apparently, to give any plausible explanation of their possession of them. I take it that a full revelation might either involve the holders in some form of criminal activity, or in income tax implications. These certificates are apparently quite numerous and, so far as the holders are concerned, are so much waste paper. The very fact that they have them would, if known, direct suspicion towards them.

I should like to find out whether the Treasury Department has established any policy with respect to such matters. Naturally the holders would like to turn in the certificates and get some form of clearance and some salvage, and yet they are afraid to attempt it. I would be obliged if you would make some inquiries of the Treasury Department, for undoubtedly they have had many such cases.

3. Gold Clause Litigation

[Payments in gold within the United States were not resumed after the banking holiday. On April 19, 1933, the international gold standard was abandoned for an indeterminate period. Payment in gold could not be enforced therefore, even in case of gold clause contracts. By joint resolution of June 5, 1933, the Congress declared that the enforcement of gold clauses was contrary to public policy and that no such provision should be included in obligations thereafter incurred.

The Gold Reserve Act of January 30, 1934, enacted after Attorney General Cummings had given the Secretary of the Treasury an opinion upholding its constitutionality (see 37 Op. Atty. Gen. 403, January 17, 1934), authorized the reduction of the gold content of the dollar. Pursuant to this act, the gold content of the dollar was reduced to about 59 percent of its former amount. This action gave rise to important constitutional questions. The courts had to determine whether Congress had the power to compel the acceptance of the new currency, dollar for dollar, in satisfaction of private contracts antedating the legislation and containing gold clauses. They had also to decide whether the government could fulfill its own gold clause contracts in the same way.

The first important case dealing with gold clauses in private contracts, involving clauses in bonds issued by a subsidiary of the Missouri Pacific Railroad, was argued and won in the federal district court at St. Louis (see *In re Missouri Pacific Railroad Company,* 7 F. Supp. 1) and then taken to the Supreme Court of the United States, as were other cases. Attorney General Cummings, contrary to the custom of many years, decided to present in person the leading argument of the government before the Supreme Court.

By the narrow margin of five to four, the government won the first group of gold clause cases (see *Norman* v. *Baltimore & Ohio Railroad Company,* 294 U. S. 240; *Nortz* v. *United States,* 294 U. S. 317; *Perry* v. *United States,* 294 U. S. 330). In the cases dealing with private contracts, the points made by the Court were substantially those which had been presented by counsel for the government. In the case of *Perry* v. *United States,* involving the constitutionality of the repudiation of gold clauses in liberty bonds, the Chief Justice, speaking for himself and three others, took the position that the government could not constitutionally violate its own obligations, because such action would destroy faith in government promises and therefore obstruct the borrowing power. The opinion seemed a thinly veiled lecture to the administration on the morality of its conduct.   No injury was done to the government by the *Perry* case, however, because of the Supreme Court's further conclusion that the claimant, as the government had argued, could show no legal damage and was, therefore, not entitled to recover.

Prior to the date of the gold clause decisions, the Attorney General, in order to be prepared in case of defeat in the suit involving gold clauses in government bonds, began studying the possibility of achieving the government's purpose by legislation withdrawing the right of individuals to sue the United States in situations of this kind.   In order to avoid being harassed by other suits and to prevent successful action against the government, the administration pressed for remedial legislation after the decision in the *Perry* case.   Attorney General Cummings gave supporting testimony before the congressional committees (see Hearings on H. J. Res. 348 before the House Committee on Banking and Currency, July 10, 1935, and before the Senate Committee on S. J. Res. 155, July 17, 1935, 74 Cong. 1 Sess.).   The measure was enacted, withdrawing jurisdiction in gold clause suits with the exception of such suits as might be instituted within a limited period of time.   A few cases arose within the period excepted, in all of which the government was successful (see *Holyoke Water Power Company* v. *American Writing Paper Company,* 300 U. S. 324, and *Smyth* v. *United States,* 302 U. S. 329).   *Ed.*]

Office memoranda to Assistant Solicitor General MacLean:

November 24, 1934

WITH regard to the gold brief:
     1. It strikes me that when dealing with the question of the sovereign power of the government, in connection with currency, we ought not only to strengthen the argument made in the memorandum I handed to you, but we ought to go into the subject a little more fully in the matter of citing authorities.   I presume there must be available some learned discussions of this subject in law publications, or elsewhere, that might be extremely helpful.   I have the general idea that in certain fields this sovereign power is well recognized and that currency is one of these fields.   If this be true, then we have a powerful argument which, in itself, is conclusive of the case.

For instance, it would hardly be doubted that Great Britain could, by Act of Parliament, have done just what the Congress has done, and that it would be binding upon the English courts, and that, if such a statute had been in existence in England, the decision by the House of Lords would have been entirely different. As I understand it, the House of Lords' decision was a mere construction of a contract, there being no statutory rule involved. If, then, England could have done what the Congress has done, then the act of Congress is either constitutional, or it must be admitted that the United States has less power in the field of currency than Great Britain has. To put it another way, we do not have sovereign power in the international sense and, in the vital matter of currency, cannot exercise the powers available to other members of the family of nations. This, it seems to me, is an intolerable conclusion. * * *

2. In connection with the consideration of sovereignty in currency matters, I am not entirely persuaded that we should forego the advantage of discussing, in the brief at least, the chaotic condition of the currency at the time the Constitution was adopted. While it may be said, as Mr. Stanley Reed suggested, that possibly the framers of the Constitution had in mind only gold and silver as money, nevertheless, the decision in the *Legal Tender Cases* settled the point that paper money was constitutional. Moreover, paper money is so essentially a part of our currency system, as well as that of every other currency system, and the impossibility of getting along without it so manifest that, whatever may have been thought of it at the time, the wisdom of the decision in the *Legal Tender Cases* has been demonstrated by events. * * *

3. Apparently plaintiff's brief admits the power of Congress in the exercise of its constitutional powers to pass enactments which indirectly destroy private contracts. I am not sure what their contention is about direct attacks upon private contracts. Apparently they make a distinction between direct attack and indirect attack. If, upon analyzing this, you find that it is a point worthy to be noticed, I should say that our brief ought to be strengthened to show that the method of direct attack is as fully warranted as the method of indirect attack. I surmise that

you would find, upon study, that the direct attack has been employed many times. I suppose it is true that a contract is property. But I suppose, also, that one of the things the government does very frequently is to destroy property. There is statutory warrant for destroying contraband property by direct action and many other illustrations will, no doubt, occur to you. In this connection, it might also be well to find out upon what theory lottery contracts are declared illegal. You might also advert to the long line of cases upholding zoning regulations and billboard legislation. I think it would be well to give some considerable thought to pertinent examples of the use, by the government, of the power to destroy property and contracts, both directly and indirectly.

4. I am handing you herewith copies of memoranda dealing with the debates in the Constitutional Convention with reference to the power of Congress to coin money, etc. * * * Whatever may be said of these ancient debates, we are perforce required to rely not upon them but upon the decisions of the Supreme Court which, after all, is the final tribunal which settles these arguments.

I think, however, there was justification for what the Supreme Court, in the *Legal Tender Cases,* said about this difference of opinion in the Constitutional Convention. Perhaps, we had better shear away from this aspect of the matter, as it cannot help us and is, after all, unimportant, but we must keep it in mind, historically at least, and be prepared to speak on the subject should the question be raised in the pending cases. * * *

5. I think also good use could be made of the language of the Supreme Court in the *Legal Tender Cases,* beginning with that quotation which states as follows: "If then the Legal Tender Acts were justly chargeable with impairing contract obligations they would not, for that reason, be forbidden unless a different rule is to be applied to them from that which has heretofore prevailed in the construction of other powers granted by the fundamental law." Later on, in the same decision, the Court said, "As in a state of civil society, property of a citizen

or subject is ownership, subject to the lawful demands of the sovereign, so contracts must be understood, etc. ＊ ＊ ＊"

Good use could also be made of the quotation which, I think, occurs in *Louisville and Nashville Railroad Company* v. *Mottley.* This case, I think, was decided about forty years after the *Legal Tender Cases* and said very explicitly, "The prohibition of laws impairing the obligation of contracts is expressly directed at state action and does not apply to Congress which may pass laws *directly* or *indirectly* impairing the obligation of contracts." The quotation is important in connection with the question of the direct attack upon the gold contracts by legislative action.

6. Also, good use could be made of the statement in *Mugler* v. *Kansas,* 123 U. S. 623 at 665, as follows: "The principle, that no person shall be deprived of life, liberty, or property, without due process of law, was embodied, in substance, in the constitutions of nearly all, if not all, of the states at the time of the adoption of the Fourteenth Amendment; and it has never been regarded as incompatible with the principle, equally vital, because essential to the peace and safety of society, that all property in this country is held under the implied obligation that the owner's use of it shall not be injurious to the community."

7. The language of Chief Justice Hughes, in the *Blaisdell* case, is important in many aspects of our case and should, I think, appear in the brief. There Chief Justice Hughes said, "Not only are existing laws read into contracts in order to fix obligations as between the parties, but the reservation of essential attributes of sovereign power is also read into contracts as a postulate of the legal order."

January 6, 1935

On page 48 of the respondents' brief in Nos. 471 and 472, it is asserted that the resolution encroaches upon the sovereign power of the states. This statement, it seems to me, is completely answered by the provisions of Article VI of the Constitution. It is also answered by certain cases we have heretofore cited, namely, the *Second Employers' Liability Cases,* and some others.

Those who insist upon the written word are insisting upon the written word in a contract dealing with gold, and gold lies at the basis of our financial structure, gold is the subject of national legislation, gold from time immemorial has been one of the chief concerns of government, gold is a thing apart—it is not an ordinary commodity. * * *

To put it another way, these contracts have invaded the federal field; it is not a case of federal activity reaching out into a private area. So obsessed are our opponents by the idea of the sanctity of contracts that they are prepared to maintain their validity even when they invade the field of the government itself.

These gold contracts are not private contracts in any real sense; they are contracts which deal with the very substance of money, which substance lies at the basis of our entire currency system. It is not safe to permit the control of this basic substance to be made the subject of private contracts not in the public interest. In other words, these gold contracts are charged with and affected by a public interest.

What was taken on June 5, 1933? Surely it was nothing more than the right to receive gold coin on the due date. The value of the property taken must, by all the rules, be estimated as of June 5. The quotations for June 4, 5, and 6, and nearby dates, show no variation in the value of the bonds as a whole. Nothing of value was taken; or, to put it another way, what was taken amounted to precisely zero. Indeed, the plaintiff makes no allegation of loss as of June 5, 1933, because he is unable to estimate any loss as of that date.

The whole case rests upon a strained effort to make an obligation something that it is not—something besides money. It is the old fallacy of commodity that vitiates their reasoning. Money is not a commodity. * * * These matters take the case outside the realm of ordinary private contracts.

January 25, 1935

With regard to what documents should be prepared in anticipation of the possibility of an adverse decision on the gold clause cases, my suggestion is that we keep at work on these matters and later on, and by that I mean in a few days, have a conference on the subject. In other words, there should be a general round-up of our forces in this matter, including the Treasury and the R. F. C. I also noticed in the paper that Congressman Sumners is doing some work along these lines. It might be well for you to have a confidential talk with him so that we may be able to coordinate our activities.

From the oral argument of the first group of gold clause cases before the Supreme Court of the United States, January 8 and 9, 1935:

ATTORNEY GENERAL CUMMINGS. If the Court please: These four cases which are now pending before this Court touch every essential aspect of the problems involved in the matter of gold obligations. In each one of these cases the program of the government is under attack upon the ground that the Congress has exceeded the powers granted by the Constitution.

The first two cases deal with railroad bonds. The third case deals with gold certificates, and the fourth case, in the order stated on the docket, deals with Liberty Bonds. Underlying these four cases are certain fundamental constitutional considerations which I think are determinative of the entire matter. * * *

Now, if the Court please, although it may seem trite to do so, I draw attention to what, for want of a better term, may be called the "presumption of constitutionality." This doctrine has been laid down in innumerable cases, some of which are cited in our briefs, but nowhere, I think, is it more effectively stated than in the *Legal Tender Cases,* in which this Court said:

A decent respect for a coordinate branch of the government demands that the judiciary should presume, until the contrary is clearly shown, that there has been no transgression of power by Congress, all the members of which act under the obligation of an oath of fidelity to the Constitution. Such has always been the rule.

But this doctrine, I apprehend, goes still further, and carries with it the proposition that this Court will accord great weight to the findings and reasons set forth by the Congress for enacting the legislation which it has passed.

The next cardinal principle is that, in selecting the means to carry out the purpose of the Congress, the Congress has wide discretion. Unless it is shown that the exercise of that discretion has been clearly arbitrary or capricious or unreasonable, this Court will not interfere with it.

I have adverted to these considerations not because they are not recognized, but because they are so well recognized that they are taken as a matter of course. We are inclined, I fear, to pay them a sort of lip service and then pass on to the consideration of matters of a more controversial character. * * * These doctrines to which I have referred are not only necessary and vital doctrines, essential to our form of government, but they surcharge the whole atmosphere of constitutional discussion. Look at the briefs filed in behalf of the government! * * * We have undertaken to carry a burden, instinctively almost, which of right rests upon the shoulders of the opposition.

Although what I have said is obvious, I want to carry it just a bit further. In these pending cases we have before us not only the resolutions of the Congress and its declarations and findings, but we have also the instructions, the declarations, and the findings of the President of the United States, as well as his public statements, his message to the Economic Conference of July 3, 1933, and, in addition to that, we have the findings, declarations, and instructions of the Secretary of the Treasury. * * *

Now, of course, if the Court please, the conditions which

existed on the sixth day of March 1933 are so fresh in our memories and have been so completely covered in the elaborate briefs which have been presented, that it seems quite unnecessary to refer to them again or at length.

The fact remains, however, and it is enough to say, that an emergency of the highest importance confronted the nation. Banks, sound and unsound, were failing or closing upon every hand; gold coin, gold certificates, and, indeed, all other forms of currency, were being hoarded in millions of dollars, and, perhaps by millions of people. Gold was taking flight either into foreign currencies or into foreign lands; and foreign trade had been brought to a standstill. International finance was completely disorganized. The whole situation was one of extreme peril. Price levels were falling. Industries were closing. Millions of people were out of work. Failures and bankruptcies were reaching enormous and, indeed, unparalleled proportions; and, with constant acceleration, our people, confessedly, were slipping toward a lower level of civilization. I undertake to say that no man of imagination could have witnessed that distressing spectacle of painful retrogression without acute apprehension and profound sorrow.

Now, in addition to that, we had the experiences of other nations; we had their example. There was not a nation on the face of the earth that was not in distress. At that time—and the time I refer to was the 6th day of March 1933—the Swiss franc, the Dutch guilder, and the United States dollar were the only coins that had not been devalued or depreciated. Country after country was going off the gold standard, and thirty countries had passed drastic legislation with regard to finance, foreign commerce, and the regulation of money. Embargoes, trade restrictions, and quotas were characteristic of the day and of the time.

So, as I say, we were confronted by an industrial and monetary and financial crisis of the most terrifying character. Amongst the various measures which were adopted to meet the situation were those which are in the group within which falls the Joint Resolution of the 5th of June 1933, which is so seriously under attack here today. * * *

In a hectic period of eleven months, a sweeping change was effected in the financial and monetary structure of our country. Our system was completely reorganized. Gold and gold bullion were swept into the Treasury of the United States; gold certificates were placed where they were readily within the control of the government of the United States; foreign exchange was regulated; banks were being reopened; gold hoarding was brought under control; parity was maintained; and a complete transition was effected from the old gold-coin standard to the gold-bullion standard, with the weight of the dollar fixed at an endurable amount.

Now, I undertake to suggest that no one can consider this series of acts without sensing their continuity and realizing their consistent purpose. Moreover, these measures must be read as a whole, and read against the background of utter national need. I think they tell the story of a nation finding its way out of financial chaos into a safer and sounder position.

Moreover, it must be remembered that in these matters two great branches of our government, the legislative and the executive, were acting in perfect harmony and for a common end. It was a sweeping change, adopted by an overwhelming majority of the Congress, and promptly approved by the President of the United States; and appealing to both as essential to the happiness and prosperity and welfare of our country.

I contend, and later shall undertake to show, that to admit the validity of the claims of those who are appearing here in behalf of the holders of gold certificates, and in behalf of the gold-bond obligations, would mean the break-down and the wreckage of the structure thus carefully erected. Moreover, it would create a preferred class who, because of a contract of a special character, are able to take themselves outside, as it were, of the financial structure of their own country.

To admit such claims to the extent of $100,000,000,000, an unthinkable sum, would be to write up the public debts and the private debts of our country by $69,000,000,000 and, overnight, reduce the balance of the Treasury of the United States by more than $2,500,000,000. It would add $10,000,000,000 to the public debt. The increased interest charges alone would amount to over $2,500,000,000 per annum, and that sum is twice the value of the combined wheat and the cotton crops of this country in the year 1930. The stupendous catastrophe envisaged by this conservative statement is such as to stagger the imagination. It would not be a case of "back to the Constitution." It would be a case of "back to chaos." * * *

The primary difficulty, as I see it, with the argument in behalf of the gold obligations, and one which vitiates it entirely, is that the question is approached without reference to this background, and is based merely upon the supposed sanctity and inviolability of contractual obligations. That our government is endowed with the power of self-preservation I make no doubt, and that a written understanding must yield to the public welfare has been so often reiterated that it is not necessary to dwell upon it any further. * * *

Those who insist upon the strict letter of the bond are insisting upon it in a matter dealing with gold, and gold lies at the basis of our financial structure. Gold is the subject of national legislation. Gold is the subject of international concern. Gold is not an ordinary commodity. It is a thing apart, and upon it rests, under our form of civilization, the whole structure of our finance and the welfare of our people. Gold is affected with a public interest. These gold contracts, therefore, deal with the very essence of sovereignty, for they require that the government must surrender a portion of that sovereignty. To put it another way, these gold contracts have invaded the federal field. It is not a case of federal activity reaching out into a private area. So obsessed are our opponents by the idea of sanctity of contracts that they are even prepared to assert their validity when they preempt the federal field. To me this seems a monstrous doctrine. * * *

Now, of course, the primary power upon which the Joint Resolution rests is that portion of article I, section 8, of the Constitution which grants to the Congress the power "to coin money, regulate the value thereof and of foreign coin, and fix the standard of weights and measures." The power also rests upon the constitutional authority "to regulate commerce with foreign nations and among the several States," and "to borrow money on the credit of the United States," and upon that "composite power" which has been referred to in that language, or in similar language, in many of our cases. * * *

It is my belief that the word "regulate" as used in the Constitution has never been completely and carefully analyzed in all of its implications. How far does the term "regulate" carry us? Manifestly it reaches to the regulation of value, and value, itself, is a relative thing. Value appears only in relation to the value of other things. And, moreover, the word "regulate" implies a continuing power, and is the same term that is used with reference to commerce, and connotes the power of adjustment. It implies the power of making the condition accord more fully with reality and with justice. But when you come to the power "to fix the standard of weights and measures," the Constitution abandons the word "regulate" and uses the word "fix." * * *

Let me pause for a moment to emphasize the proposition that the only alternative open to the Congress was a reduction in the gold content of the dollar, accompanied by a denunciation of gold clauses. In choosing this alternative, the government acted in the public interest, and it cannot fairly be contended that it acted arbitrarily, capriciously, or unfairly or unjustly, or for any improper purpose.

There can be no doubt that the gold clause was a hindrance to the borrowing power. Such obligations, if permitted to exist, would have preempted or, at least, measurably restricted, the sources from which borrowed money is obtained. There is no doubt that the gold clause likewise interfered with international obligations and negotiations; and with foreign exchange and foreign commerce. If it had been impossible to break the pre-war tie to the gold dollar, we would have been denied the privilege, open to all other civilized governments, of dealing effectively with our own currency.

No adequate reason has been advanced why the holders of interest-bearing time obligations should be preferred over holders of demand obligations, as, clearly, these forms of undertakings are of equal solemnity. The holders of $20,000,000,000 of federal gold obligations, with an annual interest charge of $700,-000,000, could, in a relatively short time, have drained all of the available gold out of the Treasury. This would have been tantamount—and I say it deliberately—to delivering the destiny of our gold reserves into private hands, and by that same token delivering the destiny of America into private hands. * * *

Should the claims of the owners of these gold obligations be approved, it would create a privileged class which, in character, in immunity, and in power, has hitherto been unparalleled in the history of the human race. I feel the walls of this courtroom expand; I see, waiting upon this decision, the hopes, the fears, and the welfare of millions of our fellow citizens. * * *

Those who framed the Constitution of the United States realized this situation, and, knowing what had happened in the colonies, took pains to see that this power, just like the power of the sword, this great attribute of sovereignty, should reside in one single authority. Hence the Constitution not only affirmatively grants this power to the Congress of the United States, but forbids its exercise by the various states.

In sweeping terms the federal government was given the power to collect taxes to provide for the common defense and the general welfare; to coin money; to declare war; to maintain armies; to provide a Navy; and, in general, to deal in these sovereign matters on an equality with the other members of the family of nations. These enumerated grants in section 8 of article I of the Constitution are set forth in representative terms, which, taken together, imply all the essentials of a comprehensive federal power over the whole subject of the medium of exchange, standards of measure and value, coinage of money, and the control of credit.   *   *   *

The history of money is fascinating. It has been tied up with the progress of the human race. There has never been an important era in which the destinies of men were at hazard where the problem of currency was not involved. Every drama in the international field involves some aspect of the money question.

In the earliest days, of course, the currency was crude in form. It developed as civilization went on. Finally we come to the period referred to in the *Mixed Money* case, where its characteristics were beginning to be understood. We then come to the early colonial days, with their chaos and their disorder and their conflict in matters of currency. And, following this, these sovereign powers of the states, which had in so many instances been unwisely used, were turned over to the federal government, and, for the first time on this continent, the control of currency was confided to a central authority.

It was then a little-understood subject—and, I must say, it is a little-understood subject now. We have passed through many vicissitudes—the Greenback Era, the period of the *Legal Tender Cases,* the experience with the double currency standard—until we reached a more or less settled status, which many people fatuously believed was the final status. The gold standard, as it was then known, survived the panic of the Cleveland administration, but it did not survive the vicissitudes of the World War. The problem moved out into international areas. Governments began to send representatives to conferences to discuss this mutually vexing problem of gold.

It would be idle to deny that things are still in a formative stage. Indeed, great things are afoot. The London Economic Conference of 1933 did not achieve its objective, but it had for one of its purposes the problem of the stabilization of the currencies of the world. On the third of July 1933 the President of the United States cabled to the Economic Conference dealing with this subject and, in the course of his message, confirmed the proposition that our broad purpose is permanent stabilization of every national currency.

We have not seen the last of international economic and monetary conferences. Already these events may be dimly seen on the horizon. I do not know when it will be. That is written in the inscrutable bosom of time. But the day will come when the

United States of America will be conferring with the other nations of the earth, with a view to the stabilization of currencies, the fixing of standards, and making those arrangements which are essential among civilized nations if we are to dwell together in any reasonable degree of harmony and prosperity.

Let nothing be said here that makes our nation enter such a conference on crutches, a cripple among the nations of the earth. * * * I ask this Court to lay down in unequivocal language the proposition that, in matters of currency, the courses of action open to other governments are not denied to this nation, and that, in employing these sovereign powers, we act upon an equality with all the other nations of the earth.

An office memorandum to Solicitor General Stanley Reed, regarding subsequent gold clause cases:

November 8, 1937

I have been examining a little more carefully the brief in the gold cases, Numbers 42, 43 and 198. It rather strikes me that Point I is adequate and persuasive and that we ought to win on that point.

With reference to Point II, I am a little troubled. I wish the discussion of it could have been more fully considered and somewhat condensed. One has an uneasy feeling that there is a valid idea in hiding in that part of the brief, but that it is never quite fully dragged out into the open. I realize the difficulty in view of the peculiar opinion in the *Perry* case. When the Chief Justice found himself unable to refrain from lecturing Congress and the Administration, he put himself in an impossible position. The favorable result apparently grew out of the theory that it was a necessary one, as the plaintiff had shown no damage, and that a contrary decision would have enabled the plaintiff unjustly to enrich himself. There was, therefore, a head-on collision between the morals of the opinion and the morals of the decision.

I assume that the *Perry* opinion must be handled with a reasonable degree of respect, but I hope we have not gone too far in acquiescing in its validity. The discussion in the brief on pages 90 to 95, and indeed from then on, is ingenious and may afford the Court a way out if it gets to the second point of the case, and very likely it would be bad tactics to be too downright about the matter.

I have always believed, and still believe, that the collective powers of the federal government set forth in Section 8 of Article I of the Constitution give to the federal government complete power over the whole subject of money, the control of credit, and incidental questions. While I do not argue (in view of the present state of our law) for an inherent sovereign power, it does strike me that in certain essential matters the government within the limits of the Constitution has a sovereign power and that the currency is one of these matters. To maintain that the Congress can make a contract concerning money which completely frustrates its later use of one of the greatest and most essential powers of government is to state what seems to me, and always will seem to me, a complete absurdity. To say that the first use of the power exhausts the second is to deny the sovereign power itself. No other civilized government on earth would tolerate such nonsense.

4. The National Industrial Recovery Act

[The National Industrial Recovery Act gave rise to complex problems of administration and litigation. The statute on which the structure for code regulation of labor and other competitive conditions was based was extremely general in its phrasing. It left to the administration the establishment of whatever machinery might be needed. A "National Recovery Administration" for the handling of activities in many fields was set up as an agency independent of any department. However, the administration of the codes of some industries utilizing agricultural products was turned over to an "Agricultural Adjustment Administration" in the Department of Agriculture; and the petroleum code and the administration of regulations based on Section 9 (c) of the National Industrial Recovery Act were allotted to a "Petroleum Administrative Board" in the Department of the Interior. Powers of enforcement were given to the Department of Justice and the Federal Trade Commission.

In the thought of the moment, however, enforcement was to be largely psychological rather than legalistically punitive. The right to display the "Blue Eagle" was given as evidence of observance of the President's Re-employment Agreement and of the provisions of the codes. The possession of the Blue Eagle was the symbol of good behavior. After consultation with General Hugh Johnson, Administrator of the National Industrial Recovery Act, Attorney General Cummings agreed to withhold action on reported violations of the law and of the codes based upon it (see Circular No. 2441, August 8, 1933). Reports of violations which were sent to the Department of Justice were regularly forwarded to the National Recovery Administration.

Popular enthusiasm for the National Industrial Recovery Act declined rapidly as business conditions improved. It became apparent that enforcement by legal process would be necessary. The several emergency agencies sought the privilege of handling their own litigation, as against leaving it to the Department of Justice where it was placed by statute and by executive order. Members of such agencies were from time to time appointed as special assistants to the Attorney General for the argument of cases, but the Department of Justice insisted on retaining control of litigation. Emergency agencies were critical of the delays which proved necessary for the adequate preparation of cases, and of the reluctance of the Department of Justice to press cases in which the basis

122

for legal proceedings seemed inadequate.   However, the Attorney General recognized the right of the National Recovery Administration to use its administrative technique of withdrawing the Blue Eagle as a mode of coercing obedience quite apart from the question of whether or not the facts were sufficient to warrant a criminal prosecution.

The prospect of winning before the Supreme Court was not easy to appraise.   Evidence of a favorable attitude on the part of the Court toward New Deal legislation was found by some people in two cases decided early in 1934 on the constitutionality of state laws.   In one, a Minnesota mortgage moratorium law severely limiting the rights of creditors was upheld (see *Home Building & Loan Association* v. *Blaisdell*, 290 U. S. 398).   In the other, while admitting that the business was not a public utility, the Court upheld price fixing in the sale of milk in New York and thereby apparently destroyed much theretofore rigid doctrine on the subject of price fixing (see *Nebbia* v. *New York*, 291 U. S. 502). Those cases seemed fairly direct precedents in support of federal emergency legislation.

In view of the speed with which new agencies were set up and put into operation for the performance of unprecedented functions, it is not surprising that some confusion prevailed which, when revealed in the litigation of the period, resulted in sharp criticism of administrative procedures, and may have been in part the cause of adverse decisions.   Cases involving the petroleum code and the administration of the "hot oil" regulations were perhaps most revealing in this respect.   The Secretary of the Interior asked and secured from the Attorney General permission to prosecute criminal cases prepared by his own subordinates against J. W. Smith and others, with the expectation that the case would provide a test of the constitutionality of the National Industrial Recovery Act.   The plan for the use of this case as a test was so criticized by other agencies of the government that the Department of Justice decided to postpone it, with the idea of superseding it with another test case if possible.   Two new equity suits were prosecuted through the Circuit Court of Appeals for the Fifth Circuit by the Petroleum Administration attorneys.   A Department of Justice lawyer began the preparation of the brief for the Supreme Court and discovered that the restrictive provision of the code had been accidentally dropped from the code and had therefore been nonexistent during the period of litigation of all the pending cases.   The criminal case was dismissed on the motion of the government, but the Supreme Court agreed to review the two cases against the Panama Refining Company and the Amazon Petroleum Corporation.   At the argument, questioning of government counsel by the justices of the Supreme Court revealed looseness of administrative procedure in failing to make available to the public, and even to other governmental agencies, administrative and executive orders having the force of law. Mr. Justice Brandeis drew from government counsel, Assistant Attorney General Harold M. Stephens, information regarding a governmental study of the possibility of establishing some form of official gazette for the publication of administrative regulations (which, it was said elsewhere, had been disapproved at the White House a few days before on the ground that the administration did not want to risk the charge of operating a "government newspaper"). In unanimous agreement on the point, the Court took occasion to criticize the administrative procedure, and on January 7, 1935, by a vote of eight to one it curbed the trend of a long line of decisions and held the grant of power to the President in section 9 (c) to be an unconstitutional delegation of legislative power *(Panama Refining Company* v. *Ryan,* 293 U. S. 388). (From this incident, it may be noted, grew the final movement which resulted not only in the establishment of a "Federal Register" but also the codification of all previously issued and generally operative regulations.)

In the meantime another test case, that of *United States* v. *Belcher* involving the lumber code, was on its way to the Supreme Court. The government viewed it with tolerance, until after the argument and decision of the oil cases. Then the question of pressing the case or asking its dismissal was debated for a number of weeks. Among the arguments for dismissal was one presented by Stanley Reed, then of the Reconstruction Finance Corporation and soon to be Solicitor General. It was dismissed. However, an unpublicized and unanticipated criminal case had been won by the United States in New York in connection with the poultry code, which was administered by the Agricultural Adjustment Administration of the Department of Agriculture. It had serious defects as a test case on constitutionality; but the persons convicted appealed, and the government was forced to defend itself in the Supreme Court. The case was argued in a period of disillusionment with the National Recovery Administration, which had become virtually inactive. The result was a unanimous defeat on the grounds of unconstitutional delegation of legislative power to the Executive and the extension of federal regulation beyond the scope of the commerce clause of the Constitution (see *Schechter* v. *United States,* 295 U. S. 495). The case brought the termination of all proceedings under the regulatory provisions of the National Industrial Recovery Act. *Ed.*]

A letter to Brigadier General Hugh S. Johnson, Administrator, National Recovery Administration, April 9, 1934:

YOU will remember that at the outset of the National Recovery Administration the Department of Justice, upon consultation with you, instructed its district attorneys throughout the United States not to institute proceedings for violation of the National Industrial Recovery Act or codes without first referring the complaint to the Department of Justice in Washington. This was so that we might consult with you with respect to each case and develop a uniform policy of enforcement throughout the country. It seems, however, upon representations made through your legal department that the enforcement program is becoming pressing and the suggestion was made that an enforcement division should be built within the National Recovery Administration, consisting of lawyers to be deputized as Special Assistants to the Attorney General to carry cases into actual trial in the courts.

We have given this matter serious consideration and, confirming the discussion by Assistant Attorney General Stephens with you today, I believe that you are in accord with the following conclusions: A divided responsibility with respect to the duties of the Department of Justice to carry on in the courts the legal proceedings necessary to enforce the National Industrial Recovery Act and codes is not advisable for either of the departments concerned. The Department of Justice should, in my view, continue to exercise its established functions and assume full responsibility for the institution and prosecution of litigation and carry these duties on through its United States district attorneys. I am of the view, therefore, that the Department of Justice should not deputize members of your legal staff as Special Assistants to the Attorney General. Exceptions made to this rule during the past year in connection with other departments have not proved satisfactory, either from the standpoint of the Department of Justice or that of the sister department concerned.

I recognize, however, the desirability, both from your standpoint and that of the Department of Justice, of screening complaints through the local compliance and national enforcement organizations of the National Recovery Administration and through its legal staff, and I am, therefore, arranging to carry out the following plan of action: I shall release the district attorneys throughout the United States from the duty, in the ordinary course, of presenting to the Department of Justice in Washington, before action, complaints submitted to them by the Director of Enforcement of the National Recovery Administration, or by its state Directors of Compliance. When such complaints are presented to the district attorneys, they will, in pursuance of their duties and at their own discretion, themselves proceed.

It is understood that before such complaints are brought to the district attorneys, the National Recovery Administration will have used its best efforts to adjust or settle the dispute involved. It is understood, also, that it is the desire of your legal staff to assemble the facts and law with respect to the prosecution of individual cases and that, in the ordinary course, requests for complaints by the National Recovery Administration to the district attorneys will be supported by evidence assembled and by legal preparation. Such preparation of both facts and law will be welcomed by this department and its district attorneys, and you will note from the enclosed copy of instructions to the latter that they are being advised of the willingness of your legal staff to assist them upon their request (see Circular No. 2538).

I am instructing our district attorneys further that, if complaints are brought to them by persons other than authorized representatives of the National Recovery Administration, they will first refer such complaints to the National Recovery Administration Local Compliance Board having local jurisdiction; and that if, after investigation by such board or by your legal staff, the complaint is deemed unwarranted and is not submitted for suit, then, if the person originally preferring the complaint still insists upon its prosecution, the question of action shall be referred to the Department of Justice in Washington.

I hope that the above plan of action will assist in accomplishing the more expeditious enforcement which is desired.

A memorandum from Special Assistant M. S. Huberman,
December 13, 1934:

The facts concerning the discovery of the mistake in the executive order of September 13, 1933, modifying the petroleum code, are as follows:

The writer was assigned the preparation of the government's response to the petitions for certiorari in the *Panama* and *Amazon* cases. The latter case alone involved the petroleum code, and in the course of preparing the government's response to the petition for certiorari in that case, it was necessary to print in the response the precise code provisions involved in the case. These provisions were Sections 3 and 4 of Article III of the petroleum code, which provide for national control of oil production. The writer had in his possession a copy of the petroleum code as approved by the President on August 19, 1933, but could not find among the executive orders which the division collects and keeps in its library a print of the executive order of September 13, 1933. The writer thereupon telephoned Mr. Fahy, Counsel for the Petroleum Administrative Board, to inquire how he could get a copy of this executive order. Mr. Fahy stated that he would send over at once a photostat copy of the original executive order. Upon receiving this copy and comparing it with the code as originally approved, the writer discovered the mistake.

So far as the Antitrust Division was concerned, there was no occasion for looking into this matter until it became necessary to prepare the response to the petition for certiorari in the *Amazon* case. While these provisions of the code were also involved in the *Smith* case, it will be recalled that the preparation of the brief in that case had been assigned to the Solicitor for the Department of the Interior, subject, however, to review and approval by the Solicitor General and the Antitrust Division. The *Smith* case was, however, put off until the October 1934 term before the Solicitor for the Department of the Interior had submitted a completed brief to the Department of Justice. Had such a brief been submitted to us for our approval, the mistake would undoubtedly have been discovered then.

You are, of course, familiar with the fact that as soon as the mistake was discovered in the Department of Justice a full disclosure was immediately made to the Supreme Court.

Circular No. 2692, to United States Attorneys, June 4, 1935:

On May 27, 1935, the Supreme Court, in the case of *United States* v. *A. L. A. Schechter Poultry Corporation et al.,* held that the provisions of Title I of the National Industrial Recovery Act relating to the promulgation of codes of fair competition were in violation of the Constitution. In view of this decision, it has been determined that no further efforts should be made to enforce the codes of fair competition heretofore approved or prescribed by the President pursuant to the provisions of the act.

You are therefore authorized and requested promptly to dismiss all criminal prosecutions and to discontinue all equity suits instituted in your district under sections 3 (f) and 3 (c) of the National Industrial Recovery Act, and to take appropriate steps to dissolve injunctions previously obtained in proceedings brought under section 3 (c) of the act.

If there are pending in your district any suits seeking to enjoin government or code officials from enforcing the provisions of codes of fair competition, please take such action as is necessary to obtain the discontinuance of such suits. This should be accomplished by stipulation of the parties whenever possible. Otherwise, the court should be informed that the government does not intend to enforce the code or codes in question and that therefore the cases are moot and present no ground for equity jurisdiction.

5. Constitutional Stress and Strain

[On May 6, 1935, three weeks before the date of the *Schechter* decision, the Supreme Court handed down its opinion in *Railroad Retirement Board* v. *Alton* (295 U. S. 330). The case involved the constitutionality of the Railroad Retirement Act of June 27, 1934, by which a comprehensive retirement scheme for railroad workers was prescribed. The Department of Justice had worked hard to win the case, but in a five to four decision, with Mr. Justice Roberts as spokesman for the majority, the Court held the plan unconstitutional and indicated that any other compulsory method to achieve the same ends would likewise be unconstitutional. Voting with him were the traditional conservatives, Justices Van Devanter, McReynolds, Sutherland, and Butler. Chief Justice Hughes wrote a vigorous dissent, deploring particularly the denial to Congress of the power to pass any form of compulsory pension act for railroad employees.

On May 27, 1935, the date of the *Schechter* decision, the Court, unanimously though not unexpectedly, invalidated the Frazier-Lemke Farm Bankruptcy Act of June 28, 1934 (see *Louisville Joint Stock Land Bank* v. *Radford*, 295 U. S. 555). In *Humphrey* v. *United States* (295 U. S. 602), on the same day, it denied the power of the President to remove a member of the Federal Trade Commission for other than specified causes, thereby greatly narrowing the doctrine of many years standing enunciated in the *Myers* case (see *Myers* v. *United States*, 272 U. S. 52). It was in the light of these controversies, involving constitutional interpretations on the part of the Supreme Court which were devastating to the New Deal program, that the Attorney General prepared his address on "The American Constitutional Method." *Ed.*]

An office memorandum from Assistant Attorney General Stephens, and two letters to the President:

March 15, 1935

I am glad to report that we apparently handled the Retirement case to the satisfaction of Labor. * * * I invited the cooperation of Mr. Frank L. Mulholland, counsel to the Association of Railway Labor Executives, representing the standard twenty-one labor railway brotherhoods, and of Mr. Herman L. Ekern, counsel to the Railway Employees National Pension Association, an organization of railway employees organized specifically for the purpose of sponsoring railway pension legislation. * * * Both of them expressed themselves as well satisfied with the brief and with the argument. They indicated Labor had reason to feel well satisfied with the work of the Department of Justice in this case. * * * I also carried out your advice * * * that we associate Mr. Harry Shulman, counsel for the Railway Labor Board, in the argument.

March 16, 1935

My dear Mr. President: The Railroad Retirement case was heard a few days ago by the Supreme Court. Judge Stephens handled the argument for the government in admirable * * * fashion. I have just received a confidential memorandum from him which I pass along to you for your information. It will be interesting as an illustration of the pains we * * * take in these various matters to avoid heartburns and recriminations.

May 7, 1935

My dear Mr. President: Attached hereto you will find certain memoranda with regard to the Railroad Retirement Board matter decided yesterday by the Supreme Court. * * * The case was always a difficult one, but the form the opinions took would seem to indicate such a marked cleavage in the Supreme Court that it may be, and probably is, a forecast of what we may expect with reference to almost any form of social legislation the Congress may enact. Apparently there are at least four justices who are against any attempt to use the power of the federal government for bettering general conditions, except within the narrowest limitations. This is a terrific handicap and brings up again, rather acutely, matters we have previously discussed, including a proposed constitutional amendment. The very vigor of the language employed by the Chief Justice in the dissenting opinion is extraordinarily significant.

From an address before The Association of the Bar of the City of New York, entitled "The American Constitutional Method," December 18, 1935, dealing with historic changes in American constitutional interpretation, the passage of "doubtful" legislation, and the propriety of criticism of judicial decisions:

In the one hundred and forty-seven years which have elapsed since its adoption, the Constitution of the United States has probably been the subject of more controversy than any other great document in human history.

The framers of the Virginia-Kentucky Resolutions of 1798 took one view of its meaning, the Federalists another. The friends of the Bank of the United States thought that the Constitution conferred powers on the federal government which the opponents of the Bank, with equal earnestness, denied. The South Carolina Nullifiers of 1833 believed that a protective tariff was unconstitutional, while Judge Story and Daniel Webster were firm in the opposite belief. After the close of the Civil War, the so-called Radicals thought that the new amendments conferred on the Congress power to protect civil rights within the several states, while their opponents gave to the amendments a narrower construction, which was afterwards confirmed by the Supreme Court.

And yet, in the face of this series of examples, which might be multiplied almost indefinitely, there is nothing more characteristic of constitutional controversy than the recurrent assumption on the part of the disputants that their own construction alone has a sole and exclusive title to correctness, and that whoever challenges that construction, or argues against it, is guilty of no lighter offense than that of laying impious hands on the Ark of the Covenant. * * *

The Constitution is a fundamental document, expressed for the most part in general principles, and couching its precepts in language designed to make possible the attainment of the great ends of government. Mr. Justice Story, in delivering the opinion of the Court in *Martin* v. *Hunter*, 1 Wheaton, page 326, said:

The Constitution unavoidably deals in general language. It did not suit the purposes of the people, in framing this great charter of our liberties, to provide for minute specifications of its powers, or to declare the means by which those powers should be carried into execution. It was foreseen that this would be perilous and difficult, if not an impracticable, task. The instrument was not intended to provide merely for the exigencies of a few years, but was to endure through a long lapse of ages, the events of which were locked up in the inscrutable purposes of Providence. It could not be foreseen what new changes and modifications of power might be indispensable to effectuate the general objects of the charter; and restrictions and specifications, which, at the present, might seem salutary, might, in the end, prove the overthrow of the system itself. Hence, its powers are expressed in general terms, leaving to the legislature, from time to time, to adopt its own means to effectuate legitimate objects and to mould and model the exercise of its powers, as its own wisdom, and the public interests should require.

A similar thought was expressed by Chief Justice Marshall in *McCulloch* v. *Maryland,* 4 Wheaton at page 407.

The result of the process of constitutional construction depends on the relative weight given to this or that factor in a chain of inference. One mind will be impressed by the need of centralized power, another by the value of local self-government; one by immediate governmental necessities, another by the danger of governmental abuses; one by the rights of property, another by the claims of human sympathy; one by the sanctity of contracts, another by the requirements of essential justice. The interplay of these conflicting concepts, and the predominance of one or another at different periods of national development, are illustrated throughout history. * * *

Shifting national needs and maturing national ideals have, at times, resulted in reversals of previous decisions. * * * The history of the Court is not free from examples of reversals, or substantial modifications, of its position in cases involving issues of wide public interest and general controversy. An outstanding illustration was the important modification of the doctrine of the *Dartmouth College* case, after a change in the personnel of the Court, by the *Charles River Bridge* case. * * * It was in this case that Chief Justice Taney voiced the memorable sentiment: "While the rights of private property are sacredly guarded, we must not forget that the community also have rights and that the happiness and well-being of every citizen depends on their faithful preservation." (*Charles River Bridge* v. *Warren Bridge*, 11 Peters 420 at 548.)

It was this decision which called forth from Judge Story on the other hand, the gloomy remark that "the old constitutional doctrines are fast fading away and a change has come over the public mind from which I augur little good." In his dissenting opinion he said that the very raising of the contentions which had received the support of the majority of the Court was "sufficient to alarm every stockholder in every public enterprise of this sort throughout the whole country." Daniel Webster complained that "the decision has completely overturned a clear provision of the Constitution" and reported that "Judge Story thinks the Supreme Court is gone and I think so, too, and almost everything else is gone or seems rapidly going." Chancellor Kent wrote that he had reperused the *Charles River Bridge* decision with increased disgust, and that "It abandons or overthrows a great principle of constitutional morality. * * * It injures the moral sense of the community and destroys the sanctity of contracts." Yet, within fifteen years, a later judge, who was himself no ineffective defender of property rights, speaking of this decision was able to say: "No opinion of the Court has more fully satisfied the legal judgment of the country and consequently none has exercised more influence upon its legislation." (Campbell, J., in *State Bank* v. *Knoop*, 16 How. 409.)

A more recent instance in which the Supreme Court, on an issue of great public importance, originally took a position from which it was later to recede is afforded by the famous *E. C. Knight* case (156 U. S. 1 [1895]), the first to come before that tribunal under the Sherman Antitrust Act. It was held that a monopolistic combination of manufacturers could not be constitutionally reached by the antitrust laws since manufacture was not commerce and, therefore, was exempt from control by the Congress. The decision, while it stood, effectively paralyzed the operation of the antitrust laws for a number of years and drew sharp criticism from many commentators. * * * Within a few years, however, the Court reconsidered its position and held that while the Sherman Act might affect local conditions it could nevertheless be constitutionally applied even to transactions local in character if they operated to effect a restraint on interstate commerce. (*Northern Securities Company* v. *United States,* 193 U. S. 197 [1904]). This decision revitalized the antitrust laws and rendered them once more serviceable.

The outstanding instance in which the Supreme Court reversed itself was the *Legal Tender Cases* (12 Wallace 457 [1871]), where it overruled its prior decision in *Hepburn* v. *Griswold* (8 Wallace 603 [1870]). The *Hepburn* case, which was decided by a vote of four to three, represented a recognition, in the minds of a majority of the Court, of a body of economic doctrines resulting from the contact of certain economists with the bullion question as it had presented itself in England at the close of the Napoleonic wars. The economic soundness or unsoundness of these doctrines was, no doubt, a question of importance for legislative consideration. To read them, however, into constitutional requirements, as the majority of the Court did, imposed an unwarranted limitation upon an essential power of sovereignty. The decision met with some favor on economic grounds, but even its supporters referred to "the impropriety of taking from Congress and committing to a court of justice a task so plainly legislative in its nature." The *New York Times* stated that "the effect of the decision if allowed to stand strips the Nation of one of its means of warfare and defense." The doctrines of the *Legal Tender Cases* were reaffirmed, in the broadest terms, twelve years later in *Juilliard* v. *Greenman* (110 U. S. 421), with but one dissent; and, in the recent gold clause cases, they have been extended still further.

In numerous instances, without overruling particular decisions, the court has shifted its emphasis from one class of guiding considerations to another. The trends which lawyers attempt to deduce therefrom are, of course, of the utmost importance in determining the law for future cases and in advising clients in pending matters. Nevertheless, the history of the decisions indicates that few such trends have been sufficiently continuous to supply a basis of certainty as to their indefinite projection into the future. On the contrary, there has been, naturally and properly, an ebb and flow, with a conspicuous lack of basis for assurance as to when the ebb will cease and the flow set in.

Outstanding examples are to be found in the construction of the commerce clause, from *Gibbons* v. *Ogden* (9 Wheat. 1) to *Leisy* v. *Hardin* (135 U. S. 100); and the course of decisions in cases of legislative price fixing from *Munn* v. *Illinois* (94 U. S. 113), to *Nebbia* v. *New York* (291 U. S. 502). In *Gibbons* v. *Ogden* the Court had plainly indicated its view that the federal power to regulate interstate commerce is exclusive, with the result that all regulation of such commerce by the states is invalid. In the *License Cases* (5 How. 504), however, the Court upheld a state regulation of liquor imported from other states. A satisfactory line of demarcation between state and federal police regulations seemed ultimately established by *Cooley* v. *The Port Wardens* (12 How. 299), but this line was again unsettled by *Leisy* v. *Hardin, supra,* which once more cast doubt on the validity of state regulations affecting articles moving in interstate commerce.

The relations of legislative price fixing to the due process clause seemed settled on the basis of public interest from the time of the *Munn* case in 1876 to *German Alliance Ins. Co.* v. *Kansas* (233 U. S. 389), in 1914, but there followed in the nineteen-twenties a series of cases like the *Employment Agency* case (*Ribnick* v. *McBride,* 277 U. S. 350), and the *Theatre Ticket* case (*Tyson* v. *Banton,* 273 U. S. 418), which seemed to stand for some narrower doctrine, until the authority of the earlier decisions was reestablished and extended, two years ago, in the *Nebbia* case. * * *

In view of the close and inevitable connection which thus exists between the questions which the Court has to decide, and the great issues which agitate public opinion, it is not unnatural that the decisions and doctrines of the Court should be the subject of widespread public interest. The Constitution is supreme simply because it expresses the ultimate will of the people. The people are, accordingly, the masters of the Constitution and their mastery is expressed in the power of amendment, which, it must not be forgotten, is as much a part of the Constitution as any other provision. This power has been exerted three times in our history for the deliberate purpose of overriding a previous decision of the Supreme Court.

The first instance occurred at the very commencement of our government when the Eleventh Amendment prohibiting suits by private parties against a state was adopted to undo the effect of the decision of the Supreme Court in *Chisholm* v. *Georgia* (2 Dallas 419). The latest instance was the adoption of the Sixteenth Amendment to make a federal income tax possible over the decision of the Supreme Court in *Pollock* v. *Farmers Loan & Trust Co.* (158 U. S. 601). The other instance was the adoption of the Thirteenth Amendment to undo the effect of the *Dred Scott* decision (19 How. 393).

In discussions of our constitutional system there is no occasion to hurry over the *Dred Scott* decision with averted gaze. It holds a lesson for us. Newspapers of the time spoke of the decision as "exerting the most powerful and salutary influence throughout the United States," as "a closing and clinching confirmation of the settlement of the [slavery] issue," and as exerting "a mighty influence in diffusing sound opinions and restoring harmony and fraternal concord throughout the country." In connection with no other opinion was there ever a greater effort, on the part of those who agreed with it, to misrepresent all public expressions of disagreement as blows aimed at the judiciary. And yet, as we look back upon that controversy, we cannot doubt that the discussion was salutary, nor can we help feeling that the sound American attitude was that expressed by Abraham Lincoln when he said at Springfield, Illinois, June 26, 1857:

> We think the Dred Scott Decision is erroneous. We know the Court that made it has often overruled its own decisions, and we shall do what we can to have it overrule this.

And, again, in his first inaugural:

> The candid citizen must confess that if the policy of the government, upon vital questions affecting the whole people, is to be irrevocably fixed by decisions of the Supreme Court the instant they are made, in ordinary litigation between parties in personal actions, the people will have ceased to be their own rulers, having to that extent practically resigned their government into the hands of that eminent tribunal.

In a time of constitutional discussion like the present, when once again, as in so many preceding periods, clashing interests and conflicting ideals are pressing for expression in governmental action, and seeking to clothe themselves with the mantle of constitutional sanction while fixing the stigma of unconstitutionality on their opponents, it is well for us * * * to resort to the steadying influence of the historic view. Such consideration should shield us from ill-considered conclusions on, at least, two questions which, for the moment, seem to be creating much confusion of thought in both professional and lay minds. The first of these has to do with the propriety of public criticism of the decisions of the courts on constitutional questions.

It seems clear, from the fragments of history to which I have adverted, that such discussion has gone on from the beginning of our government, and has repeatedly affected the character of judicial decisions or has expressed itself in the form of constitutional amendments. Of course the fact that such criticism has occurred and has produced results is, of itself, no justification of its propriety. If the Constitution imposes, in all instances, a clear and specific mandate upon the judges, leaving them no discretion, and no room within which reasonable men may differ, then obviously any criticism of decisions so compelled would be grossly misdirected. What I have said should sufficiently indicate, however, that on many great constitutional issues decisions are not thus inexorably required by the Constitution. * * *

The second question is whether the legislative branch of the government, and the Executive, in view of their oath to support the Constitution, may rightfully take any action or join in the enactment of any law, the constitutionality of which is doubtful. It has been argued that, should the Executive or a member of the Congress have serious doubt whether a proposed enactment is constitutional, he would violate his oath of office by assenting to it or voting for it.

This argument rests on a misunderstanding as to the form and nature of the Constitution and as to the function of the Supreme Court with reference thereto. If we are aware, as all students of the Constitution must be, of the sweeping language in which its provisions are couched, and of the variety of considerations to which the Supreme Court must give weight, it seems clear that practically no new legislation of a controversial character can ever be said to be free from constitutional question. Indeed, the only legislation as to which no doubt can exist is an enactment substantially identical with some previous statute already approved by the Supreme Court; and even here there is the possibility of error in view of the fact that the Court has frequently reversed itself. The theory that any member of the Congress violates his oath who votes in favor of legislation not free from constitutional doubt would entirely exclude the possibility of legislation in new fields or of novel character.

As heretofore indicated, constitutional objections have been raised as to nearly every important piece of legislation enacted since the beginning of the government. The constitutionality of a protective tariff was questioned when the first tariff act was proposed and was bitterly debated for many years; the constitutionality of national banks was contested; the constitutionality of federal expenditures for internal improvements, roads, canals, and railways, was vigorously assailed; the constitutionality of the Interstate Commerce Act was the subject of long discussion; and the constitutionality of the acts establishing the Department of the Interior and the Department of Agriculture was vehemently denied. Speaking of the bill to establish the Interior Department, John C. Calhoun said: "This monstrous bill will turn over the whole interior affairs of the government to this Department and it is one of the greatest steps ever made to absorb all the remaining powers of the States."

Certainly, no one, however, who is familiar with our history, and assuredly no lawyer, would undertake to argue that, because the Court ultimately determined that a particular enactment was constitutional, there was no reasonable ground for doubt at the outset. President Taft, for example, vetoed the Webb-Kenyon Act on the ground that his oath of office did not permit him to give his assent to an act of doubtful constitutionality. In fact, he went rather far in admonishing the Congress as to its duty in the premises. The act, however, was passed over his veto and, in due course, the Supreme Court pronounced it constitutional. (*Clark Distilling Co.* v. *Western Maryland Ry.*, 242 U. S. 311.) * * *

The correct course would seem to be that the Executive and the members of the legislative branch, when not clearly convinced of the constitutionality of a measure otherwise desirable, should not necessarily regard themselves as thereby deterred from enacting it, but should consider the advisability of leaving the doubt to be determined where it can be determined authoritatively, namely by the Supreme Court. This was the position of Senator Fessenden of Maine in the debate on the Legal Tender Acts, when he said: "I have not touched the constitutional question. * * * We may well leave that question to be settled by the courts, and not attempt to settle it ourselves." (57 Congressional Globe 767.)

It was also the position of Madison during the first Congress when called upon to vote on the bill for the encouragement of the cod fisheries. Madison felt that the bill was unconstitutional in certain respects, and favored an amendment to eliminate such provisions. The amendment failed, and it is interesting to note that notwithstanding his conscientious view that the bill was in the main probably unconstitutional, he nevertheless voted for it on its final passage. As has been heretofore noted, Lincoln was not prepared, in certain instances at least, to let such a question rest, even after the Supreme Court had spoken. * * *

The absolute theory of one and only one rational construction of the Constitution renders impossible any proper understanding of the nature of our American constitutional method and of the functions of our Supreme Court. With us, the people have established a Constitution which is supreme over all the acts of government, legislative, executive, and judicial alike, because it is the highest expression of the popular will. Of necessity, it employs broad language which leaves a wide area for legitimate differences of opinion. Within this arena of debate all voices must be heard. * * *

Our government is not a documentary, a political, or a judicial absolutism. The American constitutional method is a process of adaptation and growth, as well as a means whereby wrongs may be corrected and governmental measures may be attuned to the essentials of justice, through the orderly ways of discussion and education, as opposed to the violent changes and intolerable tyrannies by which absolute governments are inevitably characterized. Were this not true the Constitution would be a dam against which the waters of life would beat in vain, rather than a directing channel through which the stream of national existence may safely pass.

6. Statesmanship and the Law

[The government had twice ceased attempts to have the Supreme Court pass upon the validity of its "slum clearance" program (see *United States* v. *Certain Lands in the City of Louisville,* 9 F. Supp. 137, 78 F. (2d) 684, 294 U. S. 735, 296 U. S. 567, 297 U. S. 726). The decisions and the attitude displayed by the Court in the *Schechter* and other cases cast serious doubts on the constitutionality of the Agricultural Adjustment Act. An amendatory act was passed on August 24, 1935, to cure possible defects on grounds of delegation of legislative power and other points. Injunction suits against collection of the processing tax, which was a basic feature of the act, piled up rapidly until there were some two thousand. In order to prevent the recovery of taxes from the government in the event the act were found unconstitutional, the sponsors of the bill had sought to include provisions adequate to foreclose such recovery unless processors could show that the taxes had not been passed on to consumers or back to producers.

The Agricultural Adjustment Act processing tax case was prepared with great care, but on January 6, 1936, the government went down to defeat by a vote of six to three. Mr. Justice Roberts wrote the opinion of the majority and Mr. Justice Stone wrote a sharp dissent which implied that the majority had resorted to "a tortured construction of the Constitution" (see *United States* v. *Butler,* 297 U. S. 1). Thereafter, to prevent unjust self-enrichment of processors in suits recovering taxes paid but not really borne by them, Congress provided for a "windfall" tax at a high rate, the validity of which was later upheld (see *Anniston Mfg. Co.* v. *Davis,* 301 U. S. 337).

The government won a narrow victory in the Tennessee Valley Authority case, decided February 17, 1936 (see *Ashwander* v. *T. V. A.,* 297 U. S. 288). It lost again in the case to test the validity of the Bituminous Coal Conservation Act (see *Carter* v. *Carter Coal Company,* 298 U. S. 238), decided May 18, 1936, by a vote of five to four on certain points and six to three on other points. Organizations of lawyers—such as the Lawyers Committee of the Liberty League—attacked the legislative program of the administration with speeches and elaborate, widely distributed legal memoranda. Attorney General Cummings' address on "The Right Arm of Statesmanship" was delivered in this atmosphere of constitutional controversy. *Ed.*]

A letter to the President, November 19, 1935:

THE government brief in the case of *United States* v. *Butler, Receiver of Hoosac Mills Corporation,* has just been printed.

This is the outstanding case dealing with processing and floor-stocks taxes under the A.A.A. as amended.

I am well pleased with this brief. For a brief, it is rather monumental in size, running to 280 printed pages, and with the appendix running to 100 pages. It deals with every possible aspect of the question.

As in most such matters, it is the work of many hands, in which a large number of lawyers from both the Department of Justice and the Department of Agriculture collaborated. In addition to the key men who worked on this brief, there were twelve or fifteen others who had some part in it. An enormous amount of labor and research went into the work.

Statement upon the decision of the Supreme Court holding the Bituminous Coal Conservation Act unconstitutional, May 18, 1936:

A careful study of the majority opinion and of the other two opinions will have to be made before it can be ascertained what course may still be open to the government in dealing with the problems of the bituminous coal mining industry.

It should not be overlooked that the opinion of the three dissenting justices, and the separate opinion of the Chief Justice, constitute the first clear expression by members of the Supreme Court upholding the constitutionality of price-fixing for commodities moving in interstate commerce. Important, also, is the statement in the opinion of Mr. Justice Cardozo "that the prevailing opinion leaves the price provisions open for consideration in the future."

From "The Right Arm of Statesmanship," an address at a meeting of the Bar Association of the District of Columbia, December 5, 1936:

The growth of great aggregations of capital, the corporate structures that have been built up to serve them, the rich rewards that are open to all those engaged, professionally or otherwise, in these enterprises have, unless we, as lawyers, are very careful, a tendency to blunt our perception of public need. We are absorbed in personal or narrowly professional matters. Our time is intensively taken. Client relations serve to accentuate the stress laid upon private as opposed to public interests. If business finds itself meeting these unaccustomed problems with an eye primarily directed toward personal profit, it is not perhaps strange. I daresay, also, that it is equally difficult for the practicing lawyer to forget the habits of a strictly individualistic age and attune himself to the fresher outlook which he must ultimately take if he is to survive as a wise counsellor and friend.

We are not merely the advisers of those who would preserve the *status quo* at all hazards. We are servants of society, accredited representatives of a judicial system which has for its ultimate purpose the administration of justice in its highest sense. In these great areas of change and progress, would we not be better citizens, better patriots, aye, and better lawyers, if we were a little less concerned with the technicalities which have served so well in many a strategic contest and a little more given to a broader view of that movement of society which seeks to stake out a more advanced frontier of justice?

The fault is not all on one side and the exigencies of modern life have much to answer for, but the fact remains that many of our learned brethren have given less and less attention not only to public service but even to a public way of thinking while in private practice. In the meantime statesmanship has shattered the bonds of precedent and is seeking ways to fulfill the just hopes of our people. It is something of an anomaly that in the face of great problems we turn our affairs over to public servants who strive to supply the means to answer the public need, while at that very moment many of the most gifted members of our profession exercise their ingenuity and their experience to break down the structure thus created. * * *

I confess to a feeling of uneasiness when I reflect upon this state of the public mind. The public is conscious that that which was unplanned or selfishly guided in the past must take its place in an orderly governmental process and that a great cleansing and rebuilding program must go forward. It is impatient with artificial restraints and becomes irritated by those refinements of logic which are calculated to render attempts at social reconstruction sterile or abortive.

One of the unfortunate by-products of this changing point of view is a tendency upon the part of many of our people to be restive under the slow processes of the law and to cease to look upon the structure of our society as the basis of security and prosperity. This is not a wholesome situation and we must make shift to amend it. Lawyers cannot abdicate their great function as statesmen without a tragic loss to America. They must not lose their position as the friends of progress. They must not permit prejudices to accumulate against the profession. They must seek earnestly to determine how they may regain that lost prestige which was so admittedly theirs in the larger and more spacious days when America was in the making.

Questions of vast significance are moving to their solution. I doubt if there has ever been a period in our history when there was a greater need of lawyers capable and willing to give their great ability to the wise solution of our insistent problems. We not only need men of this sort in the legislatures, in the Congress, and in executive and judicial positions, but we need them in private practice where, with generous wisdom, they may advise helpfully in those processes of accommodation which are so pathetically essential in these modern days. The nation as a whole needs the service of the profession as a whole. The inward unity of America is a precious thing, and no element of our national life can afford to forget it or neglect to serve it.

Let it not be forgotten that social progress, and indeed all measures of governmental readjustment, must take on a legal form. When one considers the intricacies of modern business and the unexpected fashion in which a measure, apparently well conceived, may produce undesired collateral results, the difficulties of legislation are readily apparent. The program should not be merely the product of an administration * * *; it should be the program of America, in which * * * business, labor, agriculture, and the legal profession generously collaborate.

I am proud of the great traditions of our profession. With rare exceptions the vital documents of liberty that mark the progress of human kind have been formulated by lawyers. The charters of our colonies, the constitutions and statutes of our states, the federal statutes, the Declaration of Independence and the federal Constitution, without which America as we know it would not exist, have, to our imperishable fame, been the products of our labors. All through our history, great leaders of the bar have spoken movingly in the cause of human rights and in every era have fashioned some form of enactment to make certain of each popular advance.

Is it not appropriate that we should once more take stock of ourselves and consider again the heights to which our brethren of earlier days carried the standards of our profession? How better can this be done than by reflecting upon our duty to those innumerable, unnamed, unknown, and sometimes forgotten clients —the people of America. * * * To criticize, to debate, to litigate, all these things are very well, but the profession must not surrender its role of leadership, it must not forget that the law is the right arm of statesmanship.

7. The "Court Plan"

[After the decisions of the Supreme Court holding the National Industrial Recovery Act and other New Deal measures unconstitutional, almost every important office of the administration was flooded with suggestions as to methods of avoiding the stultifying effects of judicial review. Most of these suggestions were referred to the Department of Justice, where hundreds of them were collected. Those which seemed at all feasible were studied with care, finally reduced to a list of five, and exhaustively discussed in an elaborate, composite memorandum dated December 10, 1936. These five suggestions were: (1) that Congress declare that its own determination of fact, such for instance as what constitutes interstate commerce, should be conclusive in the courts; (2) that Congress, through its power over procedure, declare the number of judges necessary to invalidate an act of Congress, fixing the number so as to prevent the defeat of a legislative program by a bare majority of the court; (3) that Congress withdraw from the courts the jurisdiction to pass upon the constitutionality of federal legislation; (4) that the number of Supreme Court justices be increased outright so as to insure liberal decisions; and (5) that prompt retirement of judges be made attractive through the reduction of annual retirement compensation by progressively greater amounts for each year that a judge remained on the bench after the age of seventy. In the light of the analysis made, none of these proposals seemed acceptable.

The fact remained, however, that the presidential election of 1936 had retained the administration in power by an overwhelming majority, and that the vote presumably indicated widespread approval of the administration program and the desire that it should be carried forward. Yet a major segment of it had been declared void by the Supreme Court. The spending program remained, including relief and loans to private borrowers and to the states; but even here a shadow had been cast by the Agricultural Adjustment Act decision. Unless its policies could be made effective, the administration faced the prospect of discredit, even at the hands of its friends.

Under these circumstances, in a special message to the Congress on February 5, 1937, the President proposed a reorganization of the judicial branch of the government. The President's papers on this subject will appear in the volume of his "Public Papers and Addresses" for 1937 (see *The Public Papers and Addresses of Franklin D. Roosevelt, 1935,* pp. 13-14). The essence of his judiciary proposal was the appointment of an

146

additional judge for each judge of retirement age—that is, of seventy years of age or more—who failed or refused to retire (upon full salary) as permitted by law. Thus, either the courts would be increased in size or, if judges of retirement age did retire, new judges would be appointed in their places. In either event, new judges, presumably of a liberal turn of mind, would be appointed. These would either overcome or supersede the conservative majorities on most courts, including the Supreme Court. (Other items in the proposal stressed the need of more judges to dispose of crowded dockets, machinery for the special assignment of judges to temporarily congested districts, and restraints on the issuance of injunctions.)

The debates on this proposal continued through the spring of 1937 and far into the summer, with increasing bitterness in the press, in the Congress, and at the tea tables of Washington. The struggle culminated in the substitution and enactment of another measure which eliminated the highly controversial features of the bill submitted by the President. *Ed.*]

From an office memorandum to Assistant Attorney General John Dickinson, December 28, 1935:

IF IT should so happen that the Supreme Court decides adversely to practically all the so-called New Deal legislation and sets up constitutional standards which cannot be met, no doubt there will be strong pressure in many quarters for a constitutional amendment. * * *

Any number of suggestions for constitutional amendments have been made. One of the most talked of at the present time is the one I spoke to you about some days ago. This amendment is designed to accomplish the following results:

1. The conferring upon the Supreme Court of explicit authority to pass on constitutional questions, thereby setting at rest what discussion there is as to this being a usurped authority.

2. Limiting to the Supreme Court the right to pass on constitutional questions by taking away from the lower courts any authority on that score.

3. Permitting the district courts to try out questions involving constitutional issues so that there may be a factual background.

4. Permitting such courts to reserve the case for the advice of

the Supreme Court if a constitutional issue is involved that is determinative of the matter.

5. All acts of Congress to be deemed constitutional and free from attack except by the route mentioned, and to be deemed constitutional until the Supreme Court otherwise declares.

6. Should the Supreme Court declare a law unconstitutional, it is to set forth specifically in what particulars it is unconstitutional, thereby giving to the Congress the right to cure the defects if they are curable.

7. If the defects are incurable by amendment, modification, or otherwise, then the matter is to be at an end unless the Congress, at a subsequent session, a general election having intervened, shall repass the law in its original form. Such law, if approved by the President in the usual course, is to be the law of the land and no longer open to constitutional challenge. * * *

One modification suggested is that the second time the bill is passed, it must pass by a two-thirds vote.

A letter to the President, January 29, 1936:

I return herewith, as you request, the clipping * * *. It is a very discerning analysis of the situation. The writer, however, says, "What has come into view is the need for the ample revision of the foundations of the Constitution." I do not believe we have quite reached that point yet.

The real difficulty is not with the Constitution but with judges who interpret it. As long as a majority of those who have the final say in such matters are wedded to their present theories, there are but two courses open to us. We must endeavor, with all the ingenuity at our disposal, to find a way to bring helpful national legislation within the explicit terms of their decisions, or we must frankly meet the issue of a constitutional amendment.

For the present, at least, I think our proper course is along the former line rather than the latter. The hand has not yet been played out. If we come to the question of a constitutional

amendment, enormous difficulties are presented. No one has yet
suggested an amendment that does not do either too much or too
little, or which does not raise practical and political questions
which it would be better to avoid. If we had liberal judges, with
a lively sense of the importance of the social problems which have
now spilled over state lines, there would be no serious difficulty;
and the existing constitutional restraint when interpreted by such
a court would be very salutary.

All of the foregoing leads me to suggest that we might well
be giving some serious thought to an amendment to the Constitution (should we find we are forced to that point) which would
require the retirement of all federal judges, or, at least, all Supreme Court judges, who have reached or who hereafter reach
the age of seventy years. It may very well be that life tenure lies
at the heart of our difficulty and that there should be no such
thing as life tenure for any public official of any kind, executive,
legislative, or judicial. As, of course, you know, there are states
which have such a constitutional provision and it works very well.
Such an amendment would probably encounter less opposition
than almost any other I can think of. It would have the advantage of not changing in the least degree the structure of our government, nor would it impair the power of the Court. It would
merely insure the exercise of the powers of the Court by judges
less likely to be horrified by new ideas. There may be variants of
the proposed amendment which will suggest themselves as the
matter is studied. For instance, it might be coupled with a provision giving to the Supreme Court explicit power to pass on constitutional questions and taking away or denying such power to in-
ferior courts.

*From a radio address entitled "The President's Proposals for
Judicial Reorganization," February 14, 1937:*

From the beginning of President Roosevelt's first administration I have been in intimate contact with him with reference to
ways and means of improving the administration of justice. Lit-

erally thousands of proposals have been considered. In addition, the critical literature of the law has been searched, and the lessons of experience have been canvassed. Out of it have come certain well-defined conclusions. * * *

The four outstanding defects of our judicial system—delays and congestion in the courts, the chaos created by conflicting decisions and the reckless use of the injunctive power, aged and infirm judges, and the need for new blood in the judiciary—are dealt with by the President in his message of the fifth of February, in which he submits a simple, well rounded, comprehensive, and workable system which covers all these points and meets all these needs. * * *

Despite the manifest need of these reforms, despite the comprehensive and reasonable nature of these proposals, despite the long history which brought them forth, despite the eminent judges and statesmen who have either expressed views or actually proposed measures of substantially the same character, the President is now the storm center of a virulent attack. * * * We are solemnly assured that the courts are to be made mere appendages to the executive office, that the judges to be appointed cannot be trusted to support the Constitution, and that the tragedies of despotism await only the adoption of the President's recommendations.

Yet, no serious objection has been made to any one of the purposes or to any part of the plan, except its application to certain members of the Supreme Court. Why the Supreme Court should be granted a special exemption from the plan, no one has been able to explain. If there were no judges on that Court of retirement age, there would be no substantial objection from any responsible quarter. What then is the real objection? It is simply this: Those who wish to preserve the *status quo* want to retain on the bench judges who may be relied upon to veto progressive measures.

Opponents of this measure assert that it is immoral. The reason they charge that it is immoral is because they are unable to charge that it is unconstitutional. Whether the plan is immoral or not must be tested by the results it produces. If it produces a wholesome result in a perfectly legal way, it can scarcely be called immoral.

It is true that the President's proposal may possibly but not necessarily have the effect of increasing the size of the Supreme Court. But there is nothing new in that. Jefferson, Jackson, Lincoln, and Grant, together with the Congresses of their respective periods, saw no objection to enlarging the Court.

Again it is loosely charged that the present proposal is a bold attempt to "pack" the Court. * * * Every increase in the membership of a court is open to that charge, and indeed every replacement is subject to the same objection. Under the President's proposal, if there is any increase in the total number of judges, it will be due entirely to the fact that judges now of retirement age elect to remain on the bench. If those judges think it would be harmful to the Court to increase its membership, they can avoid that result by retiring upon full pay.

The Constitution imposes upon all presidents the duty of appointing federal judges, by and with the advice and consent of the Senate. * * * George Washington appointed twelve members of the Supreme Court. Jackson appointed five. Lincoln appointed five. Grant appointed four. Harrison appointed four. Taft appointed five and elevated still another to be Chief Justice. Harding appointed four, and Hoover appointed three. President Roosevelt has appointed none at all. * * *

Out of every flight of hysteria on this question there comes a further charge that the President's proposals will lead to dictatorship, through the establishment of an evil precedent. But there have been far more significant precedents than this. Jefferson ignored a subpoena issued by Chief Justice Marshall. Jackson, in a stubborn moment, told the Supreme Court to try and enforce its own decrees. Lincoln totally disregarded Chief Justice Taney's demand that the privilege of the writ of habeas corpus be restored. No one of these Presidents was a dictator, but each illustrated how powerless the courts are unless the purity of their motives and the justice of their decisions win them the popular support.

Hearings on the President's proposals; from a statement before the Senate Committee on the Judiciary, March 10, 1937 (Hearings on S. 1392, 75th Cong., 1st Sess., pp. 6-8, 11, 12):

In the course of our history the size of the Supreme Court has been changed six times, both by increasing and reducing its membership. The power to make these changes is confided by the Constitution to the President and the Congress. The exercise of a constitutional power for a wholesome purpose furnishes a sound, not a dangerous, precedent. The fact that we may abstain from using a power admittedly ours is by no means a guaranty that that same power will not be used by others hereafter. It is a strange doctrine that we must refrain from doing a good and necessary thing for fear that many years from now someone may use the same authority to do an evil thing. Let us study our own problems and solve them in the light of our own needs. * * *

Finally, it is suggested that the matter be left to a constitutional amendment. To this there are definite answers. First, no amendment is required because the proposal is clearly constitutional. What is really sought by some is a referendum, not to the whole people, but to part of the people of only thirteen states [who, under the Constitution, could prevent an amendment]. Secondly, the phraseology of any proposed amendment would be the subject of endless debate and; once submitted, might suffer the fate of the child-labor amendment, which has been pending for thirteen years. Thirdly, any amendment must, if adopted, be construed and applied by the same judges who have brought us to our present pass. In the words of Thomas Jefferson, "The attempt to make the law plainer by amendment is only throwing out new amendments for sophistry." All that is required is an enlightened interpretation of the Constitution.

From an office memorandum to Solicitor General Stanley Reed,
April 10, 1937:

I suppose you have glanced through the April number of the *American Bar Association Journal.* It looks like a propaganda magazine in opposition to the President's plan. Practically every leading article is an attack upon the President's plan, and not one article supports it. It is rather astounding to me that a publication of this type should not have included at least one article on the other side, when there are so many of them available. I notice that they even published the statement of Dean Smith, of Columbia Law School. This would seem to indicate that out of all the mass of testimony presented at the Senate hearings, the law journal deliberately selected only one statement, and that one, like all the others it printed, violently opposing the President's plan. * * * After all the *Journal* is not supposed to be a partisan publication giving only one side of a controversy of the first order. * * * However this may be, the issue is a valuable one from our standpoint as it is a rather complete exposition of about all that can be said against the President's plan. * * *

I also call your attention to Mr. Lecher's article on page 242. You will see that he is still fussing with the attempt to indicate that there may be some doubts as to the constitutionality of the bill. It is a rather strained attempt. Nevertheless, we might give it some thought. It seems rather distressing to the opposition that they have to throw up their hands and practically admit that what we propose to do cannot be challenged on constitutional grounds. They have been so accustomed of late years to challenging everything we attempt on that basis that it must give them a queer feeling to have to admit that the plan is constitutional. Every once in a while I notice an article by someone who writhes under this situation and puts forth a feeble, tentative sort of protest.

*From "Progress of the President's Plan for Judicial Reform," an
address in the National Radio Forum, April 26, 1937:*

The President's plan is direct, simple, workable—and constitutional. Of all the plans submitted, it is the least drastic. It touches no part of the Constitution. It impairs no power of the Supreme Court. It entails no disheartening delay. It enables our country to move forward to the solution of the problems that crowd upon us; and it preserves the courts and the Constitution as the workable instruments of a free people.

8. The Vicissitudes of Minimum Wage Legislation

[In the swing toward conservatism which characterized the "back to normalcy" movement of the postwar period, the Supreme Court in 1923, by a vote of five to three, held unconstitutional a minimum wage law of the District of Columbia as taking liberty and property without due process of law (see *Adkins* v. *Children's Hospital*, 261 U. S. 525). The decision was widely criticized at the time and during succeeding years, but its principles remained the law of the land. In *Morehead* v. *New York*, 298 U. S. 587, decided June 1, 1936, the Court by a vote of five to four adhered to the established precedent and placed the stamp of unconstitutionality upon the minimum wage law of the State of New York. This action indicated that the Court was not merely hostile to federal New Deal measures, but was opposed to the achievement of broad social ends by state action as well. Sharp criticism followed, from diverse political groups. On March 29, 1937, in a case involving a law of the State of Washington, the Court by a vote of five to four overruled the *Adkins* case and held the law constitutional (see *West Coast Hotel Company* v. *Parrish,* 300 U. S. 379). News of this action on the part of the Court was received with enthusiasm by the administration, though not without pointed comments on the effects of the election and the court reform movement on the trend of judicial interpretation. *Ed.*]

From a statement on the decision sustaining state minimum wage legislation, March 31, 1937:

AFTER twenty years of unabated struggle, a state minimum wage act is now for the first time sustained by the Supreme Court. Only by the shift of the vote of a single justice were the constitutional rights of the state legislatures reinstated.

So it happens that the Constitution on Monday, March 29, 1937, does not mean the same thing that it meant on Monday, June 1, 1936. For on Monday June 1, 1936, the Court stated:

> The decision [the *Adkins* decision in 1923] and the reasoning upon which it rests clearly show that the state is

155

without power by any form of legislation to prohibit, change or nullify contracts between employers and adult women workers as to the amount of wages to be paid.

While in numerous cases the Court has reversed or substantially qualified its judicial interpretation of the Constitution, it has seldom done so under circumstances so striking as in the recent minimum wage case. Indeed, in order to find so dramatic a reversal one must go back to the *Income Tax* case in 1894. There, a shift in the vote of a single justice precipitated a situation which forced the American people to resort to a constitutional amendment, while in the recent case the change of a judicial mind obviated the need of such an amendment.

It is to be regretted that four out of the nine justices have so strikingly demonstrated that they entertain a view of the Constitution which denies its adaptability to modern conditions.

This decision also throws into strong relief the futility of the suggestion made in some quarters that more careful draftsmanship of proposed legislation would avoid all constitutional difficulties. The New York minimum wage statute was drafted with the greatest care and competency to meet the objections specifically raised by the Court in the *Adkins* case. And Chief Justice Hughes, dissenting in the *Morehead* case, expressly took note of "its provisions for careful and deliberate procedure" and found that the New York statute was free of the feature so strongly denounced in the *Adkins* case. Yet the majority struck down the carefully drawn statute in the *Morehead* case with the same alacrity that it struck down the statute in the *Adkins* case. And then in the Washington case it reversed itself and sustained a statute which contains the very feature which, more than any other—so the Court stated in the *Adkins* case—stamped the statute as arbitrary and invalid. Economic predilections do not yield to skilled draftsmanship, although sometimes they yield to the pressure of events.

A statute, invalid for fourteen years, is revived by the Supreme Court; opinion to the President on the status of the District of Columbia minimum wage law, April 3, 1937:

In answer to your request of April 2, 1937, for my opinion respecting the present status of the District of Columbia minimum wage law, in view of the recent decision of the Supreme Court in the case of *West Coast Hotel Co.* v. *Parrish* overruling the case of *Adkins* v. *Children's Hospital,* 261 U. S. 525, I have the honor to advise you as follows:

The District of Columbia minimum wage law was approved and became effective on September 19, 1918 (c. 174, 40 Stat. 960). The act provided for its administration by a Minimum Wage Board to be appointed by the Commissioners of the District of Columbia. It further provided for the organization of the Board and defined its powers and duties. The Board appointed under the statute, acting in pursuance thereof, issued its order prohibiting the employment in the District of Columbia of women or minor girls in certain industries at less than a prescribed wage per month. The Children's Hospital sought to enjoin the Board from enforcing its order against the hospital. An injunction issued was sustained by the Supreme Court in the case of *Adkins* v. *Children's Hospital,* decided April 9, 1923, on the ground that the statute was unconstitutional. The effect of this decision was to suspend the further enforcement of the act.

In the case of *West Coast Hotel Co.* v. *Parrish, supra,* the Supreme Court said, "Our conclusion is that the case of *Adkins* v. *Children's Hospital, supra,* should be, and it is overruled."

The decisions are practically in accord in holding that the courts have no power to repeal or abolish a statute, and that notwithstanding a decision holding it unconstitutional a statute continues to remain on the statute books; and that if a statute be declared unconstitutional and the decision so declaring it be subsequently overruled, the statute will then be held valid from the date it became effective. * * *

It is, therefore, my opinion that the District of Columbia

minimum wage law is now a valid act of the Congress and may be administered in accordance with its terms.

From "Progress of the President's Plan for Judicial Reform," an address in the National Radio Forum, April 26, 1937:

Nearly three months have elapsed since the President submitted to the Congress his proposal for the reorganization of the federal judiciary. Now that the Senate hearings, after six weeks of spirited debate, have been brought to a close, let us briefly survey the situation. Those who testified in behalf of the plan pointed out the defects in the existing system and called attention to the unmistakable and improper invasion of the legislative field by the Supreme Court. With few exceptions even the opponents criticized the decisions of the Supreme Court, and called for effective remedies—presumably by constitutional amendment. Pitifully few of those who testified approved in whole-hearted fashion the course the Supreme Court has pursued. And now, as if to make the conclusion unanimous, the Supreme Court, albeit by a narrow margin, has voted itself a "winter garment of repentance" and has upset crucial decisions of long standing. Manifestly these events have contributed to a real understanding of our present difficulties. The need for judicial reform has been demonstrated. Only the method remains open to debate.

* * *

Twenty-five years ago, for example, the Supreme Court held valid a statute prohibiting the use of the channels of interstate commerce for the transportation of women or girls for immoral purposes. Five years later, however, the Court held that it was improper to close the channels of commerce to the products of child labor. Yet, the Constitution makes no distinction between the protection of women and the protection of children.

When another five years had passed the Court decided that even women in industry were entitled to no protection and held invalid the minimum wage statute of the District of Columbia.

In 1925 and 1936, it again struck down acts adopted to prevent gross exploitation of the labor of women. In those three decisions, five judges of the Supreme Court determined social policy and the scope of the Constitution for fifteen years. Then, less than a month ago, again by the narrowest of margins, the line of minimum wage decisions was completely reversed. Who "amended" the Constitution on March 29th last? Not the President. Not the Congress. Not the states. Not the people. The Supreme Court "amended" it by correcting its previous misinterpretation.

This bewildering history demonstrates how courts may ignore patent facts and paralyze both states and nation, by the peripatetic vote of a single judge holding office for life. It demonstrates, too, that enlightened judgment, when it comes, may hang precariously upon the social or economic views of one man. Small wonder that, in our own day, eminent lawyers and jurists have spoken of the Supreme Court as "a continuous constitutional convention."

The temper of these times demands a realistically minded court, if our institutions are to thrive—not a reactionary court temporarily in a liberal mood. It is not the Constitution that is at fault, nor was the cumbersome machinery of amendment designed nor can it serve to correct judicial mistakes one by one. Some judges, seeking to read their own views and social philosophies into our fundamental law, insist that, if their Constitution stands in the way of needed legislation, the only remedy is by way of formal amendment .And when, over their protest, constitutional interpretations are attuned to the facts of the time, such adjustments are made not by them but by their brethren. They remain fixed and immutable. When the nation moves it moves around them.

9. Repercussions of the Court Plan

[On April 12, 1937, the Supreme Court decisions were announced in a number of National Labor Relations Act cases *(N. L. R. B. v. Jones & Laughlin Steel Corporation,* 301 U. S. 1; *Associated Press v. N. L. R. B.,* 301 U. S. 103; *Washington V. & M. C. Co. v. N. L. R. B.,* 301 U. S. 142).* In and out of the administration, the act had been regarded as almost clearly invalid on precedent. The alignment of judges varied in the several cases, but the National Labor Relations Act was upheld in each case. The *Carter Coal* case was not specifically overruled with respect to the limitations on federal control over national labor relations in the production of goods intended for interstate commerce; but if the facts are studied, the former decision seems to retain little significance. On May 24, 1937, decisions were announced in cases involving federal and state social security legislation, in which the statutes were upheld in all instances *(Carmichael v. Southern Coal and Coke Company,* 301 U. S. 495; *Steward Machine Company v. Davis,* 301 U. S. 548; *Helvering v. Davis,* 301 U. S. 619).* By those decisions the way was paved to go forward with an important segment of the administration program.

It seems clear that the proposed judicial reorganization and the ensuing struggle brought about a more liberal interpretation of the Constitution. On the other hand, the labor act decisions and the social security decisions had repercussions on the Court Plan, in providing basis for the belief that constitutional interpretation had been reformed, so that drastic legislation with respect to the judiciary was no longer needed.

After the beginning of the new trend of judicial decisions and the retirement of one of the conservative judges, Mr. Justice Van Devanter, which took place June 2, 1937, the Congress itself sought to secure a judicial reconsideration of municipal bankruptcy legislation. The Municipal Bankruptcy Act of May 24, 1934, had been declared invalid on May 25, 1936 *(Ashton v. Cameron County District,* 298 U. S. 513), by a vote of five to four. A new law covering the same subject was now enacted with the possibility in mind that the court might uphold such a measure. A case based on the new act was decided by the Supreme Court after the retirement of Mr. Justice Sutherland, another of the conservatives, which took place January 18, 1938. The measure was upheld, with only two justices dissenting *(United States v. Bekins,* 304 U. S. 27). Ed.]

Statement on the decision of the Supreme Court sustaining the National Labor Relations Act, April 14, 1937:

MANIFESTLY a struggle has been going on within the Court itself, and, temporarily at least, more liberal views seem to have gained ascendency. Gratifying as these recent decisions are, it must be remembered that they are five-to-four decisions, and it is impossible to predict what will be the attitude of the Court in connection with the whole range of necessary legislation dealing with child labor, sweatshops, minimum wages, maximum hours, old age benefits, and other social matters. All these have yet to run the gauntlet of judicial interpretation. The loss of one vote in the recent cases would have made the Constitution mean something quite different from what it appears to mean now, and four members of the Court still stand as a battalion of death against all major social legislation, state and national.

It is not a wholesome situation when an administration, under a mandate to carry out a progressive program, must face a court of nine, with four votes lost to it in advance. The margin is too narrow and the risk is too great.

Radio address under the auspices of Labor's Non-Partisan League, April 19, 1937, following the minimum wage and labor act decisions of the Supreme Court:

During recent months the responsibilities of the Supreme Court in interpreting and applying the Constitution have been more thoroughly sifted and explored than ever before. It is at length becoming clear that judges do not simply lay a statute alongside the Constitution and arrive at an inevitable result by mere measurement.

Let me illustrate. Twenty years ago the Supreme Court divided evenly on the validity of an Oregon minimum wage statute for women. In 1923, the District of Columbia act was held invalid, and in 1925 the Arizona and Arkansas statutes met the same fate.   Only last June the Court reaffirmed its position in holding the New York act invalid.   But on March 29th of this year the Court completely reversed its stand of 1923, 1925, and 1936 and upheld the minimum wage act of the State of Washington.

Out of this amazing experience come three significant propositions: First, in the earlier cases, the result was reached upon a hard and fast legal theory, that bore no relationship to the actual facts of industrial life.   Secondly, neither the states nor the Congress could legislate on the evil of the sweatshop, for the Court had staked out a no man's land within which all organized government was powerless to act.   Thirdly, the vote of a single judge, holding office for life, had determined the social policy of the nation for twenty years.

A week ago another striking demonstration was afforded in the five to four decisions sustaining the National Labor Relations Act and, incidentally, upsetting the solemn pronouncements of the Lawyers Committee of the Liberty League.

And yet, the enlightened judgment, which has given us these recent decisions by the narrowest of margins, may be eclipsed tomorrow by a return to abstract theories and mistaken assumptions.   The statutes recently validated may be whittled away in their application bit by bit until nothing remains but an empty victory.

Surely this is an unhealthy condition.   The bench still lacks a sufficient number of judges whose self-restraint is predictable, judges who are willing to see the facts as they are and to decide under the Constitution and not over it.

American constitutional history is illuminated by occasional flashes such as we have witnessed in the last few weeks, but that same history is often darkened.   We find ourselves now in a moment of light.   Our problem is to keep that light burning.

Congress secures a rehearing by reenacting a municipal bankruptcy measure; a letter to the President, August 12, 1937:

I have the honor to advise you that, in accordance with your request of August 11, I have examined the enclosed enrolled bill (H.R. 5969), the purpose of which is to enact a municipal bankruptcy statute. * * *

The Municipal Bankruptcy Act, approved on May 24, 1934, was held unconstitutional by the Supreme Court in *Ashton* v. *Cameron County District,* 298 U. S. 513, by a vote of five to four. * * * The debates on the floor of the House relative to this measure indicate that it was the intention of the Congress in passing the bill to secure a reconsideration by the Supreme Court of its prior decision, in view of the fact that it was reached by such a close vote. * * * In view of the foregoing considerations, I find no objection to the approval of the bill.

10. The Public Utility Holding Company Act

[The Public Utility Holding Company Act of August 26, 1935, was proposed to prevent the continuation of abuses disclosed during the early years of the depression by the collapse of holding company mushroom structures such as the Insull domain, and similar abuses frequently disclosed when effective regulation of public utilities was attempted. After the measure was proposed in Congress the first time, it was submitted to the Department of Justice for revision of its language. After its adoption, a number of equity suits were instituted against the Securities and Exchange Commission to prevent the enforcement of the requirement of registration under the act. The Department of Justice issued circulars to United States attorneys indicating that the policy of the government was not to enforce immediately all the penal provisions of the act, but rather to find and advance as rapidly as possible a test case on constitutionality. A case against the Electric Bond & Share Company was chosen for the test.

Other utilities nevertheless sought to embarrass the government by injunction suits. The Attorney General arranged, contrary to custom, to appear in person in the Supreme Court of the District of Columbia to ask a stay of proceedings in these cases, pending the determination of the test case. In explaining his position to the court, he said that it would be cruelty to his legal staff and, indeed, a physically impossible task for the government to combat simultaneously every one of the barrage of injunction suits that had been filed. "Suits have rained upon us from every spot in the zenith," he declared. "We are literally submerged by them. No just purpose has been served by any one of them. * * * I am willing to take on any gentlemen, but I want to take them on one at a time. Even the pugilistic champion of the world would be unwilling to meet a whole ring full of opponents in one match." The court granted the stay. The Court of Appeals for the District of Columbia, however, before which the Attorney General also appeared, reversed the decision by a vote of two to one (see *North American Company* v. *Landis,* 85 F. (2d) 398) ; but the Supreme Court of the United States in a carefully limited opinion on December 7, 1936, reversed the Court of Appeals *(Landis* v. *North American Company,* 299 U. S. 248), calling attention to the advancement of the *Electric Bond & Share* case on the calendar.

On March 28, 1938, with only one judge dissenting, the Supreme Court decided the *Electric Bond & Share* case, holding constitutional the provision requiring registration with the Securities and Exchange Commission *(Electric Bond & Share Company* v. *Securities and Exchange Commission,* 303 U. S. 419). *Ed.*]

Circulars Nos. 2780 and 2786 to all United States attorneys:

November 18, 1935

THE Public Utility Holding Company Act of 1935 requires certain public utility holding companies to register with the Securities and Exchange Commission not later than December 1, 1935.

The Edison Electric Institute, a trade organization, whose membership includes a number of utility holding companies, has announced that it has retained counsel to contest the constitutionality of the act. Consequently, it is probable that a number of companies will fail to register under the act.

It is of course not the purpose of the government to harass the utility industry with a needless multiplicity of suits. Equally, however, the government does not wish to be vexed with a multiplicity of injunction suits which might embarrass and harass the government in defending the constitutionality of the act and which might result in the presentation of the issue of constitutionality on the basis of an inadequate record or a record not fairly typical of the situations covered by the act.

In enforcing the act under section 18, it is proposed that civil proceedings be instituted against one or two important companies who may violate its provisions and that the Securities and Exchange Commission will transmit evidence for criminal prosecution only when, after prior determination of the validity of the act in civil proceedings, it is satisfied that there have been violations subjecting the offenders to punishment.

In view of the foregoing, the Department suggests that you refrain from bringing or threatening to bring any criminal proceedings under the act. If any injunction proceeding is instituted against you, you will thus be in a position to disclaim any present threat of any criminal proceeding under such act. Such disclaimer should be sufficient under the authority of the *Spielman Motor Sales Co.* v. *Dodge,* 295 U. S. 89, to dispose of any restraining order which may be sought against you.

December 7, 1935

On November 26, the government instituted a civil suit in the Southern District of New York against Electric Bond and Share Company and five of its principal subsidiary holding companies to enforce compliance with the act, and shortly thereafter consented to the intervention in that suit of sixteen additional subsidiary holding companies in the Electric Bond and Share system. The major issues concerning the constitutionality of the act, in so far as such issues may legally be raised at this time, will be promptly, effectively, and fairly tested and adjudicated in this suit.

The Attorney General and the Securities and Exchange Commission have taken the position, on the authority of *Union Pacific R. R. Co.* v. *Public Service Commission,* 248 U. S. 67, *Terral* v. *Burke Construction Co.,* 257 U. S. 529, and *Power Manufacturing Co.* v. *Saunders,* 274 U. S. 490, that registration does not constitute a waiver of any constitutional rights. In its Holding Company Act Release No. 22, November 22, 1935, the Securities and Exchange Commission reiterated that "the Commission under its rule-making power expressly permits the registrant to reserve his constitutional rights," and further announced that "the Commission is prepared to go further and accept a notification that expressly stipulates that the notification of registration will at the option of the registrant be deemed void if registrant's reservation of its constitutional rights is adjudged void or ineffective."

Despite the efforts of the government to test the validity of the act in an orderly and economical manner, and in the meanwhile to safeguard every legal and constitutional right of the private interests affected, not only have a multitude of unnecessary suits been brought against government officials, but a number of stockholders' suits have been brought against various companies with a view to testing the constitutionality of the act in proceedings in which the government or its officers are not even parties. In light of the action taken by the government to safeguard the rights and interests of both registering and non-registering companies, it may be questioned whether such stockholders' suits are brought in good faith and are free from collusion as is required under Equity Rule 27 as interpreted by the Supreme Court. * * *

The government takes the position that any action by a stockholder to enjoin or to compel registration cannot bring into issue the question of constitutionality, but at most only the question of the good faith and prudent conduct of the management. The government at the present time does not plan to intervene or take any part in any action brought by a stockholder to test the constitutionality of the act.

Inasmuch as it will in many cases be impossible for the district attorneys to know of the existence of these suits, you are requested to bring this circular to the attention of the circuit judges in your circuit and of the district judges in your district so that they may be apprised of the government's position in the event that any such stockholders' suits come before them.

A letter to the President, December 11, 1935:

Tomorrow afternoon I expect to appear before Mr. Justice Bailey in the Supreme Court of the District of Columbia to present arguments in behalf of a motion to stay the proceeding in the seven holding company cases pending in that court. The matter is of pretty far-reaching consequence and, in view of its high public importance, I thought I would argue the motion in person, especially in view of the illness of the Solicitor General.

The primary purpose of the motion is to relieve the government of the pressure brought upon it by the holding companies

and to stay the proceedings until the government has an opportunity to try the suit brought by the Securities and Exchange Commission in the Southern District of New York against the Electric
Bond and Share Company and its subsidiaries and affiliates. The
government does not have at its disposal the personnel necessary
to deal with the sixty odd cases already filed in various jurisdictions, and desires an opportunity to proceed speedily with the trial
of a typical case and to secure a determination by the Supreme
Court of the constitutional questions involved as soon as possible.
The expense, delay, confusion, and embarrassment which would
be involved in attempting to try simultaneously a substantial number of cases would, it seems to me, be well calculated to break
down the processes of justice. Moreover, most of these cases
present substantially the same fundamental questions. For these
reasons I believe that there are strong equities in favor of the
motion I have made. I assume it will be resisted by one device
or another.

*An office memorandum to Assistant Attorney General Robert H.
Jackson, April 9, 1936:*

It strikes me that we might have an opportunity, after we
have received the appellants' brief in the holding company cases,
to make some headway and strengthen our position materially in
a supplemental brief of our own. I assume serious consideration
is being given to this matter already.

It occurred to me, thinking the matter over, that there were
several spots in our case that might be strengthened. I think too
that we must be careful not to be led into any bypath by the brief
which I assume will be filed by the other side shortly.

Ought we not to consider bringing the case back into focus?
I think it got somewhat out of focus as the proceedings went
along. There is a possibility that the appellate judges may be
thinking too much about what they would have done in Judge
Bailey's place. That, of course, is not the question. The real

question seems to be whether there was such a manifest abuse of power that the appellate court should interfere. This was borne in on me when I was reflecting upon the question of how I would proceed if I set myself the task of writing an opinion reversing Judge Bailey's order. I do not see how it is possible for a sound lawyer, who studies his subject, to deny that Judge Bailey had the power to do what he did. If the trial court has not abundant power in such matters, orderly judicial process is at an end. The writer of the opinion would, therefore, have to turn to the question of the abuse of discretion. How is it possible to make out a case of abuse of discretion in the face of the competing and conflicting interests and considerations involved?

Suppose you think seriously for a moment of the difficulty of writing such an adverse opinion in the face of what must be recognized as conflicting considerations of a complicated character and, let us assume, more or less legitimate upon both sides. Was this not peculiarly a question for the exercise of the wise discretion of the trial court, and is there not intelligent basis for asserting that, upon this conflicting showing, no judgment should prevail except that of the trial judge upon whom the responsibility rested? Would not the appellate court, if it reversed Judge Bailey, be substituting its own discretion for his? And has the appellate court any right to do this?

Office memorandum to Solicitor General Stanley Reed, October 15, 1936:

I note that the case of *Landis* v. *North American Company* is assigned for argument at head of call on Monday, November 9. Let me know, at your convenience, how this matter is being handled and when it is likely to be reached. * * * I do not know that there is any occasion for me to argue it in the Supreme Court.

11. The End of the Struggle over the Court Plan

[The essence of the President's proposal for judicial reform was deleted from the measure which finally passed the Congress in mid-August of 1937. The President in signing it frankly acknowledged its deficiencies. He also enumerated its accomplishments as follows: "No longer must the government stand idly by, a helpless spectator, while acts of Congress are stricken down by the courts. It expedites appeals to the Supreme Court in such matters. It seeks to improve intolerable situations created by the reckless granting by the lower courts of injunctions to restrain government officials in the operation of federal statutes. It tends slightly to relax the rigid system within circuits of assigning district judges to congested areas. All of these provisions possess merit and are either a part of, or consistent with, the plans originally submitted to the Congress." Ed.]

From "The President's Proposals for Judicial Reorganization," a radio address, February 14, 1937:

ATTACKS upon the constitutionality of measures enacted by the Congress have burdened the courts. The powers of government are suspended by the automatic issuance of injunctions commanding officers and agents to cease enforcing the laws of the United States until the weary round of litigation has run its course.

In the uncertain condition of our constitutional law it is not difficult for the skillful to devise plausible arguments and to raise technical objections to almost any form of legislation that may be proposed. Ofttimes drastic injunctive remedies are applied without notice to the government or without opportunity upon the part of its representatives to be heard in defense of the law of the land.

From a statement, before the Senate Committee on the Judiciary, March 10, 1937 (Hearings on S. 1392, Senate Committee on the Judiciary, 75 Cong. 1 Sess., p. 4):

As an immediate step the President has recommended that the Congress provide that, first, no court shall pass upon the constitutionality of an act of Congress without notice to the Attorney General and an opportunity for the United States to present evidence and to be heard; and, secondly, where the trial courts pass upon such questions there shall be a direct appeal to the Supreme Court, and that such cases shall take precedence over all other matters pending in the Court.

Letter transmitting to John N. Garner, the President of the Senate, a report, requested by Senate Resolution, on the effect of injunctions upon the operations of the government (for complete text, see Sen. Doc. 42, 75 Cong. 1 Sess.), March 23, 1937:

The report of the Department of Justice is enclosed herewith. It contains a general discussion of the cases in which injunctions, restraining orders, or other judgments have been issued, rendered, or denied in the manner described in Senate Resolution 82. These cases are classified according to the various statutes which were involved. Where individual cases present a unique situation, a statement is given with reference to each particular case. Where there are several cases or a large number of cases substantially alike, such cases are discussed as a group and statistical information is given with reference to each group. The report also shows instances of conflicts among the lower federal courts, and it indicates those instances where the granting of injunctions hampered or affected the operations of the government.

*From "Progress of the President's Plan for Judicial Reform," an
address in the National Radio Forum, April 26, 1937:*

In the matter of injunctions and suits raising constitutional
questions, I am aware of no serious opposition to the recommendation that the Attorney General be given notice and an opportunity to present the government's side of the case, with the right
of direct appeal to the Supreme Court. A measure to this effect
has already passed the House and will shortly receive the consideration of the Senate.

*Memorandum for Special Assistant Alexander Holtzoff,
August 13, 1937:*

The President has asked me for comments concerning the
bill recently passed dealing with the federal judiciary. Mr. Carusi
has the original bill and I would like to get an answer to the
President some time tomorrow.

I think what is needed is the usual analysis of the bill, indicating succinctly but with accuracy what it achieves. At the
conclusion of this analysis we might consider adding something
like this:

> This bill, it will be noted, deals primarily, and in a
> very limited way, with certain aspects of procedural reform.
> It is the outgrowth of the prolonged consideration given to
> the proposals you submitted to the Congress on the 5th day
> of February, with reference to judicial reform. Measured
> against the objectives you outlined in that message, and in
> other communications to the Congress, it is but a meager
> performance. Nevertheless, within the limits of the subject
> it treats, it presents meritorious provisions of a minor
> character.
>
> I do not find in it anything objectionable. It is a
> shadowy reminder of the effective plan you originally pro-
> posed. The challenge to which it is open is that of feeble-
> ness and inefficiency.

Under these circumstances I recommend its approval with the suggestion that an explanatory statement might profitably accompany your action in the matter.

A letter to the President, August 17, 1937:

I have the honor to advise you that, in compliance with your request, I have examined the enclosed enrolled bill (H.R. 2260), entitled, "An Act to provide for intervention by the United States, direct appeals to the Supreme Court of the United States, and regulation of the issuance of injunctions, in certain cases involving the constitutionality of acts of Congress, and for other purposes."

The bill contains the following provisions:

1. It would require that whenever the constitutionality of any act of Congress affecting the public interest is drawn into question in any court of the United States in any suit to which the United States is not a party, the court should certify such fact to the Attorney General and should permit the United States to intervene and become a party for presentation of evidence and argument on the question of constitutionality. In such event, the United States is to have all the rights of a party and the liabilities of a party as to court costs. (Sec. 1)

2. In any suit in any court of the United States to which the United States is a party, or in which it has intervened, and in which an act of Congress is held unconstitutional, a direct appeal to the Supreme Court is to be permitted. (Sec. 2) While the Congress has the undoubted right to authorize such an appeal by the government in cases in which the United States has "a legal interest," it is likely that such right will be challenged on constitutional grounds in cases in which the "interest" is merely general.

3. No injunction sustaining or restraining the enforcement of a federal statute on the ground of its unconstitutionality is to be issued or granted by any United States District Court unless the application is heard by three judges. A district judge is to

be permitted to grant a temporary restraining order pending the hearing before a three-judge court on a showing of a likelihood of irreparable loss or damage. (Sec. 3)

4. The bill proposes to reenact the present law permitting the senior circuit judge of any circuit to assign any district judge within the circuit to any other district within the same circuit, and authorizing the Chief Justice of the United States to assign any district judge to hold court in a district in any other circuit, with the consent of the two senior circuit judges concerned. The present law is permissive and provides that the senior circuit judge or the Chief Justice, as the case may be, "may if in his judgment the public interest so requires" make such designations or assignments. The bill substitutes "shall" for "may" and strikes out the clause, "if in his judgment the public interest so requires." The bill also proposes to require all such designations to be recorded on the minutes of the Supreme Court of the United States. (Sec. 4)

This bill, it will be noted, deals primarily, and in a very limited way, with certain aspects of procedural reform. It is the outgrowth of the prolonged consideration given to the proposals you submitted to the Congress on the 5th day of February, with reference to judicial reform. Measured against the objectives you outlined in that message, and in other communications to the Congress, it is but a meager performance. Nevertheless, within the limits of the subject it treats, it presents meritorious provisions of a minor character. I do not find in it anything objectionable. It is a shadowy reminder of the effective plan you orginally proposed. The challenge to which it is open is that of feebleness and inefficiency.

Under these circumstances, I recommend its approval with the suggestion that an explanatory statement might profitably accompany your action in the matter.

12. Constitutional Adaptation

[In other decisions in fields already discussed and in cases decided in other fields since the early months of 1937 when the Court Plan was under discussion, the Supreme Court has shown a lively interest in the adjustment of principles of constitutional interpretation to the needs of the present day. Opinions have been phrased no less in terms of precedents than in former times, but many present at the argument of cases and those carefully reading opinions notice a new alertness in the search for workable principles, and a lack of interest in past decisions merely because they are past decisions. This attitude, while it lasts, promises well for the success of carefully planned federal legislation enacted in the public interest. *Ed.*]

From an article on "Nature of the Amending Process" (for complete text, see the George Washington Law Review for March, 1938, v. 6, pp. 247-258; or The Congressional Record for May 19, 1938):

THOSE who have followed the trend of recent constitutional decisions are fully aware of a marked change in the judicial attitude with reference to the powers of the Congress. The Supreme Court, by a sharp reversal of viewpoint, has demonstrated anew the resiliency of the Constitution and its adaptability to new conditions as they arise. It is not presently necessary to assess the causes that wrought this change and permitted the yeast of liberalism to leaven the whole loaf. It is interesting, however, to recall the fact that when the Supreme Court controversy was at its height, suggestions were frequently made that the purposes sought to be achieved should be brought about by constitutional amendment and by that method alone. The theory was advanced that by the amending process a virtual referendum by the people could be obtained and their will thereby ascertained. * * *

Although over 2,600 constitutional amendments have been introduced from time to time, the Constitution has been amended on only ten different occasions during the 150 years of its existence—for the first ten amendments may be considered as one, while the Thirteenth, Fourteenth, and Fifteenth Amendments may likewise properly be dealt with as a single group. * * *

With but a few exceptions, on each of the ten occasions on which the Constitution has been amended the result was attributable to war or to a serious convulsion of public opinion. In the great majority of the cases the process was not only laborious but exceedingly slow, and the demands of the people came to fruition many years after public opinion had clearly manifested itself.

In the light of this history it is obvious that those who urge the amending process as a means of testing public opinion or talk lightly of it as a method of "referring the matter to the people" are speaking without knowledge and certainly without thought.

Radio address entitled "The Constitution as a Living Document," delivered before the Polish National Alliance, October 11, 1937:

This year we celebrate the 150th anniversary of the adoption of the oldest existing written constitution, the Constitution of the United States. Let us briefly consider why it has endured for so many years and why it is still a living and vital document.

Its permanence lies chiefly in the fact that it is couched in broad, general terms, happily called "the language of statesmen," and is capable of being adapted to changing conditions. The Founding Fathers realized that it was impossible for human beings of one era to foresee all of the problems that would be confronted by later generations. With prophetic vision they drafted a document that Chief Justice Marshall asserted was "intended to endure for ages to come, and consequently to be adapted to the various crises of human affairs." Justice Story, another profound jurist, observed that it "was not intended to provide merely for the exigencies of a few years, but was to endure through a long lapse of ages, the events of which were locked up in the inscrutable purposes of Providence."

If our fundamental charter had been framed like a rigid, detailed code, incapable of adjustment, it would have long ago been broken into fragments; for life has a way of disregarding forms and cannot be cast into a rigid mold.

Recent constitutional discussions have been highly educational and broadly helpful; but they have also stirred emotions that have clouded the clear course of legitimate debate. There are those who apparently regard the Constitution as embalming forever the explicit and final word of wisdom; and who feel a distaste for any critical debate as to its merits or its possible defects. They have forgotten that the Constitution is a human document formulated to serve human needs; and that it is the servant and not the master of those who created it.

Intelligent, temperate debate is the essence of free government, and it would be unfortunate indeed if the Constitution ever came to be regarded as so sacred that it could not be discussed. Every era of our national existence has been productive of some sort of constitutional struggle. These recurring controversies are but renewals of old debates and will have their counterparts in the days to come and, indeed, so long as our government endures. Such disputes are the by-products of the processes of growth and are evidences of life and not of decay.

There have been many historic occasions upon which the interpreters of the Constitution and those who were seeking to apply it in a practical manner came into collision. In each instance the conflict was resolved so as to meet the requirements of the generation in which it occurred, sometimes by a reversal or modification of opinion on the part of the judicial body possessing the power to construe the Constitution, and sometimes by the drastic process of amendment. * * *

We are living under conditions far different from those with which our forebears were familiar. * * * A century and a half ago our society was largely agrarian. There were no large industries. The machine age had not come into being and the few manufacturing enterprises then in existence were conducted by manual labor and upon a small scale. The individual workman and his employer could bargain face to face and in intimate fashion.

Life has moved on and the scene has changed. To assure the modern farmer against the vicissitudes of wide price fluctuations, to guard the wage earner against oppression in the matter of wages and hours and working conditions, to prevent the exploitation of the labor of little children, to protect the public against monopolistic practices, to cleanse our country of crime, to raise the standards and dignity of the life of our people— these and countless other problems have widened the scope and, indeed, altered the tempo and functions of government. Nearly all our problems have spilled over state lines. The forty-eight states, spread from the Atlantic to the Pacific, are closely knit together into a single unified economic fabric. As never before we think as a nation and must, of necessity, act as a nation. * * *

That such needs must and will be met is certain. We have but scant patience with those who believe that the Constitution is an unworkable document, and we are not moved by those who, in sheer blindness, strive to make it an unworkable document. It has served and it will continue to serve. The Constitution is not a stranger to justice. On the contrary, it is an instrument of justice designed, not to check the life of a great people, but rather to guide and protect it as it flows down the unending channels of history. We fervently believe that American democracy will endure, that it will justify itself in the face of a distraught world, that its problems can be solved within its constitutional framework, and, so believing, we affirm again our devotion to our great charter of liberty and our faith in the destiny of our people.

PART FOUR

REFORM OF FEDERAL PRACTICE AND PROCEDURE

1. A Dormant Reform Movement Revived

[The problem of delay and injustice arising from the complexity of procedure in actions at law in the federal courts has been one of long standing. When the federal judicial system was set up in 1789, the Supreme Court was authorized to prescribe rules for suits in equity, but the Congress failed to provide a code of practice for actions at law and simply prescribed that the mode of procedure which was used in 1789 in the state in which the court was sitting should apply. By later statutes the Congress applied the same principle to states admitted since 1789, but the conformity provision in each instance referred to state procedure in effect on some fixed date. The Conformity Act, passed in 1872, for the first time provided that the practice in federal courts, with some modification, should "conform, as near as may be" to that currently in effect in the courts of the several states.

As early as 1822 the Supreme Court promulgated rules of procedure for cases in equity. These rules, largely declaratory of existing procedure, were revised twenty years later, but it was not until 1912 that the equity procedure was thoroughly revised. Forceful agitation for the reform of procedure in actions at law, which commenced as early as 1886, came to nothing though efforts were made down through the 1920's.

In 1934, Attorney General Cummings renewed the struggle for procedural reform—after the American Bar Association, long a proponent, had given up in despair—and pressed it to a successful conclusion. Within ninety days of the time he announced his position, the Congress granted the necessary authority. Through a committee appointed and supervised by the Supreme Court, rules of practice in both law and equity were consolidated, liberalized, simplified, and made flexible as well as uniform. The statute authorizing the project provided that the rules so proposed should be submitted to the Congress at the beginning of a regular session and should not take effect until the end of such session, so that the Congress might have an opportunity to modify or disapprove the proposals. They were so submitted at the Third Session of the Seventy-fifth Congress and, no adverse action having been taken, became effective September 16, 1938. *Ed.*]

From an address at the Silver Anniversary Banquet of the New York County Lawyers' Association, March 14, 1934:

I AM persuaded that if the federal courts could reform their procedure and render it not only simpler but more responsive to actual needs, the example of such a system would have a powerful and corrective effect upon the practice in the several states.

Courts exist to vindicate and enforce substantive rights. Procedure is merely the machinery designed to secure an orderly presentation of legal controversies. If that machinery is so complicated that it serves to delay justice or to entrap the unwary, it is not functioning properly and should be overhauled.

When the details of procedure are prescribed by statute, errors can be cured only by legislation. Regulation follows regulation with bewildering multiplicity until there is created a morass of laws in which the whole profession is mired. Thus, the Field Code of Procedure adopted in New York in 1848 contained only 391 sections. It later grew to 3,397 sections. The California code was amended 340 times in ten years. Manifestly, procedural questions are too technical and too lacking in popular appeal to receive adequate consideration by any legislative body.

The Federal Conformity Act of 1872, regulating actions at law in the district courts, provides that practice and procedure in such actions shall conform, "as near as may be," to that which is followed in the state in which the court sits. Whenever the Congress has legislated as to a particular matter the statute thus enacted is, of course, controlling. The words "as near as may be," under the liberal interpretation given to them, have introduced a bewildering mass of exceptions. A litigant in an action at law in a federal district court is, therefore, compelled to study, first, the state system of practice, secondly, federal legislation relating to procedure and, thirdly, judicial decisions sanctioning departure from state practice. As the practice is not uniform in the 48 states, a serious burden is imposed upon lawyers who appear before federal courts in more than one state, and also

upon judges who are assigned to sit outside their immediate jurisdictions. Perhaps, the most vital objection is that the federal
courts are tied to the antiquated system of statutory regulation
now generally prevailing in the various states. Reform and improvement are, therefore, hopelessly stalled at the outset.

Let me turn, by way of contrast, to the manifest advantages
of a system under which rules are adopted by the courts. Clearly,
this centers authority and responsibility in qualified hands. If
changes are required, they are readily perceived by those who
function under them. Surely, rules of court can be applied with
less rigidity than statutory provisions. Under such an arrangement
we would have every right to anticipate fewer decisions based
upon technical questions of procedure while the attention of the
bench and bar could be directed to the substance of right rather
than to its form. Moreover, such a system tends to preserve the
true balance between the legislative and judicial branches of the
government, and is, therefore, in harmony with basic constitutional principles.

The policy I am advocating is not an untried, theoretical
reform. It has been in full force in England since the Judicature
Act of 1873. The English administration of justice is rightly
renowned. Legal writers attribute no small share of its celerity
and success to the fact that practice and procedure are regulated
by rules prescribed by a Rules Committee, consisting of eight
judges and four lawyers.

In our country, for more than a century, the United States
Supreme Court has been permitted to regulate practice and procedure in equity cases. The results have been highly satisfactory.
If this power could be extended to actions at law, the Court
would be in a position to unite the equity and law practice so as
to secure one form of civil action and procedure for both. This
would constitute a legal reform of the first magnitude.

For more than twenty years the American Bar Association
has advocated the granting of such power to the United States
Supreme Court. A bill of this character was first introduced in

1912 and, although it has never reached a vote, it has been brought forward in almost every succeeding Congress.

The proposal was endorsed by Attorneys General McReynolds, Gregory, Palmer, Stone, and Sargent. Mr. Elihu Root and the late Judge Alton B. Parker have personally appeared before a committee of Congress in favor of the measure. In 1921 a questionnaire submitted to federal judges disclosed that, of those replying, more than 80 percent of the circuit judges and 75 percent of the district judges favored the proposal.

Legal, commercial, and business organizations have, with striking unanimity, approved this reform. It has been endorsed by 46 state bar associations, the conference of Commissioners of Uniform State Laws, the executive committee of the Association of Law Schools, the United States Chamber of Commerce, the National Association of Credit Men, the Commercial Law League, the National Civic Federation, and the Southern Commercial Congress. It has been approved by present or former deans of many important law schools including Harvard, Yale, Cornell, and Virginia.

In 1910 in a message to Congress, President Taft sponsored the proposal. Two years later it was unofficially approved by President Wilson. In a message to Congress, President Coolidge made similar recommendations. I am authorized to say here tonight that this proposed reform also carries the endorsement of President Franklin D. Roosevelt.

Persuaded that this is the course of right and reason, I have recently communicated with the Chairmen of the appropriate Senate and House committees suggesting the reintroduction of this bill. I earnestly urge its passage.

Our one great enemy is inertia. But surely the hour has struck. Let us not confess that we are so disorganized, so indifferent, so lazy, so ineffectual, and so impotent that we cannot marshal our forces in behalf of a measure of reform which the leaders of the bar have so long and so overwhelmingly approved.

*The history of judicial rule-making; from an address entitled
"A Rounded System of Judicial Rule-Making," delivered at a
meeting of the Federal Judicial Conference of the Fourth Circuit,
June 3, 1938:*

An examination of our legal history inevitably leads one to
inquire how it came about that lawyers in this country seemed
to regard legislative enactments as the natural if not the only
source of procedure. Certainly this was not true in England.
* * * The first great legal reform movement in England culminated in the Civil Procedure Act of 1833, which specifically provided in the preamble that "the judges should make such
alterations in the rules of pleading and practice as they should
deem expedient." An even more explicit provision appeared in
the Procedure Act of 1852, which set forth that "the judges are
to retain complete power to make any rules regarding pleading
and practice that they might deem expedient, anything in the
present act to the contrary notwithstanding." And, finally, in the
Judicature Act of 1873, a schedule of rules of court was included.
The system thus created has become firmly established.

While England was adhering to the practice of fixing procedure by rule of court, the United States for the most part abandoned the theory of judicial control. The Field Code, enacted in
New York State in 1848, is, perhaps, the most sweeping illustration of this departure. While that code accomplished reforms
of the first magnitude, it accentuated the trend toward the regulation of the details of legal procedure by legislative action. This
movement has been ascribed in part to popular resentment against
the failure of the American bar and the judiciary to reshape the
old English procedure to fit local conditions, or new developments; and in part to the leadership of the legislature in the
political life of that period. It is not my purpose to discuss the
merits or demerits of the Field Code. I advert to it simply to
point out that it was a departure from the accredited system of
judicial rule-making; that historically the courts and not the legislatures were the sources of procedure; and that the recent trend

which we are now witnessing in this country is in reality a return to the basic concept which has permeated English legal development, and also governed American legal development prior to 1848. * * *

A few years ago a noted legal authority took the position that legislative rule-making was unconstitutional (as violative of the doctrines relating to the separation of legislative, executive, and judicial powers) and that all legislatively-declared rules for procedure, civil or criminal, are void except such as are expressly stated in the Constitution. It is not necessary in this discussion to go to that length. It is sufficient to point out, first, that it is entirely proper for the legislature to authorize the courts to regulate procedure; and secondly, that for reasons of policy such rules should be formulated by the judiciary.

Letters to Chairmen of Senate and House Judiciary Committees, March 1, 1934, submitting proposed legislation:

I enclose herewith a draft of a bill to empower the Supreme Court of the United States to prescribe rules to govern the practice and procedure in civil actions at law in the district courts of the United States and the courts of the District of Columbia. The enactment of this bill would bring about uniformity and simplicity in the practice in actions at law in federal courts and thus relieve the courts and the bar of controversies and difficulties which are continually arising wholly apart from the merits of the litigation in which they are interested. It seems to me that there can be no substantial objection to the enactment of a measure which would produce so desirable a result, and which, apart from its inherent merit, would also, it is believed, contribute to a reduction in the cost of litigation in the federal courts.

I request that you introduce the enclosed bill and hope that you may be able to give it your support.

From an address before the Chicago Bar Association at a dinner in honor of Lord Macmillan, August 2, 1938:

I found it desirable and helpful to approach the appropriate committees by numerous and devious methods. I think that you might be interested to know that there was a time when it was touch and go whether the rules would go through or not. I labored with the committee in the Senate and with the committee in the House, and finally by personal appeals, pathetic persuasion, and something approaching imprecations, had caused most of the opposition to dissolve. There was, however, in the House Committee of the Judiciary one recalcitrant person with whom I had extraordinary difficulty. He told me he had made speeches against the idea, that he was on record against it, and that when the matter came up in the House he would be obliged to protest.

The situation was such that only unanimous consent would permit it to pass, and one voice raised in opposition at that critical moment would have been fatal to the entire project. I labored with that man for hours, and finally we compromised. He agreed to adhere to his principles, and, in order that he might not forego them, further agreed to absent himself from the House when the matter came up.

Letter to the President, recommending approval of legislation authorizing the formulation of uniform and simplified rules of civil procedure under the supervision of the Supreme Court, June 12, 1934:

I have the honor to recommend the approval of S. 3040, "An Act to give the Supreme Court of the United States the authority to make and publish rules in actions at law." * * * It empowers the Supreme Court to prescribe by general rules, for the district courts of the United States and for the courts for the District of Columbia, the forms of process, writs, pleadings, and motions, and the practice and procedure in civil actions at law.

It further empowers the court to unite the general rules prescribed by it for cases in equity with those in actions at law so as to secure one form of civil action and procedure for both.

Since 1789, the Supreme Court has had and utilized the power to regulate procedure in federal courts for equity and admiralty cases. The result is that the federal courts have developed a simple type of procedure, uniformly prevailing throughout the United States, for suits in equity. This is also true of admiralty practice. The Bankruptcy Act confers the same power on the Supreme Court for bankruptcy proceedings, and this power has likewise been effectively utilized.

An entirely different situation has prevailed in regard to actions at law. The acts of Congress have from the first required practice and procedure in the federal courts in actions at law to conform to that prevailing in the courts of the state in which the federal court was sitting. * * * The result is that as respects actions at law, the federal courts have forty-eight different systems of practice and procedure. * * * The pending bill will make it possible to establish a simple uniform system of practice and procedure for actions at law in the federal courts.

In my opinion this measure is an important and vital step toward the simplification of legal procedure, and it will tend to reduce delays in the conduct of litigation and to eliminate controversy over procedural questions.

[Note: See an article entitled, "The New Law Relating to Federal Procedure," *United States Law Week,* June 19, 1934, p. 2. *Ed.*]

2. Formulation and Adoption of New Rules of Civil Procedure

Bar and bench unite in formulating new rules of procedure; an address at a conference of the Fourth Judicial Circuit of the United States, June 6, 1935:

ON A PREVIOUS occasion I made the statement that: "Courts exist to vindicate and enforce substantive rights. Procedure is merely the machinery designed to secure an orderly presentation of legal controversies. If that machinery is so complicated that it serves to delay justice or to entrap the unwary, it is not functioning properly and should be overhauled." This should be a measure of the task upon which we are engaged. It may very well be that because of our familiarity with certain procedural rules and devices it is more convenient for us as lawyers and judges to continue their use. That, however, is not the test which we should apply. * * *

Something which we have long done and have become used to doing may not necessarily be the best way of accomplishing the desired objective. I have frequently observed, in the contacts which I have made with procedural rules in various states, that on one side of an imaginary boundary line there may be in practice a cumbersome complicated rule, while on the other side of the line a most simple convenient one obtains. Apparently it does not occur to the lawyers of the first state that it may be possible to avail themselves of the simpler method.

The very history of the securing of the legislation which made our present effort possible provides a good example of the stultifying effect of inertia and indifference in approaching these problems. The important thing is to observe that it was accomplished in the face of prophecy of certain failure. The first step has been taken. The only problem now remaining is whether we are willing and able to carry out the clear mandate of the law. Granting a period of difficulty, while the new rules are being fitted to the judicial machinery, we should look ahead to a time two or three decades from now, when the lawyers and judges of that day will pay tribute to our work, as one of the beneficent contributions of our profession to the social structure and to the orderly functioning of government.

Lawyers as a group are looked upon as a conservative lot. We have certainly lagged behind other countries in the matter of purging our ranks of misfits and incompetents, and in removing technical procedures which delay, often for years at a time, the trial of issues on their merits. * * *

Whatever objection there may be to the great movement which we are assembled here to discuss (and in most quarters there will be none) comes largely, I think, from the inertia of some members of our modern bar—from a disinclination to devote time to the more important problems which face us as a profession, together with a feeling of local pride on the part of some which resists any change in procedural customs.

This is the sort of project in which we must have whole-hearted cooperation between the bar and the courts. I cannot help but view it as an enterprise which will test whether the bar is really entering upon the period of decadence that some critics, particularly among the laymen, have seen fit to forecast, a period in which the lawyer is no longer a leader of men but a mere caretaker of clients. To build and maintain this new system of procedure there must be an *esprit de corps* among members of the bar. The general public will watch with interest to see whether the lawyers of this country will stand united in the common effort to formulate and preserve a system which will guarantee simplicity and speed in the settlement of civil disputes.

Now it is my pleasure to be able to report * * * that from all ten circuits of the federal judicial system there has come the most hearty and willing response to the request of the Chief Justice for cooperation in this great task. His suggestion, made at the last Judicial Conference, that each Senior Circuit Judge should request the district judges to appoint, in each district, a committee of representative lawyers, or that he should, himself, appoint such a committee for the circuit, has been complied with in every instance. The committees so appointed have in turn called to their aid members of the teaching branch of the profession. You will be pleased to know that in the ten judicial circuits, more than one hundred federal judges, five hundred practicing lawyers, and many law teachers and research scholars are participating in this great project—in less than a year since the law was passed. A large mass of valuable material has been assembled, which will be placed at the disposal of the Advisory Committee recently designated by the Supreme Court to carry forward the details of this important work.

The Chief Justice in a recent address stated succinctly our objective in the task which we have undertaken, namely, to secure: "A simplified practice which will strip procedure of unnecessary forms, technicalities, and distinctions, and permit the advance of causes to the decision of their merits with a minimum of procedural encumbrances." Generally speaking, the attainment of that objective requires that the rules to be prescribed should deal with broad general provisions. The curse of procedural systems set up by legislative enactment has been the effort to prescribe minute details, which, while appropriate in each case to some situation, were entirely inappropriate to another.

We shall do well to remember that minute procedural variations which occur from state to state will tempt us to satisfy all states by writing in details. We shall do well to hew rigorously to the line of broad general principles, avoiding the morass of detail. Some of our procedural monstrosities are of such long standing that many of us first became acquainted with them as students, when, without discrimination, we attempted to encompass the whole body of law. Later, becoming ardent protagonists, we justified its idiosyncracies to the skeptics. We now find ourselves in the position of looking objectively at the whole conglomerate structure.

The rules completed; letters of the Chief Justice to the Attorney General and of the Attorney General to the Congress, submitting proposed rules of civil procedure to the Congress (for full text see House Doc. No. 460, 75 Cong., 3 Sess.):

December 20, 1937

MY DEAR MR. ATTORNEY GENERAL: By direction of the Supreme Court, I transmit to you herewith the Rules of Civil Procedure for the District Courts of the United States which have been adopted by the Supreme Court pursuant to the Act of June 19, 1934, chapter 651 (48 Stat. 1064).

In accordance with section 2 of that act, the Court has united the general rules prescribed by it for cases in equity with those in actions at law so as to secure one form of civil action and procedure for both. The Court requests you, as provided in that section, to report these rules to the Congress at the beginning of the regular session in January next.

I am requested to state that Mr. Justice Brandeis does not approve of the adoption of the rules.

January 3, 1938

TO THE SENATE AND HOUSE OF REPRESENTATIVES OF THE UNITED STATES OF AMERICA IN CONGRESS ASSEMBLED: I have the honor to report to the Congress, under section 2 of the act of June 19, 1934 (c. 651, 48 Stat. 1064; U. S. C., title 28, sec. 723c), at the beginning of a regular session thereof commencing this 3d day of January 1938, the enclosed Rules of Civil Procedure for the District Courts of the United States.

By a letter of December 20, 1937, from the Chief Justice of the United States, a printed copy of which appears as a prefix to the rules transmitted herewith, I am advised that such rules have been adopted by the Supreme Court pursuant to the act of June 19, 1934, chapter 651 (48 Stat. 1064) and that, in accordance with section 2 of that act, the Court has united the general rules prescribed by it for cases in equity with those in actions at law so as to secure one form of civil action and procedure for both; and I am requested by the Supreme Court to report these rules to the Congress at the beginning of the regular session in January, 1938.

The rules defended; from a statement before the House Committee on the Judiciary (for full text see Hearings on H.R. 8892, 75 Cong. 3 Sess.), March 1, 1938:

The Supreme Court proceeded to appoint an advisory committee composed of outstanding members of the bar and teachers of law. Every section of the country was represented. So far as the Department of Justice is concerned, it also had a committee that cooperated intimately with the advisory committee appointed by the Supreme Court. These two groups, consisting of scholarly, interested, and highly competent people, worked together with the utmost harmony.

Their work was not thrown together in a moment. They labored assiduously for almost three years. Preliminary drafts of rules were circulated among state and local bar associations, and individual judges and individual lawyers were invited to submit their views. Numerous ideas were submitted and they were carefully studied. Many suggestions, I might say, proved valuable and eventually found their way into the rules, as finally adopted. It was a searching and democratic process. It was as fine an example as I have ever known of the bar and 'the judiciary acting enthusiastically and completely in harmony. * * *

I may say this, that in my judgment the rules themselves prescribe a very simple form of pleading, practice, and procedure, with a minimum of technical requirements. The whole process of formulating these rules has been to reduce the matter to simple and easily understood terms, and to provide for the maintenance of the procedure in such fashion that even a mind of moderate capacity would easily understand what the required course might be. These rules do away with obsolete intricacies and refinements of common-law pleading through methods even more simple and more flexible than code pleading in many states. In other words, we have had the benefit of the experience of every state, and the best that could be found anywhere has been drawn into these rules. * * *

My main theme is to point out to this committee that a great work has been done. It has been done under the authority of the Congress. It has been done under the direction of the United States Supreme Court, and it has been done with the cooperation and completely harmonious action of the bench and the bar and the Department of Justice. It, therefore, comes before this committee with every presumption in its favor. To undo this work in whole or in part would be a most unfortunate reversion to outworn methods.

The rules in operation; from Annual Report to the Congress, December 31, 1938:

No adverse action having been taken by the Congress, the rules, under their terms, became effective on September 16, 1938. * * * I have directed that the Department of Justice should maintain a service for all government attorneys, United States attorneys, and the courts, containing a current compilation of all decisions, reported and unreported, construing or applying the new rules. While the primary purpose of this activity is to assist the attorneys of the Department of Justice and the United States attorneys in the field in handling government litigation, it is hoped that it may also constitute an aid in maintaining the uniformity the rules contemplate.

[Note: In the fall of 1938, lawyers' institutes were held in many parts of the country at which members of the bar heard lectures and engaged in discussions of the new procedure. See address at the Washington institute (October 6-8), printed in the *American Bar Association Journal*, November 1938, pp. 885-886.

The new rules applied to cases in the district courts. With the promulgation of the Federal Rules of Civil Procedure, it followed naturally that the same objectives should be sought with respect to the procedure of the several circuit courts of appeals. To deal with this problem, the Attorney General made a statement to the Judicial Conference, held in Washington in September, 1938, and by letter to the Chief Justice on September 27 recommended the adoption of rules by the circuit courts of appeals both to carry into effect the new rules for cases arising in the district courts and to adapt the rules to cases arising elsewhere—such as proceedings for the review of decisions and orders of administrative officers or agencies, which constitute a very considerable part of the work of the federal circuit courts of appeals. The Judicial Conference appointed a committee of circuit judges to make recommendations to this end, in collaboration with the Attorney General who in October appointed a committee consisting of Assistant Attorney General James W. Morris and Special Assistants Wendell Berge and Warner W. Gardner to cooperate in the undertaking. *Ed.*]

3. A Plea for Extension of Procedural Reform to the Criminal Field

*Address entitled "A Rounded System of Judicial Rule-Making,"
delivered at a meeting of the Federal Judicial Conference of the
Fourth Circuit, Asheville, North Carolina, June 3, 1938:*

IF I WERE asked to designate the most striking development
in procedural reform during the last fifty years, I would un-
hesitatingly single out the progress of judicial rule-making.
* * * We should, therefore, be perfectly justified in devoting this
meeting to a celebration of these gratifying achievements. I pre-
fer, however, to pursue a somewhat different course and speak to
you on still another phase of judicial rule-making. * * *

I am led to suggest that the rule-making power be extended
to criminal procedure prior to verdict.* I lay no particular claim
to credit for this suggestion. It flows rather naturally from the
previous reforms, for thus we would close the last gap in our
procedural system.

If the extension of the rule-making power to criminal procedure is a worthwhile reform—if it will make the criminal trial
less of a game and more of a search for truth—then there is no
time like the present to begin the study of its possibilities. * * *

The Conformity Act of 1872, which requires the federal
courts to conform to state practice in actions at law, does not
apply to criminal proceedings. The latter are governed by section 722 of the Revised Statutes (U. S. Code, title 28, sec. 729)
which reads as follows:

* On the recommendation of President Hoover, and with the active support
of Attorney General William D. Mitchell, early in 1933 the Supreme Court was
authorized by the Congress to prescribe rules of criminal procedure "after verdict,"
which, after formulation in the Department of Justice at the request of the Court,
were submitted in May, 1933, and promulgated two years later.

The jurisdiction in * * * criminal matters conferred on the district and circuit courts * * * for the protection of all persons in the United States in their civil rights, and for their vindication, shall be exercised and enforced in conformity with the laws of the United States, so far as such laws are suitable to carry the same into effect; but in all cases where they are not adapted to the object, or are deficient in the provisions necessary to furnish suitable remedies and punish offenses against law, the common law, as modified and changed by the constitution and statutes of the state wherein the court having jurisdiction of such civil or criminal cause is held, so far as the same is not inconsistent with the Constitution and laws of the United States, shall be extended to and govern the said courts in the trial and disposition of the cause, and, if it is of a criminal nature, in the infliction of punishment on the party found guilty.

Thus, federal criminal procedure is governed by a strange admixture of various statutes and rules of common law. * * *

However, the great majority of matters bearing on criminal procedure are not covered by any federal statute. In this situation one must look to the common law, that is the common law as modified by state constitutions and state legislation. To follow the tortuous trail of modifications is often a trying task. Under such a system there exists an inevitable element of uncertainty and confusion. But even if the trail through the forest of modifications were a clear one, the federal courts would still not be free of the entanglements of ancient common-law procedure.

Lest these observations seem like over-statements, permit me to draw your attention to the vivid words of Mr. Justice Clifford in *Tennessee* v. *Davis*, 100 U. S. 257, 299, commenting upon section 722 of the Revised Statutes:

Examined in the most favorable light, the provision is a mere jumble of federal law, common law, and state law, consisting of incongruous and irreconcilable regulations, which in legal effect amounts to no more than a direction to a judge sitting in such a criminal trial to conduct the same as well as he can, in view of the three systems of criminal jurisprudence, without any suggestion whatever as to what he shall do in such an extraordinary emergency if he should meet a question not regulated by any one of the three systems.

Of course, it is possible for those interested in modernizing our procedure to urge upon the Congress the passage of specific enactments. That has been the traditional, if somewhat haphazard, method. But such a process is necessarily patchwork. The better method is the creation, under rules of court, of a uniform, simplified, and comprehensive system.

In making this suggestion I am not unaware of the difficulties which would be confronted in drafting the rules. For example, it is not always a simple task to distinguish between procedural details on the one hand and matters which affect substantial rights on the other. While it is difficult, in close cases, to make the necessary distinctions, and while the drafters of the rules will be faced constantly with perplexing problems, these facts do not appear to me to be, in any sense, fatal to the project. The same problem was faced by the Supreme Court and its advisers in connection with the preparation of the Rules of Civil Procedure. * * * In any event, if the Court should feel that a particular problem might better be left to legislative determination, such matters could readily be excluded.

There is no reason, with the exception just noted, why such a body of rules should not run pretty fully the gamut of procedure from arrest to conviction. Much valuable information has already been compiled. The American Law Institute in 1930 completed a Model Code of Criminal Procedure, which was drafted by a distinguished group of experts. While that code was designed principally for use by the individual states, it would doubtless be of immeasurable service in any comprehensive re-examination of our federal criminal procedure. For example, the study there given to preliminary examinations in the magistrates' courts would be extremely helpful in any study of procedure before United States commissioners. The same would hold true of the sections of the Model Code dealing with the grand jury, arraignment, motions to quash and pleas in abatement, demurrers, procedure for selecting a trial jury, continuances, the conduct of the trial, and the reception of the verdict. As a matter of fact, the framers of that code had in mind its possible use in any state in which judicial rule-making had been authorized.

There are many points in our federal procedure requiring simplification. A single illustration will suffice. I would suggest, for example, the short form of indictment which prevails in many of the states but which unfortunately has been rarely used in the federal system, and then only with trepidation.

An intensive study of our procedural machinery will reveal many defects which cry for remedy. To extend the rule-making power along the lines suggested would, it seems to me, round out our federal procedure. Every reason which has impelled us to grant to the judiciary the control of procedure in civil matters and in criminal appeals is equally pertinent to the present proposal.

The American public is keenly conscious of the problems of crime control. There has been a growing demand, and a welcome response to that demand, for efficiency in the investigation and apprehension of criminals. As the public becomes increasingly alert, it is insisting upon the scientific treatment of prisoners after they are convicted. Last, but not least, it is demanding efficient disposition of criminal cases. Unnecessary delays will not be tolerated indefinitely. The average citizen has but scant patience with legal refinements that all too often cloud a criminal trial and obscure the main objective—the determination of guilt or innocence, the search for truth. We must reform or be reformed.

[Note: See article entitled "Extending the Rule-Making Power to Federal Criminal Procedure," *Journal of the American Judicature Society,* v. 22, pp. 151-153, December, 1938; also Item IV of Annual Report to the Congress, December 31, 1938. *Ed.*]

4. Administrative Procedure—
A Final Suggestion

[The sharp increase in number of federal administrative agencies of every type—commissions, boards, corporations, administrations, officers, administrators, and the like, both "in" and independently of existing executive departments—and the spread and nature of newly granted powers, have served to focus attention upon the procedure and operation of administrative officers and agencies in recent years. An imposing array of books on the subject have appeared since the World War, and articles on "administrative law" have filled legal journals for a decade or more (though no such title appears in the index to the official reports of the Supreme Court of the United States). Since 1933 the American Bar Association has had a special committee at work on the problem, and the Association's annual awards for legal discussions have been limited to the same subject. Public documents and official hearings, both congressional and executive, contain a growing body of materials. State agencies, such as the New York Constitutional Convention of 1938, have occasionally recanvassed the subject. In England, the Lord Chancellor in 1929 appointed a Committee on Ministers' Powers to consider developments in the field and make recommendations "to secure the constitutional principles of the sovereignty of Parliament and the supremacy of the Law." Its report is a standard reference.

The enforcement and defense of administrative orders or actions, in the courts, is one of the duties of the Attorney General and his staff. Thus the diverse legal phases of administration come before the Department of Justice in one form or another. As early as August 1933, in his first address before the American Bar Association, Attorney General Cummings placed this among the unusual and difficult problems which confronted the new administration (see *Modern Tendencies and the Law,* 19 A.B.A.J. 576, 578). He spoke more fully in his lectures at the University of Virginia in 1934 (see *Liberty Under Law and Administration,* Scribners, 1934). In numerous other writings, addresses and papers he touched various aspects of the problem. *Ed.*]

A letter to the President, December 14, 1938:

GREAT steps forward have been achieved under your Administration in judicial reform to the end that our courts may function with greater celerity and efficiency. I venture to bring to your attention, and to renew the suggestion which I have made publicly at different times, that there is a need for procedural reform in the wide and growing field of administrative law. Experience has proved the importance and necessity for the increasing use of the administrative process in the aid of executive, legislative and judicial functions. Government cannot perform its many and varied tasks without this efficient and flexible instrumentality. Its usefulness and increasing assistance to the functions of government necessarily depend, however, upon a procedure which affords quick and well informed action, grounded upon the fundamentals of fair play.

Different schools of thought compete for varying degrees of judicial review and for varying methods of procedure in the field of administrative law; and much has been written on the subject.

I have little doubt that many of our difficulties, perhaps the major ones, will disappear if we are able to create an efficient machine which in actual experience functions in the public interest.

The problem is one which calls for a most thorough survey of existing practices and procedure and a careful consideration by a trained body, constituted of individuals who can detect present deficiencies and point the way to improvements in the use of this process which will make it so serviceable and just that it will command the respect, and enjoy the support, of all other branches of the government and of the public at large. Of course, it goes without saying that in such procedure there should be proper safeguards for the protection of substantive rights and adequate, but not extravagant, judicial review.

The reform of the civil procedure for the district courts of the United States which recently became effective was accomplished by a somewhat similar approach. An exhaustive study was made by a representative group of the bar, appointed by the Supreme Court as an advisory committee, which was assisted in its work by representatives of the Department of Justice. The result has greatly simplified procedure in the handling of civil cases in the federal district courts and the appeals therefrom, substituting for the diverse, cumbersome and obsolescent practice, theretofore obtaining, a uniform system that apparently has met with nation-wide acclaim. Efforts are now under way to bring into harmony with the spirit of this simplified judicial procedure the review, in the several circuit courts of appeals, of orders and decisions rendered by administrative boards, agencies and commissions. Thus, it is particularly timely that attention be turned to the procedure employed by the administrative process.

In view of the many administrative bodies involved and their widely varying functions it is my recommendation that you request the Congress to authorize the Attorney General to appoint a commission to investigate and consider the whole problem, and to report to the Congress its conclusions and recommendations for such legislative action as may seem appropriate.

PART FIVE

JUDICIAL REFORM

1. The Law's Delays

[References to the all-pervading problem of delays in the operation of the federal judicial system have appeared in Part Two as the subject is involved in the administration of criminal law, and in Part Four as it is involved in the reform of procedure. In the Department of Justice judicial statistics were gathered on the subject beginning early in the administration, for presentation to the annual Judicial Conference. The inquiry into the problem led to three proposals: an increase in the number of judges; the retirement of aged or infirm judges; and the creation of an adequate administrative organization within the judiciary both to provide for the more expeditious transaction of its business and to free the judiciary from executive control in such matters as budget, supply, and assistants. Attorney General Cummings pressed for legislation to achieve each of these proposals. *Ed.*]

An office memorandum to Special Assistant Holtzoff, October 2, 1934:

I HAVE reason to believe, not only from their report but for other reasons, that the members of the Judicial Conference were especially pleased to have the exhibit indicating a survey of the courts with reference to the time elapsing between joinder of issue and actual trial in the various districts. For instance, upon the occasion when the members of the Supreme Court, the Attorney General, and the Solicitor General called upon the President yesterday, Chief Justice Hughes in discussing with the President the need for additional judges took occasion to speak of the compilation in complimentary fashion, saying it had been of much service to the Judicial Conference.

I thought you might like to know of this. I myself think that the compilation was exceedingly useful and it ought to be continued and kept up to date and made a feature of future reports.

From a letter to the President, February 2, 1937, which the President attached to his special message of February 5, 1937, proposing reforms in the judiciary:

Delay in the administration of justice is the outstanding defect of our federal judicial system. It has been a cause of concern to practically every one of my predecessors in office. It has exasperated the bench, the bar, the business community, and the public.

The litigant conceives the judge as one promoting justice through the mechanism of the courts. He assumes that the directing power of the judge is exercised over its officers from the time a case is filed with the clerk of the court. He is entitled to assume that the judge is pressing forward litigation in the full recognition of the principle that "justice delayed is justice denied." It is a mockery of justice to say to a person when he files suit that he may receive a decision years later. Under a properly ordered system, rights should be determined promptly. The course of litigation should be measured in months and not in years.

Yet in some jurisdictions the delays in the administration of justice are so interminable that to institute suit is to embark on a life-long adventure. Many persons submit to acts of injustice rather than resort to the courts. Inability to secure a prompt adjudication leads to improvident and unjust settlements. Moreover, the time factor is an open invitation to those who are disposed to institute unwarranted litigation or interpose unfounded defenses in the hope of forcing an adjustment which could not be secured upon the merits. This situation frequently results in extreme hardships. The small businessman or the litigant of limited means labors under a grave and constantly increasing disadvantage because of his inability to pay the price of justice.

Statistical data indicate that in many districts a disheartening and unavoidable interval must elapse between the date that issue is joined in a pending case and the time when it can be reached for trial in due course. These computations do not take into account the delays that occur in the preliminary stages of litigation or the postponements after a case might normally be expected to be heard.

The evil is a growing one. The business of the courts is continually increasing in volume, importance, and complexity. The average case load borne by each judge has grown nearly 50 percent since 1913 when the district courts were first organized on their present basis. When the courts are working under such pressure it is inevitable that the character of their work must suffer.

The number of new cases offsets those that are disposed of, so that the courts are unable to decrease the enormous backlog of undigested matters. More than 50,000 pending cases (exclusive of bankruptcy proceedings) overhang the federal dockets— a constant menace to the orderly processes of justice. Whenever a single case requires a protracted trial, the routine business of the court is further neglected. It is an intolerable situation and we should make shift to amend it.

Efforts have been made from time to time to alleviate some of the conditions that contribute to the slow rate of speed with which causes move through the courts. * * * The problem must be approached in a more comprehensive fashion if the United States is to have a judicial system worthy of the nation. * * * The time has come when further legislation is essential. To speed justice, to bring it within the reach of every citizen, to free it of unnecessary entanglements and delays are primary obligations of our government.

From Annual Report to the Congress, December 31, 1938:

The slow motion of litigation in the federal courts is convincingly demonstrated by a table compiled for the first time this year, showing the length of time that pending cases have remained on the dockets. * * * The table indicates that there is not a single district, with the exception of New Hampshire, in which the business of the United States district court is "current" within any proper definition of that term. The life of an ordinary piece of litigation, not complicated by unusual features, should be measured in months and not in years. This is not an impossible ideal, or an iridescent dream, but an end that it is entirely within the power of properly implemented courts to achieve.

2. The Need for Additional Judges

From a letter to the President, February 2, 1937:

REASON and necessity require the appointment of a sufficient number of judges to handle the business of the federal courts. These additional judges should be of a type and age which would warrant us in believing that they would vigorously attack their dockets, rather than permit their dockets to overwhelm them.

The cost of additional personnel should not deter us. It must be borne in mind that the expense of maintaining the judicial system constitutes hardly three-tenths of one percent of the cost of maintaining the federal establishment. While the estimates for the current fiscal year aggregate over $23,000,000 for the maintenance of the legislative branch of the government, and over $2,100,000,000 for the permanent agencies of the executive branch, the estimated cost of maintaining the judiciary is only about $6,500,000. An increase in the judicial personnel, which I earnestly recommend, would result in a hardly perceptible percentage of increase in the total annual budget.

This result should not be achieved, however, merely by creating new judicial positions in specific circuits or districts. The reform should be effectuated on the basis of a consistent system which would revitalize our whole judicial structure and assure the activity of judges at places where the accumulation of business is greatest. As congestion is a varying factor and cannot be foreseen, the system should be flexible and should permit the temporary assignment of judges to points where they appear to be most needed.

Statement before Senate Sub-Committee on the Judiciary, on the
appointment of additional judges, February 8, 1938 (Hearings on
S. 3233, pp. 1-5):

I have felt for a long time that the judicial branch of the
government is inadequately provided for in the matter of personnel and in other ways, if we consider what this country actually ought to have—a rapidly functioning and up-to-date judicial
system. I look at it not so much from the standpoint of the lawyers who appear in our courts, nor from the standpoint of the
judges themselves, but from the standpoint of the litigants—
those unfortunate individuals who are drawn into the courts.

If we are to have a system that is commensurate with the
dignity of our country and which will promote the respect for law
which we all so much desire, the law itself must move more
swiftly, more inevitably, with less friction, with less delay, and
with a higher degree of justice. We are not only concerned with
the number of cases that the judges can dispose of, but we are
concerned with the manner in which they dispose of them. I
have abundant figures to show that the district courts * * * and
the circuits * * * are undermanned or, to put it in another way,
overworked; and that the time and equipment indispensable for
consideration and research in deciding legal issues are very much
restricted in many parts of the country. * * *

Moreover, we will have to agree that an adequate judicial
personnel is indispensable if the courts are to keep pace with the
business they are required to handle. The growth of business has
outstripped the occasional increases made from time to time in
the number of judges. This is shown by the fact that during the
year ending June 30, 1913, which was the first year of the existence of the district courts on their present basis, the average number of cases filed per district judge was 276, while during the year
ending June 30, 1937, that figure had increased to 411, a growth
of almost 50 percent in the volume of business which each district judge is supposed to handle.

During this same period the average number of cases per

circuit judge filed in the circuit courts of appeals has grown from 42 for the year ending June 30, 1913, to 65 for the year ending June 30, 1937. Here again is a growth of about 50 percent.

The increase in the load carried by each judge, as reflected in the number of cases, does not, of course, tell the whole story. It must be admitted, I think, that during the same period the complexity and diversification of problems presented to the federal courts for solution have also increased. For example, jurisdiction over corporate reorganizations under section 77B of the Bankruptcy Act has resulted in a heavy burden on the district judges * * * a field which requires intensive application on the part of a judge if he is to understand the complicated matters before him, dealing, as they do, with business situations, accounting matters, and other technical details. * * *

In many instances judges, in order, ostensibly, to keep abreast of their work, approve of repeated continuances. Even in those districts in which there is an appearance of trial dockets being in what is called a "current" condition, the business may actually be in arrears due to the long interval between the final submission of a case to a judge for decision and the time when he actually makes his determination. I can cite instances of judges who sometimes take two or three or four years to decide a case after it has been submitted. Now, that is a denial of justice. * * *

The difficulty lies in the system. The judges, as I have repeatedly said, are for the most part earnest, vigorous, honest, and intelligent, and are doing the best they can. * * * They all want to do well, but they are submerged.

From Annual Report to the Congress, January 3, 1938, pp. 2-4 (for complete text, see House Doc. 378, 75 Cong. 2 Sess.):

We must not be misled by the statement that * * * the trial dockets are * * * "current." All that this means is that after the final pleading is filed in any case, the trial may be had at the next ensuing term of court if the parties and the court cooperate. It does not follow, therefore, that in such districts the business is actually "current" in any true sense, for the word "current" does not take into account the time consumed during the preliminary period before the case is in shape for trial, or the time lost between the time when a case may theoretically be tried and the time when it is actually tried; nor does it make any allowance for the fact that, in many divisions and at many places of holding court, terms are convened but once or twice a year. The interval elapsing between terms of court may alone account for a delay of as much as a year between the time the case is ready for trial and the earliest date upon which it can actually be heard. That this is an important factor may be deduced from the fact that sessions of the United States district courts are held at 376 different places. At 115 of these places there is only one term a year, while at 242 of them there are only two terms annually. At only nineteen places are there more than two terms a year. Ingenious counsel are frequently able to postpone actual trial, despite the utmost efforts of adversary parties to bring matters to a hearing. Overworked judges are at a disadvantage in their efforts to drive forward the business of the courts.

The existence of actual delay, even in districts where the trial dockets are reported to be in a so-called current condition, is conclusively demonstrated by the large number of pending cases that were filed more than two years ago and are still not concluded. For example, in New Jersey and in the Western District of Wisconsin over 60 percent of the pending cases are more than two years old, while in the Northern District of Indiana and in the Southern District of Illinois this is true of over 59 percent of the pending cases. In Delaware this is true of over 46 percent of the cases, in Vermont of over 42 percent, in the Western District of Missouri of over 39 percent, in Kansas of over 37 percent, and in the Southern District of Alabama of over 32 percent. Yet, in all of these districts the trial dockets are reported as being in a so-called "current" state. * * *

The situation that I have depicted is manifestly inconsistent with any sound idea of judicial efficiency. The problem will remain with us until we make shift to remedy the conditions that have created it. * * * The need for an increase in personnel is recognized in the report of the Judicial Conference at the session that convened on September 23, 1937, which I have the honor to submit herewith.

From Annual Report to the Congress, December 31, 1938:

In my report to the Congress submitted a year ago, I recommended that provision be made for the appointment of four additional circuit judges; one additional associate justice for the United States Court of Appeals for the District of Columbia; and 22 additional district judges—27 judges in all. Subsequent to the submission of my Annual Report, I recommend that provision be made for the appointment of one further district judge. Out of the 28 judicial positions thus recommended, 22 were created by the Congress.

Further increases of judicial personnel are indispensable if the judicial machinery is to function smoothly and expeditiously. This need is recognized in the report of the Judicial Conference, submitted herewith. * * * The need is urgent.

3. Retirement of Aged or Infirm Judges

[Under the Constitution, federal judges hold office for life and their salaries may not be reduced. They may, of course, resign or, pursuant to statute, may "retire" when they reach the age of seventy or more and have served not less than ten years. Of importance to judges, when given the opportunity of retiring upon a pension, is the security of their retirement compensation. If a judge "resigns," even though upon a "pension," the Congress may later reduce or withdraw such income. If a judge is permitted to "retire," he is still technically a judge and his compensation may not be reduced or withdrawn. A "retired" judge, moreover, may continue to render essential service in special cases or at places where additional judges are necessary because of the congestion of business. Retirement privileges, which had long been available to other federal judges, were not granted the justices of the Supreme Court until 1937 during the early stages of the struggle over the President's plan for judicial reorganization.

Voluntary retirement, however, is to be distinguished from compulsory retirement. The former, as the result of acts of Congress, is now operative in the federal courts; the latter could only be achieved by constitutional amendment. As an intermediate expedient between voluntary and compulsory retirement, it was urged in the Congress in the late 1860's and, for the lower federal courts, by two of the men who served as Attorney General in the Wilson administration that an additional judge should be appointed whenever an incumbent failed to retire at a given age. A renewal of this proposal and its application to all federal courts was the controversial feature of the President's recommendations of February 5, 1937, for judicial reorganization mentioned above in Sections 7 and 11 of Part Three. *Ed.*]

From a letter to Edwin S. Corwin of Princeton University, December 17, 1936:

QUITE apart from immediate consideration, and as a matter of general policy, I have often thought that much was to be said for a constitutional amendment requiring retirements when the age of seventy is reached. I am wondering if there would be much opposition to such an amendment if it were so framed as not to affect the present judiciary, by making it apply to future appointments only.

A letter to Hatton W. Sumners, Chairman of the House Judiciary Committee (H.R. 212, 74 Cong. 1 Sess.), February 4, 1935:

In accordance with the request contained in your letter of February 1, I have examined the bill (H.R. 5161) introduced by you to amend section 260 of the Judicial Code, for the purpose of extending to justices of the Supreme Court the privilege of retiring after attaining the age of seventy and after at least ten years of judicial service.

Under existing law (Judicial Code, sec. 260; U. S. Code, title 28, sec. 375), a federal judge other than a Supreme Court justice has the privilege of resigning or retiring after the age of seventy and the completion of at least ten years of judicial service. In either event he continues to receive his full salary for the remainder of his natural life. If he retires, however, he still remains a member of the judiciary, may be called upon to perform such judicial duties as he may be willing to undertake, and is protected by the Constitution against diminution of his salary. If he resigns, he loses the last-mentioned constitutional protection.

While Supreme Court justices have the privilege of resigning on full salary, they may not retire. The purpose of the pending bill is to extend to them the privilege of retirement and to provide that any Supreme Court justice who so retires may be called upon by the Chief Justice to perform such judicial duties in any judicial circuit as he may be willing to undertake.

In my opinion the enactment of this measure is desirable.

From "Progress of the President's Plan for Judicial Reform," an address in the National Radio Forum, April 26, 1937:

The President recommended a measure to permit the voluntary retirement of Supreme Court justices at the age of seventy, upon a pension. A bill to this effect has already been passed and is now the law of the land. The Congress has thereby recognized that seventy is a proper age for the retirement of Supreme Court justices—just as it has long been recognized as proper for judges of the lower federal courts.

Reasons for retirement of judges; from "The President's Proposals for Judicial Reorganization," a radio address, February 14, 1937:

Closely allied with the problem of the law's delays is the situation created by the continuance in office of aged or infirm judges.

For eighty years Congress refused to grant pensions to such judges. Unless a judge was a man of independent means, there was no alternative open to him except to retain his position to the very last. When in 1869 a pension system was provided, the new legislation was not effective in inducing retirement. The tradition of aged judges had become fixed, and the infirm judge was often unable to perceive his own mental or physical decrepitude. Indeed, this result had been foreseen in the debates in Congress at that time. To meet the situation, the House of Representatives had passed a measure requiring the appointment of an additional judge to any court where a judge of retirement age declined to leave the bench. However, the proposal failed in the Senate.

With the opening of the twentieth century similar proposals were brought forward. The justices of the Supreme Court however protested and the project was abandoned. When William Howard Taft, a former federal judge, left the presidency, he published his views. "There is no doubt," he said, "that there are judges at seventy who have ripe judgments, active minds, and much physical vigor, and that they are able to perform their judicial duties in a very satisfactory way. Yet in a majority of cases when men come to be seventy, they have lost vigor, their minds are not as active, their senses not as acute, and their willingness to undertake great labor is not so great as in younger men, and as we ought to have in judges who are to perform the enormous task which falls to the lot of Supreme Court justices."

In 1913 Attorney General McReynolds (now a justice of the Supreme Court) in his annual report for the Department of Justice urged that the Congress adopt a similar measure. Some judges, he argued, "have remained upon the bench long beyond the time when they were capable of adequately discharging their duties, and in consequence the administration of justice has suffered. * * * I suggest an act providing when any judge of a federal court below the Supreme Court fails to avail himself of the privilege of retiring now granted by law, that the President be required, with the advice and consent of the Senate, to appoint another judge, who shall preside over the affairs of the court and have precedence over the older one. This will insure at all times the presence of a judge sufficiently active to discharge promptly and adequately the duties of the court." In 1914, 1915, and 1916, Attorney General Gregory renewed this recommendation. Solicitor General John W. Davis aided in drafting legislation to carry out the proposal.

Instead of following this advice, however, the Congress in 1919 passed a measure providing that the President "may" appoint additional district and circuit judges, but only upon a finding that the incumbent judge over seventy "is unable to discharge efficiently all the duties of his office by reason of mental or physical disability of permanent character." This legislation failed of its purpose because it was indefinite and impossible of practical application.

The unsatisfactory solution of 1919 had been endorsed by former Justice Charles Evans Hughes, but in 1928 he made this further observation: "Some judges," he said in part, "have stayed too long on the bench. * * * It is extraordinary how reluctant aged judges are to retire and to give up their accustomed work. * * * I agree that the importance in the Supreme Court of avoiding the risk of having judges who are unable properly to do their work and yet insist on remaining on the bench is too great to permit chances to be taken, and any age selected must be somewhat arbitrary as the time of the failing in mental powers differs widely."

From "Progress of the President's Plan for Judicial Reform," address under the auspices of The National Radio Forum, April 26, 1937:

The evil * * * has been growing. In 1789, the average age of the justices of the Supreme Court was less than fifty years; half a century later, in 1841, when Harrison took over the presidency, the average had increased to sixty years; when the second Harrison assumed the office of President in 1889, after the lapse of another half century, the average age had reached sixty-five; and now, after 148 years of national history, the average age has reached the unprecedented peak of more than seventy years.

A recommendation for compulsory retirement, through constitutional amendment; from Annual Report to the Congress, December 31, 1938:

President Taft asserted that the failure of the Constitution to provide for the compulsory retirement of federal judges at the age of seventy was a defect which should be remedied. This view is held by a large number of eminent jurists and lawyers. It is also, I believe, in accord with the majority opinion of our people. So many disadvantages have resulted from the existing system that I do not pause to enumerate them. Of course, provision should be made for full pay upon such retirement. I, therefore, recommend the adoption of a constitutional amendment to accomplish the desired result. By its express terms such an amendment should be made applicable only to those appointed after its adoption.

In addition, some statutory provision (presumably on a pro-rata basis) should be made for voluntary retirement of federal judges who have become disabled prior to reaching the age of seventy. Not infrequently instances of this kind have occurred. Such a situation is unfair to the incapacitated judge and detrimental to the public interest.

4. An Independent Administrative Organization for the Courts

From a letter to the President, February 2, 1937:

A FUNCTIONARY might well be created to be known as a proctor, or by some other suitable title, to be appointed by the Supreme Court and to act under its direction, charged with the duty of continuously keeping informed as to the state of federal judicial business throughout the United States and of assisting the Chief Justice in assigning judges to pressure areas.

A suggestion; an office memorandum to the Solicitor General, October 11, 1937:

I hand you herewith a memorandum * * * relative to the status of senior circuit judges. I have been toying with the idea that there might be some advantage in legislation which would in effect recognize the status of a senior circuit judge and more clearly define his administrative powers and provide also that, upon reaching the age of seventy, his administrative authority would be passed to the next circuit judge under seventy on the same bench, and that this process should be continued so that we would always be sure of having a senior circuit judge under the age of seventy.

I do not know whether it is worth while to take up this matter at the present time. I have made no analysis to see exactly how it would work and what judges it would affect. I have merely been concerned with the principle involved which would be to have younger and more vigorous judges in charge of the actual administration of the circuit courts. I think the idea is sound as a matter of principle.

From Annual Report to the Congress, January 3, 1938 (for complete text, see House Doc. 378, 75 Cong. 2 Sess.):

Permanent additions to the judicial personnel in circuits and districts where they are urgently needed and reforms of procedure will be of enormous help, but will not entirely solve the age-old problem of the law's delays. Congestion is apt to be a temporary phenomenon, making its appearance sporadically in various districts as a result of special conditions that are not necessarily lasting. For example, the illness or incapacity of a judge or the filing of a large number of actions of special kinds such as war-risk insurance cases or suits for damages affecting a great many persons may temporarily clog the dockets. A protracted trial of a mail fraud case or a prosecution under the Sherman Act may postpone the disposition of other business and cause an accumulation of arrears that will take months to dispose of. Circumstances of this kind frequently recur, making their appearance when least expected. A system of some degree of flexibility is indispensable. It is gratifying to note that at the last session of the Congress the rigidity of the old rules was somewhat relaxed. Nevertheless, serious thought should be given to increasing that flexibility by appropriate measures that will involve a greater coordination of the judicial machinery, a better method of assembling data, and continuous oversight by the judiciary itself of its functions and efficiency.

An efficacious administrative machinery is as necessary in the courts as it is in other branches of government and in private enterprise. Individual judges must of necessity confine their time and energy principally to the transaction of judicial business. The senior circuit judges are occupied with their judicial labors and can give but scant time to the performance of administrative duties. The conference of senior circuit judges meets but once a year and continues in session only three days. It performs a valuable and useful function, but obviously it does not and cannot act as a continuous administrative body.

It is highly desirable that provision be made for a permanent administrative officer, with adequate assistance, to devote his entire time to supervision of the administrative side of the courts; to studying and suggesting improvements in the matter of handling dockets; to assembling data and keeping abreast of the needs of the various districts for temporary assistance; and to ascertaining what judges are available for such assignments, as well as performing other incidental functions. Such an officer should be appointed by the Supreme Court and act under the supervision of the Chief Justice. It is interesting to note that the appointment of an officer of this kind was recommended in England in January 1936, in a Report of the Royal Commission on the Despatch of Business at Common Law.

I believe, too, that there is something inherently illogical in the present system of having the budget and the expenditures of the courts and the individual judges under the jurisdiction of the Department of Justice. The courts should be an independent, coordinate branch of the government in every proper sense of the term.

Accordingly, I recommend legislation that would provide for the creation and maintenance of such an administrative system under the control and direction of the Supreme Court.

From a statement before the Senate Judiciary Committee on the proposal to establish an administrative officer for the courts, January 24 and 25, 1938 (Hearings on S. 3212, 75th Cong. 3 Sess., pp. 3-4, 7, 8-9, 25-28):

The country is divided into 84 judicial districts, with a district court in each district and a district court also in the District of Columbia, making 85 district courts in all. * * *

With an exception to which I shall shortly refer, each district, administratively, constitutes an independent unit. There is no general administrative officer in the district or outside of it who is responsible for the arrangement of the judicial business, the handling of the docket, or any other matters that would tend to expedite or facilitate the disposition of litigation. The law fixes the time and the place for holding terms of court. Not only is each district court a law unto itself, in a way, but each judge in a district in which there is more than one judge is practically independent of his colleagues. * * *

Now that general set-up has produced certain manifest defects of administration. Obviously a judge's first duty is the performance of his judicial functions. He has but little time—and often no inclination—to perform administrative functions. The result is, strange as it may appear, that nowhere in the whole federal judicial system is there any administrative officer charged with the duty of arranging for the facilitation of the transaction of business. * * *

There is something inherently illogical in having the budget of the courts and the expenses of the individual judges under jurisdiction of the Department of Justice. * * * The Constitution, of course, contemplates that the judiciary shall be an independent, coordinate branch of the government; and yet, administratively, it is in large part connected with the Department of Justice. * * *

The salaries of the clerks, deputy clerks, and their assistants are fixed by the Attorney General. * * * The Department of Justice fixes the number of deputy clerks and clerical assistants which each office may be permitted to employ. This results from the fact that the Department of Justice controls the budget of the judiciary. The salaries of judges' secretaries likewise are fixed by the Department of Justice because they are paid out of the appropriation for the miscellaneous expenses of the United States courts, "as may be authorized or approved by the Attorney General." Those words have appeared in the Department of Justice appropriation acts for years. * * *

The law provides for an investigation of the official acts, records, and accounts of marshals and clerks of the United States courts and United States commissioners. In order to carry out the duties required by that provision of law, we have in the Department of Justice a staff of fourteen examiners who spend their time in the field, going from one point to another, making a thorough examination of the offices of the various court clerks and United States commissioners. * * *

I have left to the last one of the most important points, and that is the preparation of the budget estimates for the courts and justifying the estimates before the Bureau of the Budget and before the appropriations committees of the Congress. All of this work is done by the Department of Justice, except that some of the judges located in the courts of the District of Columbia testify in person before the Bureau of the Budget and the appropriations committees. * * *

Let me state it this way: I cannot drive from my mind the thought that it is peculiar that not only does one of the executive departments have complete fiscal and at least partial administrative control over the judicial branch of the government but the same department appears before the courts, as counsel, more often than any other group. * * * Yet the Department of Justice, in a sense, holds the purse strings, or at least the disbursement of what is in the purse. * * *

As I have frequently said in my testimony heretofore, we have endured this anomalous situation so long that it has come to seem natural. Suppose the condition were reversed and the judiciary had control over the fiscal affairs of the Department of Justice. We would all at once say that was an impossible situation. What I am now suggesting is that it is just as illogical and unfair for the executive branch of the government to have this control over the judiciary.

Some people have said this means relinquishment of some of the authority of the Department of Justice. My answer is that I am perfectly willing to part with that authority. I do not think it belongs with the Department of Justice, and it ought not be retained there.

From Annual Report to the Congress, December 31, 1938:

I am convinced that the functions of the judiciary cannot be performed efficiently and expeditiously unless the courts are equipped with proper and adequate administrative machinery which they themselves can control and for which they will be responsible. The independence of the judiciary would seem to require that its administrative work should not be handled by one of the executive departments, or be under the control of the chief litigant in the federal courts. The sympathetic action taken by the Judicial Conference with reference to these matters is set forth as a part of its report.

[Note: As indicated in the report of the Judicial Conference following its September session, 1938, at which Attorney General Cummings discussed, among other things, the measure for the creation of an independent administrative organization for the judiciary, the Conference appointed a committee of circuit judges to make recommendations in collaboration with the Attorney General to attain the desired ends. For an interesting and somewhat related proposal to extend the Judicial Conference idea to the several circuits, based upon the results so obtained in the Fourth Circuit under Senior Circuit Judge John J. Parker, see "The Value of Judicial Conferences in the Federal Circuits," an article in the *American Bar Association Journal,* December, 1938.

It should be noted that the concept of absolute separation of executive law officers and the courts breaks down, perhaps necessarily, at various points. An interesting sidelight on the relations of the Department of Justice with the courts is illustrated in *Booth et al.* v. *Fletcher* (D. C. App., December 19, 1938) sustaining the right of the Attorney General—apparently never before exercised—to defend judges who were sued by an attorney for conspiracy to disbar him. Commenting on the decision, Attorney General Cummings said in an office memorandum on December 23, 1938: "I consider it a highly important duty, and one clearly involving the public interest, to relieve a judicial officer from the burden of such harassing litigation, a burden which otherwise he would either have to bear personally * * * or accept the gratuitous services of private counsel which would entail in some measure a sense of personal obligation that a public officer ought not to be forced to endure. A more fruitful source of harassment to conscientious judges by discontented litigants is difficult to imagine, if judges are to be denied the right of defense by public law officers."

A contrasting situation, presenting the converse of executive control over judicial administration stressed by Mr. Cummings in his testimony reproduced in the text above, is illustrated in certain Louisiana tax cases which indicate something of the problems which may arise when judges exercise the executive function of making appointments to the executive branch. The Treasury Department had requested the institution of criminal proceedings against individuals for tax evasion on income, part of which some people believed to have been diverted to local political purposes. It was charged that the cases were brought for political reasons and, to avoid complications, special counsel from other states were employed. Several defendants pleaded guilty or did not defend, and received only fines. One was tried and convicted, and another was then acquitted by the jury. Before the cases were instituted, however, a trial judge had exercised his right of making an interim appointment (U. S. Code, title 28, sec. 511) to fill the then vacant post of United States attorney for the district. After the several dispositions of cases noted above, the judicial appointee on May 11, 1936, recommended the dismissal of the remaining cases. (His grounds were that a principal witness had changed his story, that part of the tax had been paid by another person, that in one case there was no evidence on a crucial point, that in another the government had previously proved the income to have been received by someone other than the defendant, that in the one "perfect" case the jury had acquitted the defendant apparently on the ground that the funds had not been received by him for his own use, and that it was "certain" that no further convictions could be secured.) In criminal tax cases, all United States district attorneys are usually allowed wide discretion. Moreover, it was reported that the trial judge had been "distressed" when his appointee was superseded in the former trials. It was felt that a "situation of some delicacy" was thus created. The Assistant Attorney General then in charge of the Tax Division recommended that the government leave the responsibility "with the United States attorney who has been named by the court, to be handled in the regular manner." The Attorney General endorsed on the margin of the memorandum, "Course indicated is hereby approved," and the United States attorney was informed on May 26, 1936, that "these cases are subject to such disposition as you, in the exercise of your judgment, see fit to give them, and you are constituted the final and ultimate authority in such matters. You, of course, have complete knowledge of the facts in these cases, of local conditions, and in addition thereto the Treasury Department's attitude." He dismissed the cases. *Ed.*]

PART SIX

ADMINISTRATION OF FEDERAL JUSTICE

1. The Administrative Burden

[Hundreds of thousands of legal proceedings and office law matters receive attention in the Department of Justice annually. Each item must be dealt with promptly, yet with such care as to insure that it is properly handled. Politics, in the unfavorable sense of the word, must be avoided. The Attorney General functions as the general counsel of the United States. He must supervise directly or indirectly the work of both the resident and field staffs of the Department of Justice, in every type of litigation and in every field of law. The items which follow are exceedingly diverse. They are chosen not merely because of the significance of each individual document, but also because their very diversity illustrates the endless variety of matters which fill the day of the Attorney General. More or less complete data on the detailed functions and fields of activity of the Department are to be found in the annual reports to the Congress, and in the statements and testimony of all of the principal officers of the Department which are published in the reports of congressional committee hearings on Department of Justice appropriation bills. *Ed.*]

An office memorandum to Assistant Attorney General Keenan, in charge of the Criminal Division, May 9, 1935:

I suppose you have seen the practice manual for assistant United States attorneys prepared by Martin Conboy. I would be glad to have your views as to what use could be made of it in connection with our work. You also might consider the question of whether or not the Department of Justice would be justified in getting out something a little more elaborate and explicit along these general lines, which would be more formal and perhaps be in more definite and preservable shape than the circulars which we from time to time have issued. I would be glad if you would generally review this whole subject and see what there is that we can do to stimulate the work.

[Note: The "Practice Manual for Assistant United States Attorneys" referred to above was issued by United States Attorney Conboy for the Southern District of New York on April 15, 1935, as was an "Office Manual for the Office of the United States Attorney for the Southern District of New York" on October 6, 1936. At the Department of Justice at

Washington, in addition to the 827 separate circulars of instructions which were issued from March 4, 1933, to December 17, 1938, a revised compilation of general "Instructions to United States Marshals" was issued on July 1, 1934; a revision of the general compilation of "Instructions to United States Attorneys," though prepared in 1937, was withheld pending adjustments made necessary by the new rules of civil procedure (see Part Four above); revised "Instructions to Clerks of United States Courts" were in course of preparation at the end of 1938; and office manuals were issued for the Division of Records and the office of the appointment clerk in 1937 and for the Lands Division in 1938. *Ed.*]

Circular No. 2891 to all United States attorneys on the statute popularly known as the Act to Prohibit the Interstate Transportation of Strikebreakers, July 27, 1936:

On July 17, 1936, you were instructed by wire to report immediately to this Department any complaints of violations of Public Act No. 776 of the 74th Congress (approved June 24, 1936) which had come to your attention.

You are hereby instructed to continue to clear through this Department all future complaints of violations. The statute presents many difficult questions and it is desirable that there be a uniform and consistent enforcement policy throughout the United States.

Attached hereto for your information is a memorandum [of 17 pages] prepared in the Criminal Division of the Department which analyzes the statute. A few attorneys in the Department are specializing in questions pertaining to the enforcement of this act. If, following a report to this Department, any particular complaint appears to deserve a full investigation, these attorneys are prepared to assist you in conducting such investigation.

[Note: The foregoing circular illustrates the manner in which general instructions are given to United States attorneys throughout the country. *Ed.*]

From Circular No. 2946, March 4, 1937:

Certain cases have arisen recently indicating that in some instances the district courts do not appoint counsel for defendants in criminal cases who appear without an attorney unless the defendant expressly requests such appointment. * * * While it may be that the right "to have the assistance of counsel for his defense," which is guaranteed by the Sixth Amendment, may be waived, and while it may be that the practice followed in most of the jurisdictions is more than a compliance with the constitutional requirement, the Department of Justice is under a particular obligation to see that no man who needs counsel is without such assistance.

An office memorandum to Assistant Solicitor General Golden W. Bell, June 9, 1938:

Permit me to extend my congratulations to you and to Special Attorney Warner W. Gardner for the fine results achieved in the *First Federal Savings and Loan Association* case.

[Note: The item above was selected at random from similar congratulatory notes to members of the staff of the Department. The case mentioned (see *First Federal Savings & Loan Ass'n* v. *Loomis*, 97 F. (2d) 831) involved the constitutionality of the federal savings and loan system authorized by the Home Owners Loan Act of 1933. The government was not a party to the suit but, in accordance with permissible practice, Mr. Gardner successfully presented the views of the federal government as *amicus curiae* or "friend of the court" on the appeal to the Circuit Court of Appeals for the Seventh Circuit. The case was taken to the Supreme Court (83 L. Ed. 85) and set for argument in January, 1939. *Ed.*]

2. Monopoly and Restraint of Trade

[With the exception of the activities of the Bureau of Investigation in certain periods, the enforcement of antitrust legislation has usually been of greater public interest than any other phase of the operations of the Department of Justice. The most important cases have involved struggles with great corporations, the Titans of the business and industrial world. Even though the Department, understaffed and underfinanced for this form of activity, has often gone down to defeat, these legal battles have had more drama and the appearance of greater public significance than prosecutions under less conspicuous types of legislation.

During the period of the enforcement of the National Industrial Recovery Act, the emphasis of the administration was on cooperation under the regulatory provisions of codes of fair competition, rather than on enforced dealing at arm's length and the separation of business units. The Antitrust Division was engaged largely in the enforcement of emergency legislation and other commerce regulations rather than in the enforcement of the measures from which it takes its name.

After the Supreme Court decision pronouncing the invalidity of the National Industrial Recovery Act, policy remained for a time unsettled. In 1936, Attorney General Cummings directed the institution of the first successful criminal prosecutions against large industrial combinations in the history of the antitrust statutes. After that time the criminal features of the antitrust laws became the basis of a revitalized enforcement policy. In addition, a movement initiated by the Attorney General to have the laws adapted to current needs and conditions resulted in the creation of a commission by act of Congress to reinvestigate the entire subject. *Ed.*]

From a statement to the press, July 6, 1933:

THERE seems to be an impression in some quarters that the antitrust laws have been repealed or suspended in whole or in part. This is an entirely erroneous impression. It is true that the National Recovery Act provides among other things for codes of fair competition which, when approved by the President, operate to exempt conduct provided for in the codes from the provisions of the antitrust laws. It will be noted, however, that before such an exemption can become effective not only must a code have the formal approval of the President but in addition such an exemption will apply only to the particular industry concerned and only for the period during which the act and a code thereunder are in effect; and conduct under a code will be exempt only when it properly complies with the provisions thereof. Any action taken before the approval of the code enjoys no exemption whatever. * * *

Information has reached the Department of Justice that, in certain instances, in violation of existing law, sundry groups are already making and attempting to carry into effect improper restrictive agreements. The purpose of this statement is to make clear that such procedure is not lawful and will not be tolerated. * * *

A further word is perhaps necessary. A large number of industrial activities and arrangements which are prohibited by the antitrust laws do not come in any sense whatever within the purview of the exemptions contemplated by the National Recovery Act. In other words, there is a large field to which the antitrust laws apply, quite irrespective of exemptions contemplated by the statute when a code has been approved.

From an office memorandum to Assistant Attorney General Harold M. Stephens, in charge of the Antitrust Division, March 17, 1934:

Apparently we are approaching a time when we either have to proceed more fully under antitrust laws or we must devise some method of protecting the public under the N.R.A. price regulations. The whole subject is very troublesome. From the latter standpoint, it approaches pretty close to the verge of price fixing, for what we now have is apparently group price fixing by the interested parties and competitive prices regulated by competition are disappearing.

It is the old issue over again. Shall we attempt to restore or protect elements of competition, or shall the government take a larger hand in price fixing itself? Some people believe that if the present loose system prevails it will tend to stabilize the depression.

A letter to the President, April 27, 1937:

This Department has considered the question of identical sealed bids received by government agencies seeking to purchase steel products, to determine whether court proceedings should be instituted under the antitrust laws. * * * The question before us is broader, however, than that of identical bidding in the steel industry. The types of practice complained of in this instance are widespread throughout many of the basic industries of the country. The difficulty in correcting this situation raises the whole question as to the adequacy of the present antitrust laws for the solution of the monopoly problem as it now exists in the United States.

In my opinion, the time has come for the federal government to undertake a restatement of the law designed to prevent monopoly and unfair competition. This proceeds from the conviction that the present laws have not operated to give adequate protection to the public against monopolistic practices.

After 24 years' experience with the Sherman Law and its judicial interpretations, the Congress enacted the Clayton Act and set up the Federal Trade Commission. After nearly 20 years' experience, in 1933, the National Recovery Administration was established. Many other laws dealing with phases of the industrial question have been enacted and others are in contemplation. A review of the accumulated experience of the last 47 years would indicate many things to be avoided, as well as many to be accomplished, by a revision of our antitrust laws.

Moreover, these laws have been subjected to court interpretations which from time to time have limited their application, modified their meaning, and imposed upon the government impossible burdens of proof.

A long experience with the difficulties of enforcement furnishes a sound basis for improving the enforcement machinery. This Department has labored with inadequate means to enforce laws that do not provide sufficient legal weapons to make enforcement effective. In the face of a present tendency to increase prices and a necessity for a corresponding increase in the vigilance of the Department, the question is forcibly presented as to whether the country can afford to leave the enforcement of a vital economic policy so poorly sustained. The present machinery of enforcement through the Federal Trade Commission should also be made more adequate and effective, and the devitalizing effect of some of the court interpretations upon its powers should be overcome by legislation.

I therefore recommend that there be set up a committee to study the antitrust laws as to their adequacy, their enforcement, and the desirability of their amendment, extension, and clarification. The committee should have power to enlist the aid of consultant groups both within and without the government, as the studies will naturally cover a wide range, including the relation of anti-monopoly policies to such subjects as patents, taxation, commerce, manufacturing, farming, and labor.

[Note: See also Annual Report to the Congress, January 3, 1938, House Doc. 378, 75th Cong. 2d Sess. *Ed.*]

From "The Unsolved Problem of Monopoly," an address at a meeting of the Associated Grocery Manufacturers of America, New York City, November 29, 1937:

Whatever else may be said of our antitrust laws, they represent an honest attempt to preserve democratic processes. With the objectives of these laws, I assume that few responsible persons have any serious quarrel. To forbid monopoly, to preserve free competition, to insure fair trade practices, and to prevent the price range of commodities from getting beyond the reach of the consumer—these and related purposes are at once worthy and of the essence of democracy. Yet, manifestly, our antitrust laws, admirable in design and, within certain areas, reasonably successful, have failed of their major objective. * * *

The trend toward an undue concentration of wealth and economic control is unmistakable. It is estimated that in 1929, 200 non-financial corporations controlled 49 percent of the assets of all such corporations. In 1933 the percentage had increased to 56. Reports from the Bureau of Internal Revenue for 1933 indicate that nearly one-third of all the property passing by death was found in less than 4 percent of the estates. The studies made by the Brookings Institution in its 1929 report indicate that 6,000,000 families had incomes of less than $1,000 annually, and that 36,000 families in the high-income brackets received as much of our national income as 11,000,000 families with the lowest incomes. Reliable statistical information discloses that large numbers of industrial units have totally disappeared, and that there has been a progressive elimination of the small business man as a factor in American life. * * *

Moreover, the complexities of modern existence and the pressure of events have undoubtedly had their effect upon the antitrust laws, their interpretation, and their administration. If you look at the statutes, do you find the law? Not at all. Only the simple expect to find the law in the statute books. The law must be searched out, as if it were a quarry in the tangled underbrush of an almost impenetrable forest. The courts have interpreted and re-interpreted the law and have from time to time laid down doctrines of a modifying and even self-contradictory nature. It is a case of "confusion worse confounded."

When the Sherman Antitrust Act came before the Supreme Court in 1895 in the famous *Knight* case, it was held that the sugar refining business of the country "bore no direct relation to commerce between the states or with foreign nations." It is hardly to be doubted that this decision devitalized the Sherman Act to a marked extent, and for many years thereafter monopolistic practices went forward under judicial sanction. We have come a long way since that time, as you may readily see by comparing the reasoning in the *Knight* case with the reasoning of Chief Justice Hughes in the *Jones & Laughlin* case. * * *

The Robinson-Patman Act, the Miller-Tydings bill, and enactments like the Wagner labor relations law, the Walsh-Healey Act, and the Guffey coal bill affect business methods in many essential ways, with results which we have not yet fully appraised. In the meantime, various decisions have been rendered by our courts which have tended to curb the power of the Federal Trade Commission and limit the scope of its useful activity. * * *

Despite the difficulties and uncertainties to which I have alluded, there still remains an extensive area within which antitrust proceedings, even under existing laws and procedure, may be highly fruitful. This we have demonstrated by many successful actions dealing with such matters as unfair methods of competition, harmful restraints of trade, and ruthless suppression of small business by unethical methods. * * *

Nevertheless, it is literally impossible, with the limited personnel of the Antitrust Division, to give attention to every complaint or to prosecute all the cases that ought to be brought to the attention of the courts. Roughly speaking, it costs the government not less than $100,000 per year to prosecute one sharply contested antitrust suit. Under the conditions that now prevail, it is only by working under extreme pressure that we are able to investigate the most urgent of current complaints and keep three or four large cases moving simultaneously. Moreover, the Department of Justice should be supplied with a staff especially qualified for economic analysis. Practically all of the difficult antitrust cases involve intricate economic and business problems. Manifestly, no suit against an American enterprise should be instituted without the most careful preliminary investigation. No responsible person would desire the Department to file suits on popular rumor and suspicion, without adequate check or preparation and without an eye to ultimate results. * * * It is idle to pass new laws or to revise old ones without realizing that their administration is fully as important as their formulation; and that to enact ambitious laws and not to provide the means of their enforcement is to "keep the word of promise to our ear and break it to our hope."

In what I have said it has been my primary purpose to state a problem, to indicate roughly its outlines, and to stress its importance. We have built up a body of law that is at once difficult to understand and well-nigh impossible of practical application in many of the urgent situations of modern times. A thorough overhauling of these laws is imperatively required. This is necessary, not only from the standpoint of the government and the public, but from the standpoint of business as well.

Naturally, I deprecate a "slap-dash" approach to the subject. In my judgment, there should not only be serious study but extensive hearings, so that every interested element of our national life may be represented and so that it may not be contended that any legitimate considerations have been ignored. Adequate consideration of the matter must of necessity cover a wide range of inquiry which should touch such subjects as mergers, holding companies, financial control, federal incorporation or licensing, base-point bidding, price leaders, identical bids, patents, and taxation. * * * Competing considerations should be given their appropriate weight so that the resultant may gain general respect, for there is nothing in the world more futile than to enact laws which public opinion and the courts are not prepared to support.

We should determine how far wrongful intent is to be considered as a criterion when actual restraint of trade has been shown, and whether the so-called "rule of reason" requires redefinition. We should consider whether we are chiefly concerned with the form of competitive practices, or whether the accent is to be placed on the control of the supply and price of the product with the resulting mastery of the market.

A sinister intent is difficult to establish, whereas an economic result stares one in the face. The establishment of rebuttable presumptions, within reasonable limits, would tend to relieve the government of many almost insupportable burdens in the matter of affirmative proof that now has to be drawn from reluctant or adverse witnesses.

Monopolistic practices could undoubtedly be more clearly defined. This would be helpful in the interest of enforcement and would be a protection to those who honestly endeavor to comply with the law. Consideration might well be given to an increase in the authority of the Federal Trade Commission to act as an advisory body.

No doubt, in rewriting the antitrust laws, thought should be devoted not only to strengthening them and making them more intelligible, but attention should also be given to providing protection and encouragement to legitimate efforts of enlightened business men to increase production and employment, to improve working conditions, to eliminate waste, to provide more effective methods of distribution, and to supply better services to consumers and to the public. Nor should we overlook the fact that recalcitrant minority groups may, by ill-considered methods, impair or destroy the orderly conduct of business, with incidental injury to labor and to the public. * * *

The American people will not permanently tolerate monopoly or its evil fruits. Every business group understands this full well, and, indeed, those who maintain conditions that are tantamount to monopoly are opposed to every monopoly except their own. Complaints under the antitrust laws usually originate with business men and are directed against other business men. In this welter of things, nothing is more obvious than the fact that "big business," if I may use that term, is moving blindly but with accumulating acceleration down the road leading to ultimate government supervision. Indeed, there are those who are persuaded that economic groups that in one way or another have arrived at a position of dominance in any essential line of activity are likely candidates for regulatory treatment—and that this is especially true with reference to so-called natural monopolies or lines of business dealing with national resources. The problem has been so long with us that unless it is frankly considered and firmly grasped, it will get quite beyond control and lead to remedies of a character that few really desire.

A letter to Hatton W. Sumners, Chairman of the House Judiciary Committee, to which impeachment matters are referred, December 18, 1937:

I feel it my duty to call to your attention the conduct of United States District Judge Ferdinand A. Geiger of the Eastern District of Wisconsin, who yesterday at Milwaukee discharged a grand jury without permitting it to report after a three months' investigation of the automobile finance industry. Before discharging the grand jury and thus preventing criminal proceedings, Judge Geiger had taken an attitude which made it impossible for this Department to obtain a civil decree which would have given immediate relief to consumers from the payment of excessive reserve charges, relief to dealers from coercion by automobile companies, and relief to independent finance companies from unfair competition and restraint of trade.

Many months ago, upon complaints, this Department instituted an investigation of the automobile finance industry, chiefly centered in three large companies which were identified in interest with General Motors Corporation, the Ford Motor Company, and Chrysler Corporation. The complaints of violation of law were as follows:

1. That the automobile companies were discriminating against the independent finance companies, and dealers who patronize them, by offering to their associated finance companies and dealers who patronize such companies services and the facilities for the wholesale financing of automobile purchases while at the same time denying such facilities and services to the other finance companies and dealers.

2. That the automobile companies and their associated finance companies were compelling dealers to do their retail financing with the associated finance company, by various coercive

devices including the termination or threatened termination of the franchises of recalcitrant dealers.

3. That the associated finance companies were requiring the inclusion of excessive reserves concealed from the purchaser in the time sales price of automobiles, which reserves were paid over to their dealers as a secret profit upon the payment in full of the paper.

4. That in the case of one of the automobile manufacturers, these coercive and discriminatory practices were aggravated by the ownership of all of the stock of its associated finance company, and in the case of a second manufacturer through a contract under the terms of which the manufacturer agreed to recommend the use of the associated finance company in consideration of a substantial percentage of the profits of the associated finance company.

After the grand jury began its investigation, this Department was approached by representatives of some of the companies involved who extended assurance that the abuses of which the government complained could be remedied by civil decree, that the automobile companies had engaged in such practices under more or less compulsion from competition and from economic conditions, and that criminal proceedings at this time would be detrimental to the automobile industry. It was therefore strenuously urged by these representatives that conferences be held to determine whether a civil decree could be agreed upon. The Department did not feel warranted in declining to hear such representations and to hold conferences for such a purpose.

From the outset, this Department took the position that it would not enter into a compromise decree but would consider only a decree which corrected all of the above abuses. It also took the position that it would not consent to any decree unless the representatives of the independent finance companies, who had filed the original complaints, agreed that it was adequate to prevent further abuses, and unless those companies themselves agreed to be bound by the terms thereof. The Department also took the position that it would not approve any decree which favored any one competitor over any other.

In these conferences the companies' representatives were advised that the government could give no assurances as to what action the grand jury might take, and that the government was undertaking only to discuss a civil decree which, if agreed upon, would be presented to the grand jury for its consideration along with the evidence already before it. It was, however, anticipated that if satisfactory consent decrees could be agreed upon which eliminated the foregoing abuses, it might not be necessary to go through the prolonged ordeal of criminal trials.

No agreement was reached, but a tentative proposal for a decree was drawn up which the attorneys for two of the groups represented at the conference agreed to submit to their clients for consideration. The proposed decree would have enjoined both the automobile and finance companies from discriminating against independent finance companies and dealers who patronize them, and from coercing dealers. It would have abolished the system of excessive reserves and relieved the consumer from that burden. It would have eliminated control by the automobile companies of their associated finance companies through stock ownership or otherwise. In short, it would have given all of the relief that could have been anticipated as a result of successful litigation.

While the tentative draft of the decree was under consideration by the companies, the Department was advised by Mr. Russell Hardy, the special assistant in charge of the grand jury presentation, that Judge Geiger had called him in and commented unfavorably on the fact that conferences were being held, taking the position that there should be no conferences between the Department and the companies affected, even though the terms of the decree might grant essential relief to an important American industry and avoid a great deal of litigation. This Department deferred to Judge Geiger's wish and canceled all conferences.

Having accomplished this much, Judge Geiger was not satisfied. He had prevented the government from obtaining a satisfactory and far-reaching civil decree. Arbitrarily and against the protests of government counsel, he recessed the grand jury and summoned the companies' attorneys to advise him about the conferences held with the Department. He then proceeded to absolve the companies from prosecution by discharging the grand jury, although advised that the grand jury had voted to return indictments.

The net results of Judge Geiger's unwarranted interference with this Department and with the grand jury have been: first, to free the companies from any present necessity for correcting the objectionable practices; second, to save them from indictment for past violations of the antitrust laws; and third, to discredit the efforts of the government to correct abuses in the industry.

This is not an isolated instance of arbitrary, unjust and unfair conduct on the part of Judge Geiger. Your attention is directed to certain criminal tax cases which came before Judge Geiger in April, 1935. The cases were *United States* v. *Volland, United States* v. *West, United States* v. *Branigan, United States* v. *Lubar, United States* v. *Tarnof,* and *United States* v. *Pokrass.* All six of these cases were dismissed by Judge Geiger because in *one* of them an agreement had been made—pursuant to section 3229, Revised Statutes, by the Commissioner of Internal Revenue, approved by the Secretary of the Treasury, and sanctioned by the Attorney General—whereby the defendant was to pay the full amount of taxes, penalties, and interest, and enter a plea of guilty to one count of an indictment. In the *Volland* case, in which the compromise agreement had been accepted, Judge Geiger completely repudiated and disregarded section 3229 of the statute. In the other five cases no compromise had been accepted and in four no offer had even been made. Judge Geiger nevertheless dismissed these indictments also.

This course of conduct is so obstructive to the administration of justice that I could not justify a failure to bring it to your knowledge. This Department stands ready to submit to your committee all of its pertinent documents, and its staff will appear at any time to answer any questions concerning the foregoing matters.

[Note: Hearings were held before the House Judiciary Committee (see Hearings, Official Conduct of Judge Ferdinand A. Geiger, 75th

Cong. 3 Sess.), which took no action. The automobile financing cases were then presented to a grand jury in Indiana, which returned indictments. Negotiations were resumed at the request of the Ford and Chrysler companies, consent decrees were agreed upon and entered, and the indictments were dismissed. The criminal proceeding against General Motors awaited trial. *Ed.*]

A report to the President, February 10, 1938:

So much is being said and done about the antitrust situation that I have caused to be prepared a memorandum of the principal cases and investigations now pending in the Antitrust Division, with discussions as to the problems involved. I enclose it herewith. If you will glance over it you will get a bird's-eye view of what is going on in that Division.

A statement to the press, May 18, 1938:

The Department of Justice recently announced a policy under which there would be issued a series of public statements throwing light on the prosecution policy with respect to antitrust laws. The necessity for making such public statements with respect to antitrust prosecutions arises from the fact that they present a problem different from the enforcement of other criminal statutes. In antitrust cases the rule of reason necessarily requires the exercise of judgment on the part of the prosecuting arm in order to give the general principles of the antitrust laws an equitable and economic application to unlike cases and dissimilar industrial situations. A guide to businessmen as to prosecution policy should be furnished by the Department wherever possible.

There is set forth below an outline of the general form which future statements of this character will take:

1. *Form of Statements.* The statements will be issued in the form of announcements signed by the Assistant Attorney General in charge of the Antitrust Division, and approved by the Attorney General.

2. *Purpose of Statement.* The aim of these statements in connection with any particular proceeding or investigation is to serve (1) as a guide to businessmen who seek information on the probable action of this Department in similar circumstances, (2) to aid the Department itself in formulating a consistent policy of antitrust law enforcement, (3) to serve as a warning to those engaged in similar illegal practices, and (4) to call the attention of the Congress to the interpretation and application of antitrust laws by the Attorney General, as they may have a bearing upon contemplated legislation.

3. *Contents of Statements.* These statements on prosecution policy will not discuss the guilt or innocence of particular defendants; they will not interfere with the presumption of innocence which defendants have in a criminal case or the advantage of the burden of proof which they enjoy in a civil case. They will be confined to the reasons for departmental action. It may be assumed as a matter of course that the Department would not take action unless it had in its possession evidence which in its judgment warranted it in proceeding. Under such circumstances, the Department is under a public duty to present such evidence to an impartial judicial tribunal.

In general, the statements will cover (1) the conditions which the Department believes to exist in the particular industry which create monopolistic control or restraint of trade, (2) the reason why the particular procedure was followed, whether a civil suit, consent decree, criminal prosecution, acceptance of pleas of *nolo contendere,* or dismissal of the proceeding, and (3) the economic results which are to be expected from its action in the particular case.

3. Taxation

[Pursuant to that portion of the executive order of June 10, 1933, which transferred to the Department of Justice such functions of conducting litigation as were not then performed by it, a Tax Division was set up in the Department to prosecute or defend all income tax cases in the courts. Such proceedings, except for criminal cases, theretofore had been handled largely by Treasury Department attorneys.

Illustrative of these duties were cases against former Secretary of the Treasury Andrew W. Mellon. Shortly after taking office, Attorney General Cummings determined to use the full powers of his office to bring to an end the practice of claiming losses from fictitious or "wash" sales, which had been freely indulged in by taxpayers to escape their full share of the tax burden. Pursuant to this policy, a substantial number of cases were submitted to grand juries for determination by them as to whether or not criminal prosecution should be had—among them that of Mr. Mellon, which led to criticism and claims of political persecution although similar cases submitted involved both Democrats and Republicans. The grand jury did not return an indictment against Mr. Mellon. However, in civil proceedings before the Board of Tax Appeals the government, represented by General Counsel of the Bureau of Internal Revenue Robert H. Jackson, was successful as to part of its claims (see *Mellon* v. *Commissioner of Internal Revenue,* 36 B.T.A. 977), and, before the case was carried further, the Treasury Department accepted a substantial settlement. Frank J. Hogan, who later became President of the American Bar Association, was chief counsel for Mr. Mellon.

Another development of major significance in the tax field was the decision in *James* v. *Dravo Contracting Co.,* 302 U. S. 134, December 6, 1937, in which the Supreme Court permitted state taxation to reach the gross income of government contractors who had previously been exempt upon the theory that they were "federal instrumentalities." This conclusion had been urged by the Department of Justice in a brief filed by the Attorney General as *amicus curiae* at the invitation of the Court. Following up the movement thus given impetus, on April 25, 1938, the President transmitted to the Congress a message recommending the enactment of legislation which (1) would subject to the federal income tax the interest paid on future issues of federal, state, and municipal bonds and the salaries of state and municipal employees, and (2) would permit state taxation of holders of future issues of federal bonds and of federal officers and employees within the taxing jurisdiction. An intensive study was thereupon undertaken in the Department of Justice and completed on June 24, 1938. The report of that study, an exhaustive treatment of the legal phases of the problem, was furnished to the President, the Treasury Department, and the several interested committees of the Congress. It is illustrative of the work of the Department of Justice involved in conducting studies of broad legal questions. *Ed.*]

The Mellon tax case; a longhand note to Assistant Attorney General Frank Wideman, in charge of the Tax Division, May 1, 1934:

IF I CONSULTED my personal comfort I would be disposed to drop the matter—but I do not see how I can do this unless the whole attempt to stop "wash sale" devices is to be given up. I do not think we should put the Department of Justice in the position of approving such practice, and when the question of good faith is involved, and no satisfactory offer of compromise is proposed under the statute, the fairest way is to let the grand jury pass on the case. We shall have performed our duty if we submit such cases with scrupulous regard for the rights of *all* concerned. Perhaps this will let us in for criticism—but I do not see how we can help that. I haven't the disposition to get after the little fellows and treat the big fellows on a different basis. In the long run this is the fairest course to pursue. Our one safety is to treat all alike. The Morris * memo is a good one, and I appreciate the thoughtful suggestions.

A statement to the press, May 8, 1934:

It was for the Grand Jury to say whether or not the facts disclosed, and fairly and impartially submitted, required further proceedings. Evidently they reached the conclusion that there was not sufficient evidence of improper motive to warrant an indictment. This was a function entirely within their province and there is no disposition to challenge the result. * * * Mr. Mellon * * * was treated like anyone else in a similar situation.

* Special Assistant James W. Morris, later an Assistant Attorney General.

State taxation of federal instrumentalities; from a press release, September 14, 1937:

In a brief filed on behalf of the United States in three cases, the Supreme Court has been asked to overrule a number of its prior decisions and to end the immunity from taxation accorded to those doing business with the federal and state governments. The brief was filed in response to a request by the Supreme Court that the Attorney General present the views of the United States on the question of whether taxes by states on gross receipts of contractors building dams for the federal government were a burden on the federal government. The brief takes the position that the state taxes, being non-discriminatory, are not an unconstitutional burden on the federal government and urges that they be upheld. If the position taken in the brief for the United States is adopted by the Supreme Court, the immediate result will be that private individuals selling to or contracting with the federal government will be subject to all applicable non-discriminatory state taxes. * * *

The brief points out that no express statement is to be found in the Constitution to the effect that either the states or the federal government should be exempt from taxation by the other, but that such immunity has been recognized by judicial decision on the ground that it is necessary to protect our dual system of government. According to the brief, the immunity doctrine, as expounded by Chief Justice Marshall in 1819, was much more restricted than it is today. The present expanded immunity dates from the decision in *Collector* v. *Day* in 1870, where it was held for the first time that Congress could not tax the salary of an officer of a state. * * *

Although admitting that a decision restricting the exemption doctrine and upholding the state taxes would increase the expenses of the federal government, the brief states that the United States cannot complain of being required to enter the market place on a par with all other purchasers. It is pointed out that the increased taxes which would be collected by the United States, if the exemption of individuals is restricted as asked in the brief, would at least partially offset any additional cost to the federal government. The brief estimates that the states would benefit from a restriction of the immunity to a greater extent than the United States, and suggests that the additional revenue received by the states should have the natural effect of lessening the claims of states for federal aid.

The brief contends that any increase in the expenses of the federal government by reason of state taxes, if the exemption is restricted, may be regarded as proper payment to the state for the facilities, such as roads and schools, maintained by the state which assist the federal government in building and carrying on its projects. * * *

In summarizing the position of the government, the brief states: "Our position, then, is that any tax should be held valid which is imposed upon the contractor rather than the sovereign, and which does not discriminate against the sovereign or affect the performance of the project in any way as distinguished from its costs."

A letter to Assistant Attorney General James W. Morris in charge of the Tax Division, July 2, 1938:

I have been examining with intense interest the bound set of the report and the six volumes of appendix covering the study made by the Department of Justice, under your direction, in connection with the legislation recommended by the President in his message of the 25th of April. * * * In my judgment it is one of the finest productions that has come out of the Department of Justice in a long time.

I congratulate you most sincerely upon this work and would be glad if you would convey my personal thanks to those who cooperated with you.

4. The Criminal Law

[In contrast with Part Two of this volume, which deals with the broader aspects of federal crime control, the items of this section illustrate the day-to-day administration of criminal law, which involves countless situations in all parts of the United States and often in foreign countries.

Some of the most troublesome criminal law enforcement problems develop in connection with labor disputes, in which there is interference with interstate or foreign commerce or with the mails. In one such case, thirty-six persons in Illinois were convicted on charges of systematically destroying railroad property. In another case, striking sailors on the S. S. *Algic* were convicted of mutiny. Ohio strikers fell afoul of the law when picket lines resisted the passage of mail trucks. Attorney General Cummings is reported to have expressed tersely the attitude of his Department in these matters by saying, "The ships must sail; the mails must move; and the railroads must run."

Another type of enforcement problem having to do with labor is illustrated by prosecutions in Arkansas and Kentucky. In Arkansas, persons guilty of securing forced labor through framed convictions of workers were convicted under an old anti-slavery statute. In Harlan County, Kentucky, the jury disagreed in cases against mine operators for violating a post-Civil War statute which penalizes conspiracies to deprive persons of their rights under federal law, which in this instance was the National Labor Relations Act. The cases were then set for retrial. *Ed.*]

From an office memorandum to Assistant Attorney General Brien McMahon, July 17, 1937:

I HOPE that intensive consideration will be given to the Post Office interference cases in Ohio. * * * As you know, I am much interested in this matter and feel that, in view of the pressure that may be brought upon government witnesses either directly or indirectly, unusual care should be taken not only to protect them but to see that the case is fairly, vigorously, and earnestly presented.

From an office memorandum to Special Executive Assistant Gordon Dean, December 27, 1937:

I draw your attention to an article appearing in the *Washington Star* of December 26, 1937, entitled "LATEST WIRE TAPPING DECISION CONFUSES LAW ENFORCEMENT." In view of what is said in this article, and also in view of the importance of the subject, I would be glad if you would collaborate with a view to working out a policy. (1) Consideration should be given to the latest decision and its scope. (2) I should like to know whether the District of Columbia is included or not. In other words, whether the statute as interpreted affects interstate commerce and communications within the District of Columbia and the possessions of the United States. (3) I would like to be assured as to the distinction, if any, between receiving or obtaining information and actually publishing it. (4) Consideration should be given to the question of whether an amendment to the law should be suggested.

[Note: The decision in *Nardone* v. *United States,* 302 U. S. 379, occasioned the foregoing inquiry, which is typical of many flurries in the enforcement of the criminal law. *Ed.*]

Letter to Assistant Attorney General Brien McMahon, in immediate charge of the trial of the Harlan County cases at London, Kentucky, July 13, 1938:

I quite appreciate the difficulties under which you labor, and whatever the outcome may be I have every confidence that you and your associates will do all that possibly can be done to bring about a successful conclusion of the case. I hear nothing but praise of the manner in which you are handling yourself and it makes me very proud to know that this is so. Please present my greetings and best wishes to your associates. They are all fine fellows and doing a grand piece of work.

A confession of error in the case of some college students convicted of burning their fraternity house, December 26, 1934:

CONFESSION OF ERROR

Comes now the Attorney General on behalf of the respondent in the above-entitled case and confessing error in the judgment therein sought to be reviewed, as to appellants' assignments of error, Nos. 7 and 8, in respect of the failure of the trial court to direct a verdict in favor of each of the defendents, moves the court to reverse the judgment herein. * * *

The Attorney General, having personally reviewed the record and evidence in this case and having confirmed his conclusions by a supplemental investigation of various phases of the case, does not feel justified in asking that the judgment be affirmed and suggests to this court that the judgment of conviction below should be reversed. * * *

The Attorney General is of the opinion that the evidence adduced at the trial did not justify a submission of the case to the jury, and, in view of all the circumstances involved, is satisfied that the defendants are innocent of the crime of which they were convicted. He, therefore, requests the court to reverse the judgment.

[Note: The foregoing confession of error was filed in the Court of Appeals for the District of Columbia on an appeal from a conviction for arson. The court, however, did not accept the confession of error but reversed the case on the ground that certain evidence had been improperly admitted by the trial court (see *Parlton* v. *United States,* 75 F. (2d) 772). The Department of Justice, of course, did not retry the case since the defendants were believed innocent. Confessions of error in the criminal field are the comparatively rare admissions by public prosecutors that persons convicted of crime are not guilty. *Ed.*]

5. Public Lands and Indian Wards

A letter to the President, December 12, 1938:

IT HAS occurred to me that you, as the Chief Administrator as well as Chief Executive of the nation, may be interested in the attached book of instructions and procedure for one of the divisions of the Department of Justice. You know, better than any of us, both the necessity and the difficulty of attaining simple and effective administrative organization and procedure.

This volume indicates something of the whole mechanism of the Department of Justice as well as the detailed operations of one of its several divisions. Indeed, the Lands Division is an excellent subject for several reasons. It is the largest litigating unit of the Department of Justice, the functioning of which is responsible for a third of the mail which passes through our departmental record division. Its jurisdiction is more varied and extensive than that of other federal law offices and involves huge sums of money, to say nothing of values in property. More than three billion dollars in ascertainable claims alone are now pending there. Its sphere of activity includes subjects traditionally the source of severe public scandal, such as oil and gas, Indian affairs, huge grants or reservations of land or minerals, and the custody and protection of public real property interests of every kind. The obscure and technical origins of the law so administered seem peculiarly susceptible to delay and misdirection, possibly because most lawyers have little inclination to explore the mysteries of these ancient but fascinating and certainly important fields of the law.

With these factors in mind, I have taken some interest in a reorganization of our extensive functions centered in the Lands Division. Its organization took its present shape in November 1937. As proof that the system and the instructions described and embodied in this volume are not merely red tape, it is significant that the tremendous load of unfinished land business pending from day to day has been cut in half during the last fiscal year and is still being reduced at a uniform rate. It disposes of from three to four hundred cases a week and undertakes between two and three hundred new cases each week. Its duties are performed in workmanlike and effective manner.

In making this progress, Assistant Attorney General McFarland is entitled to commendation. Of course, no unit of government can achieve method, organization, and successful operation without the high type of personnel which we have insisted upon for this work.

"Hoover" or "Boulder" Dam? Correspondence with Secretary of the Interior Harold L. Ickes:

January 17, 1935

Dear Homer: On page 4 of the bill of complaint in the case of *The United States of America, Plaintiff,* v. *The State of Arizona, Defendant,* there is a reference to "water discharged at Hoover (Boulder) Dam." Having gone to great lengths to give to Boulder Dam its original and proper name which my predecessor in office attempted feloniously to take from it, for which praiseworthy and meritorious public act I have been roundly condemned by reactionary Republican papers in all parts of the country, I may say that the reference in this bill of complaint to "Hoover Dam" gives me nothing at all to cheer about. I should have been glad to point out what was undoubtedly merely an inadvertence but I lacked the opportunity, since I did not see the bill of complaint until after it had been printed and filed with the Supreme Court.

January 21, 1935

Dear Harold: This acknowledges your letter of the 17th of January about Boulder Dam, and I am not surprised by your perturbation. Even in the midst of great events, the misuse of a cherished name is apt to be upsetting.

The difficulty in this particular instance seems to grow out of the fact that, while the term "Boulder Dam" is used as often as possible and scattered somewhat promiscuously in strategic places in the bill of complaint, nevertheless the drafters of that document seemed to feel it necessary in describing the dam to use the title employed by the Congress in the acts appropriating money for its construction. I believe these acts refer to the dam as "Hoover Dam" (see 46 Stat. at Large 1146; 47 Stat. at Large 118; and 47 Stat. at Large 535). Moreover, the dam is referred to as "Hoover Dam" in the contract between the United States and the Metropolitan Water District, under which contract, I understand, the dam is actually being constructed.

Our Department was not aware that you had officially rechristened the dam, or that there had been any change in its technical name since the order of Secretary Wilbur made on the 17th of September, 1930.

I rather doubt whether it is feasible to do anything about the matter at this late day, even if it were deemed appropriate so to do. In other words, it looks to me very much like water over the Hoover (Boulder) Dam. When I see you, I shall extend my commiseration in person.

The last of "Teapot Dome"; from Annual Report to the Congress, January 3, 1938, p. 110:

In connection with leases of public oil lands, the executors of the estate of Edward L. Doheny paid the United States $100,000 in settlement of one claim against them, and in a suit previously instituted against Doheny for fraudulently securing the execution of certain leases of public lands they paid $3,000,000 in settlement, ending fourteen years of litigation and bringing the government's recoveries arising out of the so-called "Teapot Dome" scandals to a total of $31,141,322.62.

6. Claims Against the United States; War Risk Litigation; Customs

Another echo from the Harding administration; press release on the decision of a trial court of the District of Columbia in the matter of a claim against the United States, January 27, 1937:

PLAINTIFF brought suit for approximately $680,000 interest on an Alien Property Custodian claim for $7,000,000 which had been allowed and paid in 1921. The government counterclaimed the $7,000,000 on the ground that the original claim was fraudulent, and that its allowance had been secured in joint conspiracy of Thomas W. Miller, former Alien Property Custodian and Harry M. Daugherty, former Attorney General. * * *

Miller, who was the Alien Property Custodian who recommended the allowance of plaintiff's original claim in 1921, and Harry M. Daugherty, who was the Attorney General who ordered the allowance of the claim, were indicted as a result of this transaction and prosecuted in New York in 1927. Miller was convicted but the jury disagreed as to Daugherty, and the indictment against the latter was dismissed. A portion of the liberty bonds making up a part of the property paid over to the plaintiff under its claim in 1921 were traced into the possession of Thomas W. Miller. In the same case the government claimed to have traced similar bonds into the hands of Mr. Daugherty. The defense presented in behalf of Mr. Daugherty, who did not testify at his trial, was based on the claim that his name was used by others as a dummy and that he knew nothing about the bond transaction.

Proof adduced in the present trial was to the effect that the bank in which the proceeds of the sale of the bonds had been deposited in Harry M. Daugherty's name had failed, and that in 1930 Mr. Daugherty filed verified proofs of claim for that particular account, alleging under oath that he was its true owner.

There was further proof that he had received liquidating dividends from the receiver of the bank as late as September 1935.

[Note: See *Cummings* v. *Societe Suisse pour Valeurs de Metaux,* 85 F. (2d) 287 (1936) ; decided, after retrial, on January 27, 1937; and affirmed by the Court of Appeals for the District of Columbia, 99 F. (2d) 387, July 25, 1938. The claimant requested the Supreme Court to review the case. *Ed.*]

A memorandum to Assistant Attorney General Sam E. Whitaker, in charge of the Claims Division, September 23, 1938:

I am greatly pleased with your recent report concerning the activities of your Division and thank you for sending it to me. In view of the succinct manner in which it stated the situation, I sent a copy of it to the President with a memorandum which I attach hereto. I did not have time to consult you about the details of the *Societe Suisse* case and, therefore, had to give my impression of it from memory.

A recommendation to liberalize the law permitting suits against the United States for damages; from Annual Report to the Congress, December 31, 1938:

Many years ago the Congress waived the sovereign immunity of the United States in respect of actions for breach of contract, and claims founded on the Constitution or a law of Congress. * * * The immunity of the government from suits in tort is, however, still in effect. As a result, claims of the latter type are handled by special legislation. Numerous private bills are introduced in each Congress relating to one or more specified claims. It must be remembered that no such private law can be passed without discriminating against all other persons falling in the same category. The Claims Committees of the Senate and House are flooded with matters that should properly be handled by a judicial tribunal. * * *

Many of these claims arise out of alleged negligence on the part of drivers of government vehicles. In principle and as a matter of abstract justice, it would seem to be as reasonable to permit a person who has sustained property damage or personal injuries as a result of the negligence of the driver of a government automobile or truck to sue the United States as it is to allow suit to be brought under similar circumstances against the owner of a car belonging to a private individual or corporation. Special legislation is a matter of grace. Claims of this sort should be placed on a basis of right.

A letter to the President, November 5, 1934:

Attached hereto is a summarized statement of the War Risk Insurance litigation statistics for the first quarter of the fiscal year 1935. You will note that 923 cases were disposed of, that the total savings to the United States amounted to $10,419,957.33, and that the government was successful in 91.77 percent of the cases handled. On the whole, a very satisfactory record.

A search for more expeditious disposition of customs litigation; a letter to Special Assistant Mac Asbill, November 27, 1937:

I have your memorandum of November 24, 1937, with reference to the studies going forward in the matter of expediting customs litigation. I think it would be an excellent idea for you to go to New York as you have already planned, with a view to following up the studies and seeing if there is anything in the mechanics of the situation that can be improved. * * * At my suggestion, a change was made by the President in the set-up of the court. Acting under provisions of existing law, he designated Judge McClelland as presiding judge. This change, and the activity of Assistant Attorney General [Joseph R.] Jackson [in charge of the Customs Division] has, in my judgment, contributed in marked fashion to the improvement in the state of business in that court.

7. Legislation—Advice to Congressional Committees and to the Chief Executive

[In matters affecting the administration of justice, the Attorney General is called upon by congressional committees for views and often submits drafts of needed measures to members or committees of the Congress. The Chief Executive requests comment on bills presented for his approval. During the Roosevelt administration, the duties of the Attorney General and his staff with respect to legislation were greatly expanded in number, scope, and subjects. From March 4, 1933, to December 7, 1938, the Department drafted and sponsored 126 measures, made requested reports to congressional committees on 797, reviewed 144 prepared in other departments and agencies, and commented on 511 submitted to the President for approval. This function is illustrated in numerous items in other parts of this volume. The Attorney General, however, is not a legal adviser to the Congress or its committees and, for more than a hundred years, has with more or less consistency refused to give advice to the Congress except upon questions directly affecting the operations of the Department of Justice. Occasionally, memoranda are submitted or oral views given. Notable instances in recent years have been testimony before congressional committees by Assistant Attorney General John Dickinson on the validity of the amended National Bituminous Coal Conservation Act and of Assistant Attorney General Robert H. Jackson on the validity of the so-called "wages and hours" bill. *Ed.*]

Circular No. 2516, January 18, 1934:

HEREAFTER, all requests or recommendations for legislation shall be submitted to The Assistant to the Attorney General before being presented to Congress. This applies to any official expression of opinion, whether written or verbal, regarding pending or proposed legislation.

In order that the Department of Justice may comply with the provisions of Circular No. 49, as amended, issued by the Bureau of the Budget upon order of the President, it is directed that hereafter all requests for new legislation and opinions relative to pending legislation shall be officially transmitted to Congress through The Assistant to the Attorney General. All such matters will be submitted by The Assistant to the Attorney General to the Assistant Attorney General or other official having jurisdiction over the subject matter for the preparation of a memorandum and recommendation upon the subject. Such memorandum and recommendation shall be transmitted to The Assistant to the Attorney General, who will submit the matter to the Bureau of the Budget for recommendation to the President. When the Department is informed whether the request or measure is in accord with the financial program of the President, Congress will be advised to that effect and as to the attitude of the Department toward the legislation.

Bills referred to the Attorney General by the President for advice as to possible objection to their approval will be handled in the same manner as are requests or recommendations for legislation and official expressions of opinion regarding legislation pending before or to be presented to Congress, as provided above. All bills so referred by the President will therefore be first submitted to The Assistant to the Attorney General. By him each such bill will be routed to the official of the Department having jurisdiction over its subject matter for the preparation of a memorandum and recommendation, which will be transmitted to The Assistant to the Attorney General as a basis for a report to the President.

A letter to Henry F. Ashurst, Chairman of the Senate Judiciary Committee (Senate Report No. 202, 75 Cong. 1 Sess.), May 7, 1935:

I have your letter of March 27, requesting my views relative to the merits of the bill (S. 2155) to grant relief to persons erroneously convicted in courts of the United States.

This measure proposes to permit any person who has been convicted of any offense against the United States and who is thereafter found innocent of the crime, or receives a pardon on the ground of innocence, to bring suit against the United States in the Court of Claims to recover compensation for the pecuniary injury that he has sustained as a result of his erroneous conviction. The bill contains a maximum limitation of $5,000 on the amount that may be recovered in such a proceeding.

I doubt whether a person who has been convicted and whose conviction is reversed before he has served any part of his sentence should receive any compensation. Ideal justice would seem to require that, in the rare and unusual instance in which a person who has served the whole or part of a term of imprisonment is later found to be entirely innocent of the crime of which he was convicted, some redress should be made. On the other hand, reversals in criminal cases are more frequently had on the ground of insufficiency of proof or on the question as to whether the facts charged and proven constituted an offense under some statute. Consequently, it would be necessary to separate from the group of persons whose convictions have been reversed those few who are in fact innocent of any offense whatever. * * *

The bill in its present form seems to be fraught with some danger. If limited and amended * * * I think its enactment will make a desirable addition to the statutory law of the United States.

[Note: The proposal finally became law (see 52 Stat. 438). *Ed.*]

A letter to Hatton W. Sumners, Chairman of the House Judiciary Committee (House Report No. 2357, 74 Cong. 2 Sess.), February 29, 1936:

Modern developments have rendered obsolete the common-law rule governing the admissibility of certain types of documentary evidence. Yet at times the application of the rule has resulted in a miscarriage of justice and has stood in the way of a successful prosecution of meritorious criminal cases.

The old common-law rule requires that every book entry be

identified by the person making it. This is exceedingly difficult, if not impossible, in the case of an institution employing a large bookkeeping staff, particularly when the entries are made by machine. In a recent criminal case the government was prevented from making out a prima-facie case by a ruling that entries in the books of a bank, made in the regular course of business, were not admissible in evidence unless the specific bookkeeper who made the entry could identify it. Since the bank employed eighteen bookkeepers and the entries were made by bookkeeping machines, this was impossible.

The United States Circuit Courts of Appeals for the Second, Fourth, Seventh, and Eighth Circuits, and many district courts, as well as a number of the state courts, have recognized the necessity for modifying the rule and have adopted the doctrine that, in order to make it admissible in evidence, it is sufficient to show that the entry is contained in a book of regular entries maintained in the establishment, without producing the particular person who made the entry and having him identify it. Owing to the failure of some federal courts, however, to adopt the modern rule, legislation appears to be necessary to secure uniformity in this matter and to keep the rules of evidence in line with modern developments.

I enclose a draft of a bill to accomplish the above-mentioned purpose, and shall be glad if you will introduce it and lend it your support. I also enclose a memorandum, dated January 28, 1936, discussing the questions involved in greater detail.

[Note: The proposal was adopted by the Congress and approved by the President (see 49 Stat. 1561). *Ed.*]

A letter to the President recommending the veto of a measure, February 10, 1936:

I have the honor to advise you that in accordance with your request I have examined the enclosed enrolled bill (H.R. 4178), for the relief of the International Manufacturers' Sales Company of America, and the accompanying reports from the Secretary of State, the Secretary of the Treasury, the Acting Director of the Bureau of the Budget, and the Comptroller General.

The bill provides for the payment of the sum of $900,000 to the International Manufacturers' Sales Company in compensation of a loss that it sustained in connection with a sale of shoes in Siberia in the years 1918 and 1919.

The claimant is a New York corporation which was engaged at that time in the export business. In October, 1918, it had on hand at Vladivostok a large stock of shoes which it had previously shipped from the United States. At that time President Wilson adopted a plan for extending economic aid to the Siberian population. The task of carrying out the plan was entrusted to the War Trade Board. Arrangements were made whereby the agent of the War Trade Board at Vladivostok aided in disposing of the shoes to the people of Siberia, particularly in the matter of transportation and delivery. This assistance was rendered and the claimant corporation sold the shoes in various parts of Siberia in December, 1918, and January, 1919. Payment was made by Siberian municipalities in rubles, the money being deposited to the credit of the claimant corporation in certain Siberian banks. The exchange value of the rubles at that time was in excess of $900,000.

In February, 1919, the Federal Reserve Board adopted a regulation prohibiting the exportation or importation of Russian rubles. Apparently this fact precluded the claimant corporation from procuring American exchange for the rubles thus on deposit. Later, the assets of the banks in which the money was on deposit were confiscated by the Soviet government when it came into control of Siberia, and all the Russian currency issued prior to the Soviet regime was cancelled. The result was that the claimant lost the money that it had realized in connection with the disposal of the shoes.

While the Secretary of State in his report submits no recommendations, he attaches a letter written by Acting Secretary of State Cotton, dated April 5, 1930, in which the suggestion is made that there are grounds which, in equity, might be considered in determining the advisability of granting indemnification to the company. The Secretary of the Treasury, the Acting Director of the Bureau of the Budget, and the Comptroller General unite in recommending that the bill be vetoed. I concur in their recommendation.

There was no contractual relationship between the United States and the claimant company upon which any legal claim can be predicated. It is asserted, however, that the regulation of the Federal Reserve Board creates a moral obligation on the part of the government to grant compensation for the loss resulting from its application. This can hardly be so, for it was but the exercise of a sovereign right which does not contemplate compensation for incidental injury. Nor is it clear that the loss sustained by the claimant corporation was due to the action of the War Trade Board, which merely rendered assistance in carrying out transactions which the claimant company desired to consummate.

The action of the Federal Reserve Board was not the proximate cause of the loss. The direct cause appears to have been the acts of the Soviet government in confiscating the assets of the banks and canceling the rubles. To pay the claim in question would be an unwarranted extension of the rule ordinarily applied to claims based on assertions of a moral obligation.

[Note: The President vetoed the bill (see Cong. Rec. v. 80, pt. 2, . p. 1817). *Ed.*]

A letter to the President recommending the veto of a crime bill, August 24, 1937:

I have the honor to advise you that, in compliance with your request of August 23, I have examined the enclosed enrolled bill (S. 1375) to provide for the punishment of persons transporting stolen animals in interstate commerce.

The bill proposes to impose a penalty of imprisonment not exceeding five years, or a fine not exceeding $5,000, or both, on anyone transporting in interstate or foreign commerce any animal, or the carcass or hide or any part of the carcass or hide of any animal, knowing the same to have been stolen. * * * It will be observed that the scope of the measure is so broad as to bring within its terms numerous offenses of the petit larceny type. It seems best that cases of this class should be handled by the local authorities, as they have been heretofore, and that federal jurisdiction should not be extended to them.

Cattle and poultry depredations on a large scale in instances involving interstate transportation can be prosecuted under existing law, as the National Stolen Property Act (Act of May 22, 1934, 48 Stat. 794; U.S. Code, title 18, secs. 413-419) penalizes the interstate transportation of any stolen property of the value of $5,000 or more. The present act contains an element of flexibility, in that if a defendant is charged in the same indictment with two or more violations of the act then the aggregate value of all the property referred to in the indictment constitutes the value for the purposes of prosecution. In other words, if the same person ships stolen goods on several occasions, federal jurisdiction attaches if the aggregate value of all of the shipments equals $5,000 or more, even though the value of each shipment is less than this amount. * * *

The measure could not be enforced without a large increase of the personnel of the Federal Bureau of Investigation and a considerable additional expenditure of funds. This would hardly seem warranted under the circumstances. * * * Moreover, the bill is not well drawn, for it subjects the thief who steals one chicken and carries it across the state line to the same penalty as a person guilty of depredations on a large scale.

I recommend that approval of the bill be withheld.

[Note: The President vetoed the measure (see Cong. Rec. v. 81, pt. 8, p. 9613). *Ed.*]

8. The Federal Bureau of Investigation

[The Federal Bureau of Investigation, which is the "secret service" arm of the Department of Justice, is treated in Part Two above in connection with the broader aspects of the problem of crime control. The Bureau performs quite as important services in civil matters, although these activities are less spectacular. The following items are largely illustrative of what may be called the personal side of its functions. *Ed.*]

A telegram to Special Agent F. J. Lackey, Kansas City, Missouri, June 20, 1933:

I DESIRE to express to you my best wishes for your rapid recovery from the wounds received by you in line of duty and to commend you for the courageous manner in which you conducted yourself under the most trying circumstances.

[Note: The special agent mentioned was severely wounded in the so-called "Kansas City Massacre" in which two agents—the other, Reed Vetterli—were wounded and two local officers were killed in taking the notorious gangster, Frank Nash, to Leavenworth. Mr. Lackey continued in the service. *Ed.*]

A letter to William B. Bankhead, Speaker of the House, May 4, 1938:

William R. Ramsey, Jr., special agent of the Federal Bureau of Investigation of the Department of Justice, died early yesterday morning in a hospital at Danville, Illinois, as a result of gunshot wounds inflicted the day before by a bank robbery suspect whom he was endeavoring to arrest near Penfield, Illinois.

Special agent Ramsey, accompanied by another special agent and several local officers, had proceeded to a point near Penfield to arrest three men suspected of the burglary of the State Bank of Lapel, Lapel, Indiana. The arrest of one of the suspects had been effected. The officers then entered a farmhouse, approxi-

266

mately three miles northwest of Penfield, Illinois, for the purpose of arresting one Joe Earlywine, another of the suspects. Earlywine opened fire on the officers, mortally wounding Special Agent Ramsey, and in the exchange of bullets which followed, Earlywine was also killed. * * *

Mr. Ramsey courageously met his death in the unflinching performance of a dangerous duty. He left a widow and a baby nine months old, who because of this circumstance are entitled to every possible consideration at the hands of the government.

From time to time within recent years the Congress has enacted bills to compensate the widows of special agents of the Federal Bureau of Investigation of the Department of Justice who were killed in the performance of their official duties, the amount of compensation awarded in each instance being $5,000 (see the acts of August 21, 1935, 49 Stat. 2156; May 4, 1936, 49 Stat. 2268; April 6, 1938, Private No. 434, 75th Cong.).

Accordingly, I enclose herewith a bill which has been drafted in this Department to provide compensation for Mr. Ramsey's widow in the sum of $5,000 as was done in the other cases to which I have referred. I recommend its enactment.

[Note: The requested measure was introduced in the Congress (H.R. 10564, 75th Cong. 2 Sess.), but had not passed at the close of the session. The Congress has uniformly adopted such measures in these cases. In addition, it is the custom of the special agents to make up a fund, to which each contributes ten dollars, for presentation to the families of special agents killed in the course of duty. *Ed.*]

A letter from J. Edgar Hoover, Director of the Federal Bureau of Investigation, January 25, 1938:

Upon my return to Washington I did want to tell you personally how much I appreciated your telegram which reached me at St. Paul upon my arrival there. It meant so much to me to have your commendation. I read the contents of it to the agents who were with me, and they all were most appreciative of your thoughtfulness and kindness in sending such a fine message.

I know that you would have been just as proud as I was to

have seen the fine standards to which the agents of our Bureau measured up during the terrifically trying days of the last week. The agents who were engaged upon this case went many days and nights without sleep, and several days without food, and endured physical hardships in the North Woods of Minnesota and Wisconsin. * * * The temperatures were way below freezing and the snow in most places had a depth of from three to four feet. They had to mush through this for miles and miles, and I am happy to report to you that not a single man faltered or wavered in the enthusiasm to carry through and bring to a successful consummation the solution of one of the most vicious and atrocious crimes of this decade.

[Note: The foregoing is selected at random from among numerous similar communications from the Director. The matter referred to is the successful search for the body of Charles S. Ross, who had been kidnapped and killed by John H. Seadland. The latter, who confessed, had been apprehended in California. The ransom money, part of which had been buried, was recovered in the course of search. *Ed.*]

9. Prisons, Parole, and Pardons

[The broad outlines of the prison program are given in Part Two above. From 1933 to 1939 the complex and detailed problems of parole, probation and prison labor were studied, policy was formulated, legislation was secured, and administration was coordinated and developed. In the field of executive clemency, all applications were personally reviewed by Attorney General Cummings, after investigation. From March 4, 1933, to December 7, 1938, a total of 7,944 applications were filed, 3,028 recommendations submitted by the Attorney General were considered by the President, and 4,583 were disposed of in the Department of Justice under presidential regulations. These matters include full pardons, the restoration of civil rights, commutation of sentences, respites, and remission of fines, costs, and penalties. In the closing months of 1933, Attorney General Cummings recommended a general amnesty proclamation to restore civil rights to those convicted of violating the war-time Espionage Act and the Selective Service Act. The President issued the proclamation on December 23, 1933. *Ed.*]

An office memorandum to Sanford Bates, Director of the Bureau of Prisons, June 4, 1935:

I WAS at Alderson, West Virginia, on the 31st of May and had ample opportunity to look over the federal institution [a prison for women]. It was a highly enjoyable and stimulating experience. * * * The impression I received was distinctly favorable.

There are certain matters which, at your convenience, I would be glad to talk over with you. When you write to Doctor Harris please present my congratulations and best wishes. Later on I shall write her a personal note of appreciation.

Office memorandum to Executive Assistant Ugo Carusi, June 5, 1935:

When I was at Alderson, the attached letter from Eva May Jones was handed to me together with the memorandum attached thereto.

Eva is a very tall, gangling sort of colored girl. My understanding is that she attempted to shoot someone and missed the mark. The shot, however, terminated the career of someone else, hence the long sentence of thirty-six years.

I would be obliged if you would have the matter looked into and let me have a report about it, and return the attached memorandum to me with your report. I gathered that she was in a great state of excitement, bordering on instability, for quite a long while after she was sentenced, but has more or less come out of this condition and now seems peaceable and reasonably well disposed. I would like a pretty thorough report as to all of the facts of the particular crime and the mental history as well.

An office memorandum to Executive Assistant Ugo Carusi, June 6, 1935:

I return herewith the file in the matter of James F. Putthoff. If it were not for the statement made to the accused at the time he pleaded guilty, this case would offer me no difficulty. I doubt very much whether a promise was made, at least as interpreted by the prisoner. Nevertheless, something was said to him which led him to believe that his term might be reduced. In other words, the record from the standpoint of the government is not entirely satisfactory. * * * Naturally, I would like to take such a course as would straighten this out, if possible. * * *

Before taking final action, I would like a little more information. I therefore return the papers to you and ask you to inquire more fully into the man's record, conduct, and general psychology, with a view to determining what kind of a risk he is. Perhaps you will find it desirable to talk the matter over with the members of the Board of Parole. It would also be helpful to have access to the medical reports and the reports, if any, of the psychiatrist. * * * The record apparently contains nothing to give me any idea of what would happen to him if he should be released. What honest vocation could he follow? What opportunities for employment has he? What are his family connections? Who would look after him?

Office memorandum to Special Executive Assistant Henry Suydam, June 10, 1935:

I see no objection to having the attached [prison population] statistics published. They are not only a bit of useful information, but they indicate clearly the increasing perplexities of our prison problem and probably will be helpful in aiding us to work some solution. Our prisons are filling up pretty rapidly and, if the present increase continues, the situation will become quite serious.

Office memorandum to The Assistant to the Attorney General, William Stanley, June 17, 1935:

I am somewhat disturbed by the jail situation and the rapid manner in which our institutions are filling up. I am wondering how you and Mr. Bates are getting along in connection with the attempt to secure more jails. It strikes me that this is a matter that ought to be pressed with great vigor. Moreover, if there is any danger of our program failing, we should enlist the cooperation of the War Department and, if the funds cannot be obtained along the lines now in mind, it would seem to be a matter calling for an appropriation.

10. Opinions—Advice to the President and Cabinet

[The Judiciary Act of 1789, in creating the office of Attorney General, required him only to represent the United States in the courts and give opinions on questions of law to the President and heads of departments. The opinion function has grown with the years until it now requires a special staff of assistants. From March 4, 1933, to December 8, 1938, the Attorney General rendered 851 opinions, passed upon the form and legality of 1,706 executive orders and 270 proclamations, and approved or rejected 813 important compromises of law suits (minor cases being disposed of by other officers of the Department). In addition, he examined informally many hundreds of questions which occur from the countless legal details of public law and administration. Assistance in these several types of duties is furnished chiefly by the office of the Assistant Solicitor General. Legal studies of large problems—such as immunity from state taxation, federal incorporation, and the use of troops in cases of domestic violence—are distributed among appropriate units of the Department. *Ed.*]

Office memorandum to Assistant Solicitor General Golden W. Bell, November 27, 1936:

QUESTIONS have arisen as to the rule of law involved in the appointment of cabinet officers. Amongst the points raised are the following: (1) Is there any rule of law requiring a President who has been reelected to submit to the Senate the names of the cabinet he desires to have serve with him, if it is his wish to retain the old cabinet? In other words, are reappointments and reconfirmations necessary? (2) How long does a cabinet officer by law hold office? (3) On what legal basis is founded the provision in the commission that a cabinet officer serve at the pleasure of the President? I think all the commissions have some such language, at least in substance. (4) Is there a distinction in the matter of Postmaster General? It has been said that there is a provision of law that, for some reason, puts the office of Postmaster General on a slightly different basis. What is this distinction, if any, and are there any other distinctions as between various cabinet posts?

[Note: The foregoing is an example of numerous informal queries on legal questions which arise in public administration. In reply to the inquiry, the Attorney General was advised that the heads of all departments, with the exception of the Postmaster General, hold office at the pleasure of the President and that it is unnecessary for them to be reappointed and reconfirmed by the Senate at the beginning of a new presidential term. There are numerous instances in which cabinet officers have held over after the inauguration of a new President, without reappointment—as, for example, when all the members of President Jackson's cabinet, who were in office when his term expired, continued to serve under President Van Buren without new commissions. On April 18, 1929, Attorney General Mitchell advised President Hoover that it was unnecessary for him to reappoint Secretary of the Treasury Andrew W. Mellon who had been appointed by President Coolidge and continued to serve under President Hoover (see 36 Op. Atty. Gen. 12). The statute under which the Postmaster General is appointed, however, provides that "the term of the Postmaster General shall be for and during the term of the President by whom he is appointed, and for one month thereafter, unless sooner removed." *Ed.*]

Constitutional questions; an opinion to the President, March 26, 1937:

In response to a request from the Federal Home Loan Bank Board that you obtain my opinion on "the constitutionality of the creation of the federal home loan banks under the Federal Home Loan Bank Act" (July 22, 1932, c. 522, 47 Stat. 725; U. S. C., title 12, secs. 1421 *et seq.*), you submitted the matter to me, and suggested that, if I knew of no objection, I comply with the request. I expressed reluctance to do so because of a well-settled practice to which I shall hereafter refer at greater length and which, it seemed to me, ought not to be abandoned. Thereafter, with your letter of January 5, 1937, you transmitted to me a letter addressed to you by the Chairman of the Board under date of

December 31, 1936, resubmitting the question for further examination.

Save in exceptional cases it has been the practice of Attorneys General to refrain from rendering opinions as to the constitutionality of enactments of the Congress after their approval or disapproval by the President. While the bill which became the Federal Home Loan Bank Act was awaiting executive action, my predecessor was asked to let the President know whether, in his judgment, there were any objections to its approval. Under the established practice, my predecessor's report is not available to the public, but I think I may say, subject to your approval, that it suggested no constitutional or other objection to the bill—nor do I find any.

I think I should take this occasion, however, to stress the soundness of the rule which I have mentioned and the grave objections to the rendition of opinions by the Attorney General upon requests from the heads of the federal departments and independent establishments concerning the constitutionality of laws they have been appointed to administer. There is no warrant for such requests as the presumption of validity is binding upon them and they must act accordingly.

In my opinion of August 16, 1935 (38 Op. 252), to the Secretary of the Treasury, concerning the duty of disbursing officers to make the payments required by the Agricultural Adjustment Act, I said:

> Ordinarily, I think, it does not lie within the province of a ministerial officer to question the validity of a statute which, in so far as he is concerned, merely imposes upon him a proper duty and has no bearing upon his constitutional rights. As stated by the Supreme Court in *Aikins* v. *Kingsbury,* 247 U.S. 484, 489, "he who would successfully assail a law as unconstitutional must come showing that the feature of the act complained of operates to deprive him of some constitutional right." It is not sufficient that the statute may adversely affect the rights of others; and it can make no difference that others who claim to be injured are assailing its constitutionality.

The head of a department is under no duty to question or to inquire into the constitutional power of the Congress (36 Op. 21, 25). Such matters arise in the Congress, or with the President, and are not "questions of law arising within the administration of a department," within the contemplation of the statute under which the heads of the departments are authorized to require my opinion (U.S.C., title 5, sec. 304). This provision has been long construed as limiting the scope of opinions to specific cases, actually arising, in which the head of a department is authorized to make some determination, or to take some action, in connection with which some guidance is required.

Assuming, therefore, that in the administrative branch of the government only the President ordinarily can have proper interest in questioning the validity of a measure passed by the Congress, and that such interest ceases when he has expressed his approval or disapproval, it necessarily follows that there rarely can be proper occasion for the rendition of an opinion by the Attorney General upon its constitutionality after it has become law.

Necessarily when the Attorney General, at the request of the President, is considering pending legislation, he must often point out doubts and uncertainties of varying degrees of merit and must deal with the matter in a practical and, at times, argumentative fashion. Since such opinions are merely for the assistance of the President and are ordinarily regarded as confidential, the Attorney General may state his views fully and freely, with advantage to the President and without embarrassment to any one. To illustrate the manner of treatment sometimes required, I quote below from two unpublished opinions rendered during a former administration on proposed legislation, connected in no way with the legislation which has drawn forth this letter.

(A) The question is one which has been debated back and forth by lawyers, legislators, and writers on constitutional law * * *. Substantial arguments have been adduced on both sides of the question. The strict constructionists take the view that Congress has not the power and those inclined to more liberal views reach the opposite conclusion * * *.

It is one of those questions where a little statesmanship must be added to legal arguments to reach a sound conclusion. * * * Practical considerations lead to the conclusion that the liberal view, sustaining the power, should be adopted. * * * I do not believe the Congress would pay any attention to an opinion of an Attorney General to the effect that the power does not exist.

(B) In my judgment it would not be wise to base objection to this measure on constitutional grounds. * * * This measure falls into a class with innumerable others that have been enacted by Congress since the organization of the government and which, if constitutional at all, would have to be sustained under the so-called general welfare clause because there is no specific authority elsewhere in the Constitution. The question as to the extent of authority of Congress under the general welfare clause has never been decided by the Supreme Court of the United States and is not likely to be. An attack on this measure on the ground that it is not authorized by the Constitution would be met instantly with the argument that many measures open to the same objections have been approved during this and prior administrations; and to single out this one measure for constitutional criticism would result in inconsistency which could not be defended.

The situation is fundamentally different when the Attorney General is asked to pronounce upon the constitutionality of a statute after it has been passed by the Congress and approved by the President. Both then have evidenced their determination that the measure is constitutional. What before remained in the sphere of debate has now been elevated to the domain of law. Should the Attorney General now vouchsafe his opinion holding the legislation unconstitutional, he would set himself up as a judge of the acts of the Congress and of the President. Moreover, should a practice of rendering opinions upon requests such as that submitted in this instance prevail, the occasion surely would arise when, entertaining doubts which he could not conscientiously put aside, he would be compelled to declare, with disturbing public effect, the invalidity of a statute, while in effect voicing only a personal view that might ultimately be rejected by the courts. Of course, if the Attorney General should regard a statute as clearly constitutional, an opinion to that effect might not be immediately harmful—aside from the fact that he might later be called upon to defend the statute in the courts under such tactical disadvantage as may flow from a prior public exposition of his position. Often, however, although the Attorney General should conclude in favor of the constitutionality of a measure, he could not deny the presence of doubt; and yet, as the government's chief advocate in the courts, he would hesitate publicly to express misgivings which would only supply an issue that he must later meet in the performance of his official duties.

Even assuming the existence of some doubt about the validity of enacted legislation, it should always be remembered that its constitutionality may never be drawn into question, or may be questioned only in a particular aspect in its application to a specific set of facts. Just as it is not the function or the practice of the courts to make moot determinations of the constitutionality of entire statutes but to decide actual cases arising under specific factual situations to which the statutes may relate, so there would seem to be no reason why the Attorney General should rule upon such broad, abstract questions—especially when, as I have stated, the constitutionality of the statute may never be challenged.

I think that the duty of the Attorney General, in connection with inquiries from the heads of the departments and independent establishments as to the constitutionality of statutes, is correctly indicated by the following excerpt from the opinion of May 6, 1919 (31 Op. 475, 476), rendered by the Attorney General to the Secretary of the Treasury, concerning the taxation of judges' salaries:

> Ordinarily, I would be content to say that it is not within the province of the Attorney General to declare an act of the Congress unconstitutional, at least, where it does not involve any conflict between the prerogatives of the legislative department and those of the executive department—and that when an act like this, of general application, is passed it is

the duty of the executive department to administer it until it is declared unconstitutional by the courts.

It is interesting to observe that, notwithstanding this statement, the Attorney General proceeded to examine and pass upon the question, with consequences which emphasize the futility of such a practice. He concluded that "the act requiring the salaries of the officials in question to be included as a part of their gross incomes for the purposes of the income tax is valid and constitutional." Later the Supreme Court adopted a contrary view. *Evans* v. *Gore,* 253 U. S. 245. His opinion, given as an exception to the rule which he expressly recognized, clearly accomplished nothing of substance.

It is true that many opinions of the Attorney General have dealt with constitutional questions arising in connection with enacted legislation. Some of them have interpreted general statutes in the light of the Constitution, applying the principle that ambiguous language is to be construed, if possible, so as to avoid imputing to the legislature an intention that would transcend prescribed restrictions or raise serious constitutional questions. Some opinions have examined Supreme Court decisions and stated, for administrative guidance, the apparent scope thereof and the resulting effect upon the statutes under consideration. Others come within the recognized exception concerning statutes presenting possible conflict with prerogatives of the executive department. Very few have discussed constitutional authority in sweeping terms. I shall not further attempt to distinguish or classify these prior opinions, but they are to be sharply distinguished from the one requested in the present instance. The practice which has generally prevailed in the past is salutary and departures from it should be viewed with concern. * * *

I suggest, therefore, that in the present instance the request of the Federal Home Loan Bank Board be withdrawn.

11. Changing Personnel

[During the calendar year 1936 alone, there were 7,896 personnel changes in the resident and field staff of the Department of Justice and 1,764 in the staff of the judiciary, a total of 9,660 upon which the Attorney General was required to act. Two thousand of these were new appointments. Some sixty thousand such changes occurred between 1933 and 1939. They include appointments, transfers, resignations, cancellations, suspensions, terminations, leaves without pay, and increases and reductions of salary affecting the executive offices and their staffs, United States attorneys and marshals and their assistants, judges' clerks, law clerks, and commissioners. Attorney General Cummings discussed, briefly, some of the aspects of this function in the statement included above in Section 2 of Part One. *Ed.*]

Correspondence with Senator T. J. Walsh, Attorney General designate:

February 22, 1933

Dear Homer: Giving some thought to the organization of my force in the Department of Justice, I should very much like to have you take the place of [the] Assistant who handles all patronage matters, appointments of judges, district attorneys, marshals, and other officers of like character. Your experience as a practitioner in the conduct of important lawsuits, as well as your familiarity with the country at large, fits you, as I think, peculiarly for the place.

February 24, 1933

Dear Friend Walsh: It was very gracious of you to tender so important a place in the Department of Justice. * * * It just so happens, however, that Governor Roosevelt has tendered me the appointment as Governor General of the Philippine Islands and I have indicated to him my willingness to accept. This, of course, makes it impossible for me to accept your very flattering invitation.

279

A statement issued by the President-elect in his own hand, through
Secretary Stephen T. Early; a note from the latter transmitting a
photostat of the statement; and a reply:

March 2, 1933

Mr. Roosevelt had expected to announce today the selection
of Mr. Homer Cummings of Connecticut to be the Governor General of the Philippines. Because of the untimely death of Senator
Walsh, he has asked Mr. Cummings to assume the post of Attorney General for a few weeks before going to the Philippines.

January 10, 1938

Dear General: It has been a long "few weeks"—March 1933
to January 1938—and I know why he still wants you here.

January 12, 1938

Dear Steve: It was fine of you to send me the photostat of
your first press announcement. I cannot tell you how I appreciate your thoughtfulness. It brings back very vividly the memories of that hectic day.

A letter from Solicitor General Stanley Reed, upon his resigna-
tion to become a justice of the Supreme Court of the United States,
January 27, 1938:

Attached is my letter of resignation as your Solicitor General.
While it is only a formality, it saddens me, for it marks the end
of a service with you that has been filled with work of the kind
every lawyer enjoys. You have been patient and understanding,
beyond words, in the innumerable achievements, disappointments,
defeats, and victories which we have gone through together, just
as you have been quick and sure in action when my personal interests were at stake. For all of these things, I am forever grateful.

A letter from Thurman Arnold, selected to head the Antitrust Division, March 6, 1938:

I do not suppose you need this letter after my acceptance of your appointment to the Antitrust Division over the telephone. I write it however so that if by any chance you need a written statement you will have it on Monday morning.

I write it also for another reason. No possible way of announcing the appointment could have pleased me more than the one you took—to introduce me to the public as "an old time good friend" of yours.

A letter to Senator Joseph C. O'Mahoney, Chairman of the Sub-Committee of the Senate Judiciary Committee to consider the confirmation of the appointment of an Assistant Attorney General, March 8, 1938:

Since I shall be absent from Washington, I have requested Honorable Joseph B. Keenan, The Assistant to the Attorney General, to present to the Committee of which you are Chairman, my reasons for recommending Mr. Thurman W. Arnold as Assistant Attorney General in charge of the Antitrust Division. * * *

I selected Mr. Arnold, first, because he has been a successful practicing lawyer, used to the trial of cases and familiar with the practical side of litigation. * * * The second reason for my recommendation is that Mr. Arnold combines with his wide practical experience a first-hand acquaintance with the traditions of scholarship and research found in our best law schools. * * * My third reason for recommending Mr. Arnold lies in his wide experience with the problems of government administration. * * *

My final reason is my intimate, friendly acquaintance with Mr. Arnold since he came to Connecticut. I am confident that he may be relied upon to conduct the affairs of his office with vigor and fairness. * * * I have persuaded Mr. Arnold to accept this appointment because I feel that his duty to public service should outweigh all other considerations.

A letter from Frank Hogan, President of the American Bar Association, November 24, 1938:

The press dispatches reporting the tender of your resignation as Attorney General did not surprise but really did grieve me. They were not a surprise because I recall your telling me, nearly a year ago, of your determination to lay down the burdens of public office and to resume private practice; and I recall, too, the reasons you gave for that determination. I knew also that only the President's persuasion had kept you in office during the past year. But the reports grieved me because, frankly, I had hoped that the President would succeed in holding you longer. I have said publicly over and over again that close observation and past experience had combined to make me know the high degree of efficiency that had been achieved throughout the Department of Justice under your administration, and the ability and impartiality of that administration.

There are those who will criticise as well as those who will praise the administration of any great department of the government; and none is more apt to receive criticism than the Department of Justice. This is inherent in its functions. Any one who would say to you or of you that he agreed with everything you had stood for and found no exception to be taken to anything you had done would be a dealer in fulsomeness and a peddler in flattery. You and I have taken opposite views on questions of public importance and in cases which have attracted attention, but these have simply contributed to my opportunity to judge and appraise your administration as a whole. * * * I think history will include you among the nation's outstanding Attorneys General. I have no doubt of it. More important than that, however, certainly to citizens who are brought to deal with your Department, is the unquestionable and I think unquestioned fact that you have run the Department, not only well, but extraordinarily so. * * *

Your restoration of the rule-making power to the Supreme Court, resulting in the new Rules of Civil Procedure from which so much good is now rightly expected; your common-sense contribution to the movement to give the federal judiciary control of its own expenses, the handling of its own appropriations, and the administration of its own business; your getting under way the inevitable granting to the federal judiciary of control over the procedure applicable to criminal cases; and the magnificent advancement made under your direction in the healthy enforcement of the country's criminal laws, are only a few of the things which make me so confidently appraise even now the place history will accord you among the nation's chief law officers.

A letter from Herbert Harley, Secretary of the American Judicature Society, November 29, 1938:

Like all others interested in strengthening our judicial system, I regret that we are not to have the benefit of your leadership much longer, although I fully appreciate your claim to relief from an arduous position. I can speak with full confidence when I say that you have done far more for the federal judiciary than anyone in the entire history of the country.

A letter to the staff, December 27, 1938:

TO MY FRIENDS AND ASSOCIATES IN THE DEPARTMENT OF JUSTICE: * * * It is a source of sincere regret that in leaving the Department of Justice I cannot personally say good-bye to each and every one of you. As I look back over the last six crowded years I feel more than ever grateful to those whose loyalty and cooperation have made my stay here pleasant and, I hope, fruitful. * * * I think we may all feel a just pride that the burdens of recent years have been successfully carried and that solid and permanent gains have been made. * * * What we have built has been the work of many hands and many minds, laboring for a Department whose honor we cherish.

APPENDIX

Politics and Humanity

[Most public officers in policy-making positions are under pressure to deliver addresses on many subjects before many types of organizations. Attorney General Cummings spoke before bar associations, law schools, meetings of various types of organizations, colleges, religious convocations, encampments of Boy Scouts, and clubs, as well as at political assemblies and banquets and over the radio. However light the demands of the occasion, he used his speeches as vehicles for ideas in such a way as to make them of much more than temporary significance. *Ed.*]

Education, science, and government; from an address at Rollins College, Winter Park, Florida, February 26, 1934:

IT IS the nature of man to break down frontiers. As the scouts of our early days passed with the conquest of prairie and mountain, there arose * * * the scouts of science, clearing the path for their fellows through the frontier of knowledge. Great institutions of higher learning developed, first in the classics, then in pure science, finally in applied science and the various arts. Physics, chemistry, biology, economics, sociology, and, indeed, all the physical and social sciences were developed and applied to the myriad uses of man. As the Thirteenth Century was essentially an age of religion, so our age is largely one of science—of scientific accomplishment and of scientific method, of collection and classification of data, of formation and testing of hypotheses, of reaching conclusions and building thereon, of checking one discovery against another so that, ultimately, isolated findings become a part of the pattern of all. * * *

And yet, a short twelve months ago, our transportation facilities were largely idle; our abundant crops were rotting in the warehouses; our factories were closed or running upon pitifully

285

short time; thirteen million people were idle; and our elaborate and carefully constructed banking system had entirely ceased to function. We were confronted with the puzzling paradox of starvation amidst plenty. * * *

Education and science, if they are to be useful to government, must function within government as they have functioned outside of it. It is a sad commentary that we have used science least where we needed it most. To transportation, communication, agriculture, industry, medicine, sanitation, architecture, finance, and business, we have applied science and the fruits thereof— but not to government. There has been learning, yet it has gone unused. Economists, sociologists, historians, students of politics there have been and, like their brothers in the pursuit of truth, they have sought and they have found. In the books of the dead and the activities of the living, * * * in the great laboratory of life down the ages, they have seen the trial and error of collective life. All this knowledge they have stored * * * —and we have not used it. * * * Remember—as educated men and women, as scholars, as scientists, as citizens—that education and science must be for, not merely in, democracy.

The New Deal; from "The Law and the Prophets," a radio address, July 9, 1934:

The New Deal is economic rather than political. Its very terminology is that of finance, accounting, budgeting, crop production, labor distribution, costs of living, costs of production, margins of profit, price levels, and the like. The measures thus operating seek to adjust the economic factors of our life so as to produce efficiency in that sense of the word which means the abolition of idleness and poverty in a land of plenty. * * *

To those reactionaries to whom every new step appears a ghastly peril, each departure from the course to which they have been accustomed seems a fatal step. They felt that way when Jefferson departed from the concept of an Atlantic seaboard nation and purchased the Mississippi valley. They felt that way when our jurisdiction was extended to the Pacific Ocean. They were. confident that confiscation lay ahead when we adopted the income tax as a means of raising revenue, and some of them were positive that it was the end of financial individualism when we erected the Federal Reserve banking system. Time has a way of dealing with such critics and life passes them by.

The economics of the 1920's; from an address before The Commonwealth Club of California, San Francisco, August 17, 1934:

We have been passing through difficult times. The boundless resources of our country and the capacity for converting these resources to human account have been so completely relied upon in the days gone by that we have been careless of the heritage that is ours. We have learned to our cost, in the years since the World War, what havoc the recklessness of unwisdom may create. Careless of moral values and even of business prudence, our country entered upon an era of ill-ordered production, unwise spending, sheer business libertinism, and almost universal gambling. And it paid the price.

The chaos of March, 1933, and the remedies; from an address at Stamford, Connecticut, October 30, 1934:

I recall well the fourth day of March, 1933. I recall well the abject terror that had overtaken the greatest of our leaders of finance. I recall how the captains of industry were turning their eyes toward Washington, how the managers of every bank in America, sound or unsound, were looking for help. I recall how the panic that had seized upon our people had led to the withdrawal of vast sums from our financial institutions until even the best of them were upon the brink of collapse.

I remember well the thirteen million people out of work,

those millions who were eating the bitter bread of charity and shuffling along the streets of our cities and the country lanes, pleading for work, only to be turned away. I remember the multitudes of our little children who were grievously under-nourished, and the despair in great areas in our agricultural states as farm families at the rate of 200,000 a year were evicted from their homes. I remember the pleas that were being made from every quarter of the country for a courageous leadership that would take America out of the dark pit into which she had fallen. * * *

The memory of man is short. We have already moved so far from the horrors of that experience that there are those who have forgotten, or who want to forget or want others to forget, and who desire to restore the conditions that produced the perils from which they have so narrowly escaped.* * *

The genius of the New Deal lies in the application of science to government, and it contemplates the reapplication of the doctrines of cooperation. The Agricultural Adjustment Act is a planned attack upon unbalanced production, The National Recovery Act upon unbalanced employment, and both upon our diminished purchasing power. * * * The Agricultural Adjustment Act complements the National Recovery Act. The Public Works feature sustains both. Thus, production, consumption, and capital goods industries are being aided simultaneously. The Civilian Conservation Corps, the Civil Works Administration, the housing program, the Home Owners Loan Corporation, the Farm Credit Administration, and various other emergency measures are component parts of a seriously thought-out program. The banking structure is undergoing a necessary rehabilitation. Price adjustments and dollar stabilization are sought by the scientific method of trial and error and not by arbitrary fiat. A cleansing of the public service and a campaign against crime have been undertaken as matters essential to a healthy national life. * * *

Which of these measures would our critics desire to repeal? In the Public Works program, 750,000 bread earners are directly employed, and as many more indirectly. In the Civilian Conservation Corps are 300,000 of our young men, who otherwise would be idle in the streets or wandering from coast to coast, branded as vagrants in their hopeless search for work, or drifting, perhaps, from unemployment to various forms of depredation. They have been gathered together in the conservation camps, where they have received instruction and food, have had opportunity to build up their health and their bodies, and have worked in preserving the natural resources of our country.

Despite its confessed defects, which are in process of being remedied, the National Recovery Administration has found new places for four million men and women; and on the first day of August, 1934, industrial wage earners were receiving seventy-two million dollars per week more than at the close of the last administration. Collective bargaining has been recognized, improvement in working conditions has kept pace with the rise in wages, the sweat shop has been outlawed, and child labor has been abolished. Business failures have been cut in half, and have reached the lowest level in twenty years.

The farm income for 1934 will exceed that of 1932 by one billion six hundred million dollars; and over four hundred thousand farm homesteads have been saved from foreclosure. The banking structure has been so revitalized that the people of our country have no concern as to the safety of their deposits. Secret security affiliates, formerly connected with the banks of our country, have been abolished so that it is no longer possible to gamble with the funds of the depositors. Stock market regulations have been established which protect the public in the matter of sales literature, which now, under penalty of the law, must state not only the truth but the whole truth in connection with securities offered to the public for sale. The Home Owners Loan Act has already prevented over nine hundred and thirty thousand foreclosures. The credit of the government has been so strengthened that government bonds, which in January 1933 were selling at eighty-three cents on a dollar, are now selling above par.

*The Salvation Army; from an address upon the occasion of America's tribute of farewell to Evangeline Booth, Madison Square
Garden, New York City, November 1, 1934:*

To the equalization of the opportunities and rewards of the
individual, governments in all parts of the world—each according to its own ideas—have been devoting their scrupulous attention, but none, so far as I am informed, has found a method of
accommodating man to the strain of his intricate, modern environment.   But meanwhile, to alleviate human burdens and to restore
faith to human hearts, religious and other organizations have
stepped in where governments have hesitated to tread or have
trod with laggard feet.   One of the greatest of these is the organization whose new head we are gathered here tonight to
honor. * * *

Into that perpetual twilight of the poor that seems so remote
to us who think ourselves secure in our hold upon the material
things of life, the Salvation Army marched with its baskets and
its banners.   It has given shelter to the stricken, protected the
little child in the warmth of its mother's arms, shod the barefoot, and built fires for those who were cold.   Under the street
lamps on a thousand corners this organization has sung and told
its message.   The sound of its trumpets and its drums has risen
above the clamor of traffic, the cries of trade, and the jeers of
the skeptical and the contemptuous.

Into the dark regions of despair this noble woman has borne
the lamp of hope.   Into the house of hunger she has carried
bread.   Her touch has soothed the sick, the naked she has clothed,
and in the hour of death she was not absent.

*Perspective in government; from an address of welcome at the
opening session of The Imperial Council of the Masonic order
commonly known as the "Shrine," at Washington, D. C., June 11,
1935:*

You find us installed in a magnificent series of new buildings, rising on the banks of an historic river. These buildings
are more than a superb expression of the perfection of mechanical
processes and the genius of art. In them even the least imagina-
tive spectator can discern a reflection of the enduring grandeur
of his government and those imperishable aspirations for which
it stands. * * *

Behind those walls and in those buildings are men. * * *
Those men are human, attempting to bring to bear upon such
problems as few generations have ever had to meet their wisest
judgment, their shrewdest counsel, their most industrious application—all not untouched, I hope, with the trace of good humor
that leavens the heaviest loaf. Without these qualities government is dull and dead; with them—and above all with a sense
of perspective—government becomes a less desperate and somewhat calmer business.

*Justice; from an address at the John Marshall College of Law,
Jersey City, New Jersey, June 19, 1935:*

In this imperfect world we cannot hope for perfect justice
nor can we know precisely what it is. Yet, if reason fails to tell
us what justice is, we realize, by a certain sort of intuition, what
injustice is; and we are moved accordingly. If today * * * the
springs of needed faith are running low, it is because men feel
that somehow common justice is not functioning as it should.
For the moment, society has become more aware of its weaknesses
than of its strength, more conscious of its outgrowths of human
injustice than of its lasting foundations of organic truth. * * *

In our fault-findings we are disposed to think of injustice
as due largely to defects of legal justice. * * * The truth is that,

while legal justice may be imperfect, its operation is in fact more practical and more effective than that of many other institutions within the range of our social system. Its principles, standards, and techniques are well established. These are the priceless fruits of endless years of trial and error, which, moreover, offer dependable guarantees of substantial fairness. In our government, under its wise division of powers into legislative, executive, and judicial, the technical standards and rules of action are well defined.

Yet the vast and ever-continuing changes which the years have wrought in the nature of human society have disclosed many areas of our common life in which something more than mere legal justice must function. It is especially in these areas that justice takes on new and various aspects. It is here that government, in its wider sense, must often guide by canons summoned from deeper sources than the letter of the law. * * *

These considerations have intrigued the world's greatest thinkers from the beginning of history, though probably no one ever penetrated deeper into the mystery of what justice is than did the humble Carpenter of Nazareth whose divine teachings so many of us venerate and so few of us follow.

Religion and Crime; from an address entitled "Organized Religion and Crime Prevention," read before the Williamstown Institute of Human Relations, Williamstown, Massachusetts, August 29, 1935:

There has been no more difficult problem in the whole field of prison management than that of securing inspiring religious services and religious instruction. This has been due in large degree to the fact that, when a clergyman associated himself with a penal institution in the capacity of chaplain, he became an officer of the prison in the eyes of his fellows and in the eyes of the inmates, and in so doing he lost something of his character as a clergyman.

The Department of Justice has enlisted the cooperation of the Federal Council of the Churches of Christ in America and The Council for the Clinical Training of Theological Students. The Federal Council of Churches will nominate qualified men, who have been especially trained for the duties of a prison chaplain, to fill vacancies which occur in the Protestant chaplain service. Once a man is appointed these organizations will supervise his work, keep in close contact with him, and keep him in close contact with the church. A somewhat similar plan has been worked out for the Catholic chaplains. The Bishop of the diocese in which the institution is located will designate a priest for the position and the School of Social Work of Catholic University is offering special training for the men so designated to fit them for their duties. Representatives of leading Jewish organizations cooperate with us in the selection of Jewish chaplains.

* * *

In the community of a hundred years ago, and even more in the community of two hundred years ago, the church played a dominant part in the exercise of those disciplines which operate to preserve social order and to eliminate crime. Many of the offenses now known to our statutory law were left to the administration of the church—at an earlier time through the formal procedures of the ecclesiastical courts and later through the informal disciplines of church administration. Even after the separation of the American colonies, the place of the church in this disciplinary process was well recognized. In the earlier Colonial laws, we even find citation of Old Testament texts as authorities for the major criminal provisions.

Peace movements; from a radio address on the "World Peace Ways Program," November 21, 1935:

Those who expected that the dream of international peace would be realized without serious effort, and in some immediate and miraculous manner, have been grievously disappointed.

Moreover, there are a large number of people who seem to resent the idea that war can be prevented, and insist that human effort in this direction is futile. There are also large groups in all lands who appear to take a perverse delight in crying "failure" when peace movements prove abortive or when treaties are threatened or broken. Yet nothing could be more ill-advised than the thoughtless cry of "failure" in connection with these great adventures.

[Note: In 1938, Mr. Cummings was selected by Argentina and Chile to arbitrate their conflicting claims to the Beagle Channel Islands. *Ed.*]

Political freedom and crisis; from an address at the dedication of the new law school building, erected in honor of John Randolph Tucker, at Washington and Lee University, Lexington, Virginia, June 11, 1936:

It was well for Washington and Lee University that those men, who were its earliest sponsors, did not share the view of one of the most celebrated of the Colonial Governors, Sir William Berkeley, who, in his report to the Commissioners in London some three-quarters of a century after the birth of the colony of Virginia, said: "I thank God we have no free schools or printing, and I hope we shall not have for one hundred years, for learning has brought heresy and disobedience into the world, and printing has divulged them and libels against the best governments. God help us from both." * * *

We hear much talk of being in the midst of a crisis; but in this environment * * * need I stress the fact that every era is one of crisis and that each age is, and ever has been, one of change? Who, for example, better than the man to whom this building is dedicated, would appreciate that in the midst of a man-made world, just now suffering from a sense of moral frustration, no problem of government is so difficult as the attempt to establish a true balance between the rights and duties, both individual and collective, that in the end determine the scope

and operation of justice? Who, better than he, would understand that justice in the modern state is a fabric of infinite pattern, and that the unending effort to grasp and apply its elusive
significance should inspire us with hope instead of despair?

*Change and the Constitution; from an Independence Day address
at a meeting of The Society of Tammany or Columbian Order
of the City of New York, July 4, 1936:*

Implicit in the revolutionary phrases of the Declaration of
Independence are the sanctions of all just governments, as well
as the stirring concept that such governments are the servants and
not the masters of human need. Of necessity, such a government as ours was an experiment; but it * * * stands today as
the hope of modern civilization. In many quarters there are
those who, pointing to the swift and even fundamental changes
that have overtaken other peoples in other parts of the world,
freely predict a break-up of the foundations of our institutions.

These forebodings of disaster were especially frequent in
1932 and during the early part of 1933, when our country found
itself in a bewildering period of industrial and financial chaos.
* * * Sheer necessity gnawed at the roots of democracy. * * *
In large areas of our country, among disillusioned and embittered
groups of our people, serious outbreaks were recurring with
alarming frequency. Hunger and fear, the twin breeders of
revolution, stared at us with menacing eyes. Since that time,
* * * hunger has been appeased, fear has been banished, hope
has reentered American homes, orderly governmental processes
have been restored, and a great cleansing and rebuilding program
is proceeding towards its legitimate conclusion. These achievements are fresh tributes to American statesmanship and to the
resilience and patience of our people. They demonstrate of what
stout stuff America is made, but they teach us, too, how essential
it is that the freedom our fathers won should not be forfeited
by a complacent acquiescence in the face of old evils that recur
in new forms. * * *

The theory of our government has not changed, but the times have changed and invention has altered the scope and tempo of our life. There are many influential and intelligent citizens who are disturbed by these things and indulge fears, largely artificial, that something terrible is happening to America. They seek to interpret the law and the Constitution as a check rather than as a guide to the flow of life. They fling themselves athwart the currents of existence and order them to pause. These futile gestures bring only disappointment and bitterness to those who indulge them. Nothing is happening to America except that it is growing and that it is insisting that it shall not lose its freedom in the process. * * *

No living institution is ever finished; no rigid formula for the solution of human problems is ever apt to be devised. The teachings of history repeatedly admonish us that what one period regards as radical another comes to consider as conservative. The equity stirring today becomes the law of tomorrow.

The shrines of Washington; from an address of welcome at the opening session of a national encampment of the Boy Scouts of America at Washington, D. C., June 30, 1937:

You are encamped at the feet of shrines erected to the memory of those who performed glorious deeds in the public service. Upon this land have trod the feet of our most eminent patriots. Even the river which borders these hallowed grounds holds for us all a deep significance. * * *

You stand within the shadows of the past. This place is sacred with tradition, and yet for ten days you will live in the midst of a modern whirl, on a patch of ground surrounded by the surging, busy life of the Capital. * * * Like many visitors to Washington you will scurry from building to building, from monument to museum. In days to come you will be asked * * * just what Washington meant to you.

Let me leave with you this thought. Washington is a city

of symbols. Do not be content to ascend the Washington Monument without at the same time catching something of the spirit which inspired that monument. Do not leave the shrine of the Great Emancipator without resolving to do your part in the emancipations yet to come.

You are encamped in a setting of complexity. Here you may feel the pulse of a giant among the nations—hear the beat of its heart. We are a people in transition. We are continuously working out a civilization. You share it. You will improve upon it. That is the undimmed glory of youth. That is the challenge of our times.

Organized resistance to new legislation; from "Preserving Democracy," an address at the Jackson Day Banquet, Chicago, Illinois, January 8, 1938:

Do not for a moment assume that it is a simple task to preserve democracy and to make it an efficient instrument of government. Great reforms do not come easily. Even after the people have determined upon them, the attempt to enact them into law precipitates a terrific struggle.

Let me tell you a brief but significant story. Those who stood amid the wreckage of the Hoover administration will recall that 6,067 banks had been forced to close their doors. Simultaneously, there was a great demand for money of all kinds for hoarding, not only in safe deposit boxes but in mattresses and in holes dug in cellars.

Early on Monday, the 6th of March, 1933, President Roosevelt issued his first proclamation which suspended the operation of all our banking institutions and preserved them from destruction. Thereafter, the President, acting in close cooperation with the Congress, approved a series of acts and promulgated executive orders that effected a sweeping change in the financial structure of our country. Moreover, the administration secured the enactment of a law insuring deposits to the extent of $5,000 each in all of the banks within the federal system. Fifty-eight million accounts come within the protecting folds of that beneficent law; and their owners no longer lie awake nights worrying about their deposits. These measures were but a part of the inspiring story of a troubled nation finding its way successfully out of financial chaos. * * *

When the anti-gold-hoarding measures were promulgated, there was a great hue and cry in ultra-conservative quarters. They were assailed as wicked and unconstitutional encroachments upon private rights. But surely there can be no right to hoard in time of national peril any more than there can be a right to seize the best lifeboats in a storm at sea, or sequester food in a city under siege. * * *

The same forces that fought the gold clause legislation were active and recalcitrant as each new reform was put forward. They lobbied in the Congress, they advertised in the newspapers, and they fought in the courts. For fully three years municipal power projects have been blocked in 23 states by the injunctive process. The national will as expressed in the public works legislation, the desires of the affected communities, and the hopes of those who counted upon work or planned to sell materials were alike set at naught while this unwarranted litigation dragged its weary length through the courts. * * *

To prevent the operation of the Public Utility Holding Company Act, seven major suits were brought simultaneously in the District of Columbia and over forty similar suits in twelve different judicial districts, when one test suit would have served every legitimate purpose. There seemed to be, and I say it with regret, a deliberate purpose to engage the government upon so many fronts that effective defense would be rendered difficult or impossible.

In September, 1935, a group of fifty-eight eminent lawyers solemnly admonished the nation that the Wagner Labor Relations Act was unconstitutional and not worthy of obedience. They formulated an elaborate opinion covering one hundred and twenty-six pages, published it in the newspapers everywhere, sent copies of it to lesser legal lights, and did incalculable harm in fostering litigation and disregard of law. They spoke as if from on high, they entertained no doubts, they acted with superb confidence, and, as the opinion of the Supreme Court subsequently disclosed, they were completely wrong. * * *

Naturally there is a growing distaste for the elaborate tactics of obstruction that make it so difficult for a democracy to function. * * * And still the struggle goes on. So long as there are evils to be corrected, there will be beneficiaries of evils to resist the measures of correction.

Of late years there has been an increasing trend toward an undue concentration of wealth and economic control. It is a situation of which any responsible government must take notice. While our antitrust laws have checked the growth of monopoly, they have not prevented it. We have come into an era of price control by concerted group action and that, I undertake to say, is an intolerable situation. We cannot be expected to permit such practices to impair our prosperity or to throw it out of balance.

A nation as capable as ours of producing an abundance of wealth is not adequately using its powers if there is an insufficient distribution of such wealth among the masses of the people. If their incomes are depleted by unjust prices and inequitable wages, there will be precisely that much less to spend for the good things of life. The purchasing power of the future lies in the standard of living of those on the lower rung of the ladder; and there will be found the answer to our hope of a well-ordered national home.

Mass production and all the advantages that flow from operations on a large scale may be, and often are, the sources of great public service. That fact has been demonstrated over and over again. Indeed, it is one of America's outstanding achievements. It must not be forgotten, however, that the control of the vast power involved carries with it not only high responsibilities, but also dangers of misuse against which we must safeguard our democracy.

In dealing with these problems our purpose should be constructive, not merely destructive. * * * I say with all the earnestness at my command that until agriculture, labor, and capital, with the aid of the government, have learned the lesson of friendly and intelligent cooperation our democracy will not rest on a safe foundation. * * *

No tribune of the people ever stored up love for himself in the House of Privilege. Every great leader we have ever had has been the victim of calculated slander and reckless invective. All of our great Presidents have had their detractors. Washington knew them; Jefferson knew them; and so on down the list of the illustrious men who gave all they had in the service of their country. No one knew them better than the Great Emancipator, whose body lies not far from here and whose mighty spirit still broods over a troubled people. He knew them in all their meanness, all their malice, and all their venom. These wretched traducers proclaimed him a tyrant, a dictator, and a usurper. They said that he had loaded the country with intolerable taxes and had "piled an enormous debt incalculably high." They said that he was an enemy of our form of government and had "torn the Constitution to tatters."

The struggles of Andrew Jackson with political and financial privileges, his sturdy attempts to make the doctrines of Jefferson living and breathing things, his titanic battle with Nicholas Biddle and the Bank of the United States, and the unbridled criticism to which he was subjected have their counterparts today.

The Declaration of Independence; from an address on the occasion of the Fourth of July Celebration of the City of Washington, July 4, 1938:

Tonight we are met to celebrate the signing of America's compact with liberty. * * * Since then, 162 years have swept by. We, the heirs of that great experiment in democracy, meet tonight—a people 135 million strong, rich with unbounded resources and favored with the countless blessings of free government. Great social and political transformations have marked the shaping of this child among the nations to become a giant among the nations.

America was not finished when the Declaration of Independence was issued. That was the day when America began. Every decade since that time has presented its insistent and peculiar problems; and every decade has known its own triumphs. * * * Our work is never done. No living institution is ever finished. * * * And yet we turn, again and again, with increasing gratitude, to the Declaration of Independence. Its far-seeing philosophy, its friendly, human touch, its faith in the future of mankind—these things cheer and strengthen us amid the problems of a modern world and confirm us in the belief that we, as a people, are destined to enter wider fields of freedom and happiness than we have thus far known.

International relations and domestic law; from informal remarks at a dinner of the Chicago Bar Association in honor of Lord Macmillan, August 2, 1938:

I have often thought that unless we could create a condition wherein our homes were safe from invasion and the sanctity of human life was in some degree respected, unless the administration of both the civil and criminal law could move on in an orderly fashion, it would be well-nigh impossible for the government to deal successfully with the intricate and difficult domestic problems which always vex a great * * * people. Without order we cannot progress; and I think that is true of international affairs as well. * * * Peace is not a gift; it is an achievement, and the world will have peace when men deserve it. This we know—that life is the common adventure of all mankind and, under the complexities of modern existence, also a common destiny. There can be no peace except a peace common to all the world, and no lasting prosperity that is not shared by all. It has sometimes perplexed me * * * to realize that art is international, literature is international, science is international, but law is not international. Somewhere hidden in that thought is the answer to many of our difficult problems.

The American Way; from "Making Democracy Work," an address at York, Pennsylvania, October 29, 1938:

Many of our most vocal statesmen, who criticize the New Deal and can see no virtue in it, are undoubtedly sincere, but they are strangely lacking in vision. * * * They dread change, they fear new things, they think in terms of the past. * * * They remind me of the old story of the United States Patent Commissioner back in the 1850's who, in making a formal report of the business of his department, solemnly recommended that the Patent Office be abolished on the ground that everything that could possibly be invented had already been invented. He was the Herbert Hoover of his day. Since that time we have known the telephone, the electric light, the bicycle, the automobile, wireless telegraphy, the airplane, the submarine, the radio, the moving picture, and countless other devices that are part of the daily life of our people. * * *

Dictatorship, revolution, bureaucracy—these have been the cries, the constant and invariable answers to every effort to eliminate injustices and restore some measure of equal opportunity to the people of this country. In recent months we have heard a phrase, originally invented by Mr. Landon and since reemployed by Republican spokesmen—"The American Way." No one has defined it nor attempted to translate it into an understandable program. Without such clarification, are we not justified in assuming that by the "American Way" they simply mean the America of 1929, or the America of 1932, or some other bygone era? * * * Does the "American Way" mean sweat shops, child labor, slums, stock frauds, monopolies, interstate crime, starvation wages to laboring men, and starvation prices to farmers? * * *

Today the United States stands out among the countries of the world as the testing place, the proving ground, the ultimate hope of democracy. Every rumbling of war should be a warning to the people of this country to bring democracy to its highest working efficiency. We have come a long way in these past five years, but much remains to be done. The time in which we will be permitted to do it is all too short. Let us bend ourselves to the task of putting our house in order and making our civilization so strong, so fair, so just, so powerful, so prosperous, so happy, that the waters of discontent and the floods of alien propaganda will beat against it in vain.

The old regime; from "America Must Not Turn Back," an address at Greenwich, Connecticut, November 5, 1938:

Recently Mr. [Herbert] Hoover suddenly reappeared in Hartford, for all the world like Banquo's ghost at the banquet table of the Republican Party. He exhibited his political wounds, received in the house of his friends, and appealed for vengeance. * * * It is as though a perturbed spirit had arisen from the period of financial and social ruin to warn the living that the cause of death is the way of life. Mr. Hoover suggests that the country might well take the next two years to "stop, look, and listen." Now there is a program of progress for you! Mr. Hoover asserts that whatever the New Deal has accomplished in the way of preventing business abuses is all very well, but he hastens to add that "We do not need to pull down the temple of liberty to catch a few cockroaches in the basement." Assuming that this is the language of statesmanship and that Mr. Hoover is an authority on entomology, I still inquire, what parts of the temple of liberty have been torn down? He fails to particularize. That there were bugs in the basement he admits. But I am sure that they were less like roaches skipping

harmlessly over a marble floor, than like termites secretly under-
mining the foundations. There were termites and plenty of
them: child labor, sweat shops, industrial strong-arm methods,
long hours of labor, starvation wages, fraudulent stock schemes,
closed banks, disillusioned youth, foreclosures of homes and
farms, insecurity, poverty, hunger, and despair.

*The attributes of a great jurist; from an address in the memory
of Benjamin N. Cardozo, before the Supreme Court of the United
States, December 19, 1938 (which was the occasion of the last appearance of Homer Cummings in the Supreme Court as Attorney
General):*

A great judge leaves his mark not only on the law which
he serves but also on the life of the people. Not until future
generations of scholars have traced the course of the law in its
constant search for justice will the full scope of his great service
be revealed. But we can today with all certainty say that Mr.
Justice Cardozo opened ways along which a free people may
confidently tread. * * *

The peculiar influence of Cardozo * * * spread far beyond
the conference room. To lawyers and to courts his opinions
were more than a record of the judgment. They spoke with
the majestic authority of an analysis which reached to the bed
rock of the learning of the past and yet was attuned to the
needs of the living. And always the opinions spoke in tones of
rare beauty. They might deal with things prosaic, but the
language, lambent and rich, was that of a poet. * * * Signifi-
cantly, his most notable contributions to the common law are
found in fields which had long before settled into fixed forms.
No other judge of his time was so deft in weaving the precedents
of centuries into a new shape to govern a new society. This
is the heart of the common law process, but only a master can
fashion a new rule and yet preserve the essential truth of older
decisions. * * *

Few men have, with such whole-hearted humility, practiced that tolerance for human experimentation which many feel must be the hall-mark of a great constitutional jurist. None knew better than Mr. Justice Cardozo that, when the question was one of personal liberty rather than the economic judgment of the legislature, vigilance rather than obeisance must be the order of decision. Of freedom of thought and speech, he wrote in one of his last opinions for the Court, "one may say that it is the matrix, the indispensable condition, of nearly every other form of freedom." He has elsewhere said: "Only in one field is compromise to be excluded, or kept within the narrowest limits. There shall be no compromise of the freedom to think one's thoughts and speak them, except at those extreme borders where thought merges into action. * * * We may not squander the thought that will be the inheritance of the ages." * * *

Thus far I have spoken of our friend as a lawyer and a judge. This imperfect tribute leaves untouched the far reaches of his mind and character. * * * They are so intimate and so beautiful that they quite transcend the limits of our common speech. * * * Mr. Justice Cardozo has reached the end of his journey. It has been a journey of loving service to the law and to those who live under the law. * * * So long as our common law and our Constitution persist, men will pay tribute to the memory of this shy and gentle scholar, whose heart was so pure and whose mind was so bold.

INDEX

A

Adams, Abigail, 25.

Adams, John, 25.

Adkins v. *Childrens Hospital,* 155-156, 157 (*see* Minimum Wage Legislation).

Administration, burden and routine of, xxi, xxii, 18, 229-283.

Administrative Assistant to the Attorney General, the, 15.

Administrative Division, 14.

Administrative law, new problems, 11; *see* Administrative Procedure.

Administrative procedure, 123-124, 127-128, 195, 200-202.

Agricultural Adjustment Act and Administration, xxiv, 98, 122, 124, 141-142, 146, 288.

Alcatraz, 19, 29-35, 73.

Algic, SS., 250.

Alien Property Bureau and Custodian, 14 n., 20, 256-257.

Amazon Petroleum Corporation, 123-124, 127.

Amendments, *see* Constitutional Amendments.

America Must Not Turn Back, an address, 303.

American Bar Association, 67, 92, 97, 153, 181, 183, 194 n., 200, 225, 282.

American Constitutional Method, The, an address, 131.

American Institute of Criminal Law and Criminology, 92.

American Judicature Society, 92, 283.

American Law Institute, 48, 92, 198.

American Prison Association, 92.

American Way, The, an address, 302-303.

Amicus curiae, 231.

Amnesty proclamation, 269.

Automobile finance cases, 240-244.

Anniston Mfg. Co. v. *Davis,* 141.

Annual reports to the Congress, 12, 42 n., 194, 207, 211, 213, 218, 221, 225-226, 255, 257.

Antitrust laws, policy, and Division generally, xvii, xxi, xxii, xxiii-xxiv, xxv, 14, 16, 17, 232-245, 281; automobile finance cases, 240-244; base-point bidding, 238; competitive practices, 238; concentration of wealth, 236; control of supply, 238; criminal prosecutions, 232; effect of N.R.A., 232-234; enforcement, cost and burden of, 237-238; financial control, 238; federal incorporation or licensing, 238; holding companies, 238; identical bids on government purchases, 234, 238; intent, 238; interpretation of statutes, 236-238; mergers, 238; monopolistic practices, 239; origin of complaints, 239; patents, 238; price leadership, 238; problem, 299; revision of laws, xxv, 234-240; rule of reason, 238; statements, 244-245; statutes, uncertainty, 236-239; taxation, 238.

Appointment clerk, 230; *see* Personnel.

Argument of Gold Clause cases, 112.

Arkansas forced labor cases, 250.

Arnold, Thurman W., 14 n., 281.

Asbill, Mac, 258.

Ashton v. *Cameron County District,* 160.

Ashurst, Henry F., 57, 260.

Ashwander v. *T.V.A.,* 141.

Assistant to the Attorney General, The, 17, 259-260, 279.

Assistant Attorneys General, 5, 16.

Assistant Solicitor General, 15, 16, 20, 272.

Associated Grocery Manufacturers of America, address before, 235.

Associated Press v. *N.L.R.B.,* 160.

Association of American Law Schools, 184.

Association of the Bar of the City of New York, address before, 131.

Association of Juvenile Court Judges of America, address before, 77, 93.

Association of Railway Labor Executives, 129.

Attorneys, *see* United States attorneys; Department of Justice; Lawyers.